International Political Economy

International Political Economy

AN INTELLECTUAL HISTORY

Benjamin J. Cohen

PRINCETON UNIVERSITY PRESS

PRINCETON AND OXFORD

Published by Princeton University Press, 41 William Street,
Princeton, New Jersey 08540
In the United Kingdom: Princeton University Press, 3 Market Place,
Woodstock, Oxfordshire OX20 1SY

All Rights Reserved

Library of Congress Cataloging-in-Publication Data

Cohen, Benjamin J.
International political economy : an intellectual history / Benjamin J. Cohen.
p   cm.
Includes bibliographical references and index.
ISBN 978-0-691-12412-4 (hardcover : alk. paper)—
ISBN 978-0-691-13569-4 (pbk. : alk. paper)
1. International economic relations. 2. Economics—History—20th century. I. Title.
HF1359.C643 2008
337—dc22   2007025705

This book has been composed in Sabon

Printed on acid-free paper. ∞

press.princeton.edu

Printed in the United States of America

1   3   5   7   9   10   8   6   4   2

For Jane

Once more, with feeling

CONTENTS

ILLUSTRATIONS

ACKNOWLEDGMENTS

As USUAL, many debts of gratitude have been accumulated in the course of this project. I am especially grateful to the friends who took time from their busy schedules to read some or all of this manuscript while it was being drafted. These include Bob Cox, Marc Flandreau, Bob Gilpin, Joanne Gowa, Eric Helleiner, Miles Kahler, Peter Katzenstein, Bob Keohane, John Odell, Lou Pauly, Ronen Palan, and John Ravenhill. Special thanks goes to Nita Rudra, whose comprehensively detailed comments saved me from many an error of omission or commission.

I am also grateful to the many others who provided help along the way, including Rawi Abdelal, Peter Andreas, Mark Blyth, Jeff Chwieroth, Randy Germain, Barry Gills, Richard Higgott, Jonathan Kirshner, Ulrich Krotz, Anthony Payne, Tim Sinclair, David Stasavage, and Geoffrey Underhill. At various points in the text some of these colleagues are quoted without attribution, as are a few others who prefer to remain anonymous. In all such cases, the comments and observations are reproduced faithfully from private communications.

Jesse Russell provided valuable research assistance at the earliest stage of this project. Heather Arnold performed miracles during the lengthy period while the manuscript was being written. Both deserve recognition for their speed, efficiency, and initiative.

From the start, Chuck Myers of Princeton University Press has been a great source of support and inspiration for this project. I am also indebted to the Press's Peter Dougherty for his enthusiasm and encouragement.

Finally, a most special thanks goes to my wife, Jane Sherron De Hart, whose own writing projects did not prevent her from playing a critical role as adviser, sounding board, and cheerleader. She is my muse.

ABBREVIATIONS

APSA	American Political Science Association
BISA	British International Studies Association
CBI	central-bank independence
CFIA	Center for International Affairs (Harvard)
CIS	Commonwealth of Independent States
CMH	capital mobility hypothesis
GATT	General Agreement on Tariffs and Trade
GPE	Global Political Economy
G-7	Group of Seven
HST	hegemonic stability theory
ILO	International Labor Office
IMF	International Monetary Fund
IO	*International Organization*
IPE	International Political Economy
IPEG	International Political Economy Group
IR	international relations
ISA	International Studies Association
LSE	London School of Economics
MIT	Massachusetts Institute of Technology
OEP	Open-Economy Politics
OPEC	Organization of Petroleum Exporting Countries
PTA	preferential trade agreement
RIPE	*Review of International Political Economy*
URPE	Union for Radical Political Economics
UCLA	University of California at Los Angeles
WTO	World Trade Organization

INTRODUCTION

Miss Prism. Cecily, you will read your Political Economy
in my absence. The chapter on the Fall of the
Rupee you may omit. It is somewhat too sensa-
tional. Even these metallic problems have their
melodramatic side.
Cecily. (*Picks up books and throws them back on table.*)
Horrid Political Economy!
—Oscar Wilde, *The Importance of Being Earnest*, act 2

HORRID? After more than four decades of university teaching, I must concede
that I have known students who seemed to agree with Cecily, though they did
not often express their feelings in quite so forceful a manner. But I have also
known many others who learned to appreciate the value—perhaps even the
melodrama—that came from reading their political economy. Not everything
in political economy may be as sensational as the fall of a currency, whether
the rupee or any other. But much of political economy is indeed dramatic and
just about all of it is important.

This book is about the academic field of study known as International Political Economy—for short, IPE. More precisely, it is about the *construction* of
IPE as a recognized field of scholarly inquiry. Following standard practice, the
term IPE (for the capitalized words International Political Economy) will be
used to refer to the field itself, understood as an area of intellectual investigation. The field of IPE teaches us how to think about the connections between
economics and politics beyond the confines of a single state. Without capital
letters, international political economy refers to the material world—the myr-
iad connections between economics and politics in real life.

As Oscar Wilde's witty dialogue suggests, sharp observers have long understood that such connections do exist. As a practical matter, political economy
has always been part of international relations (IR). But as a distinct academic
field, surprisingly enough, IPE was born just a few decades ago. Prior to the
1970s, in the English-speaking world, economics and political science were
treated as entirely different disciplines, each with its own view of international
affairs. Relatively few efforts were made to bridge the gap between the two.
Exceptions could be found, of course, often quite creative ones, but mostly
among Marxists or others outside the "respectable" mainstream of Western
scholarship. A broad-based movement to integrate market studies and political
analysis is really of recent origin. The field today has been described as a

"true interdiscipline" (Lake 2006). IPE's achievement was to build new bridges between older, established disciplines, providing fresh perspectives for the study of the world economy.

An academic field may be said to exist when a coherent body of knowledge is developed to define a subject of inquiry. Recognized standards come to be employed to train and certify specialists; full-time employment opportunities become available in university teaching and research; learned societies are established to promote study and dialogue; and publishing venues become available to help disseminate new ideas and analysis. In short, an institutionalized network of scholars comes into being—a distinct research community with its own boundaries, rewards, and careers. In that sense, the field of IPE has existed for less than half a century. This book aims to offer an intellectual history of the field—how it came into being, and why it took the shape that it did.

WHO CARES?

But who cares? Why would anyone be interested in an intellectual history? Could anything be more dull? Or as Cecily might put it, could anything be more horrid?

In fact, there are three main reasons for an intellectual history of IPE. The first one is the practical importance of the subject matter. We are all affected, daily and deeply, by the nexus of economics and politics in international affairs. The gasoline that powers the world's cars comes mainly from nations like Saudi Arabia and Iran. Can anyone doubt that politics plays a critical role in determining the cost and availability of energy? The shirts and socks that can be bought at Wal-Mart come mainly from China. The largest part of U.S. grain production is sold in Europe and Asia. More than half of all Federal Reserve banknotes circulate outside the United States. The most popular car in the United States is produced by Japan's Toyota. Is there any question that all these market relations have political ramifications? IPE can be found every day in the pages of our local newspaper.

The second reason is the inherent allure of ideas, on which we all rely, consciously or unconsciously, to interpret the world around us. An academic field rests on ideas. Essentially, it is a mental construct that teaches us how to *think* about our experience—how things work, and how they may be evaluated. An intellectual history adds to our understanding by teaching us where a field's ideas come from—how they originated, and how they developed over time.

An intellectual history also reminds us that the construction of a field like IPE is never complete. History does not mean closed. A field of study in social science reflects the world in which we live, and since the material world is always changing, so too is the way we examine and evaluate it. Ideas and events are forever interacting and evolving. Our understanding, therefore, can always be improved. The construction of IPE has been an investment in intellectual progress. The field is also very much a work in progress.

At issue are profound questions of what scholars call *ontology* and *epistemology*. Ontology, from the Greek for "things that exist," is about investigating reality: the nature, essential properties, and relations of being. In other contexts, ontology is used as a synonym for metaphysics or cosmology. In social science, it is used as a synonym for studying the world in which we actually live. What are the basic units of interest, and what are their key relationships? Epistemology, from the Greek for "knowledge," has to do with the methods and grounds of knowing. What methodologies do we use to study the world? What kinds of analysis will enhance our understanding? The construction of a field of study requires development of a degree of consensus on both ontology and epistemology—a shared ("intersubjective") understanding of the basics. Whatever differences specialists may have on particular matters of substance, they must craft a common language in which to communicate. The process is never easy.

Finally, there is the *human* quality of the IPE story, which involves real people in real time. Ideas do not combat each other in some abstract, ethereal void. Ideas are the product of human imagination, pitting one scholar against another in verbal jousting or printed debate. Intellectual history is also a personal history. As we shall see, the key individuals involved in the construction of IPE have been anything but dull.

Diversity

The field of IPE is united in its effort to bridge the gap between the separate specialties of international economics and IR; that is its common denominator. But IPE is hardly a monolith. The bridges are many and varied, making for a colorful interplay of ideas. Indeed, as a practical matter, there is no consensus on what precisely IPE is all about. Once born, the field proceeded to develop along divergent paths followed by different clusters of scholars. One source characterizes IPE today as "a notoriously diverse field of study" (Payne 2005, 69). Another describes it simply as "schizoid" (Underhill 2000, 806). Too often, students are exposed to just a single version of the field. One purpose of this book is to remind readers that there are in fact multiple versions, each with its own distinct insights to offer. Another purpose is to help readers understand why, among different groups of scholars, some ideas have come to enjoy greater weight and influence than others.

Globally, the dominant version of IPE (we might even say the hegemonic version) is one that has developed in the United States, where most scholarship tends to hew close to the norms of conventional social science. In the "American school," priority is given to scientific method—what might be called a pure or hard science model. Analysis is based on the twin principles of positivism and empiricism, which hold that knowledge is best accumulated through an appeal to objective observation and systematic testing. In the words of Stephen Krasner (1996, 108–9), one of the American school's leading lights, "International political economy is deeply embedded in the standard methodology of the social sciences which, stripped to its bare bones, simply means stating a proposition and testing it against external evidence."

In U.S.-style scholarship, most of the emphasis is placed on midlevel theory building. In contrast to macrotheory (or metatheory), midlevel theory eschews grand visions of history or society. Rather, work tends to concentrate on key relationships isolated within a broader structure whose characteristics are assumed, normally, to be given and unchanging. (Economists would call this partial-equilibrium analysis, in contrast to general-equilibrium analysis.) The American school's ambition has been self-consciously limited largely to what can be learned from rational, empirical inquiry.

Even its critics concede that the mainstream U.S. version of IPE may be regarded as the prevailing orthodoxy. Perched at the peak of the academic hierarchy, the U.S. style largely sets the standard by which IPE scholarship worldwide is practiced and judged. The American school's history, it is fair to say, is the story of the *core* of the field as we know it. Because of its acknowledged primacy, the U.S. version is the one that will receive the most attention in this book.

The U.S. version, however, hardly represents the only way that the field could have been constructed. The uniqueness—some would say the idiosyncrasy—of the U.S. style must also be stressed. In practice, the American school's self-imposed limitations have been challenged in many parts of the world and in many different languages. In France, more emphasis is placed on regulatory issues; in Germany, on institutions; and elsewhere, on various elements of Marxist theory. The range of alternative approaches, in fact, is remarkably broad—regrettably, too broad to encompass in a single brief history.

For want of space, this book will concentrate on work in the English language—in particular, on an alternative approach that has emerged in Britain and outposts elsewhere in the former empire, such as Canada or Australia. In these locales, scholars have been more receptive than in the United States to links with other academic disciplines, beyond mainstream economics and political science; they also evince a deeper interest in ethical or normative issues. In the British style, IPE is less wedded to scientific method and more ambitious in its agenda. The contrasts with the mainstream U.S. approach are not small; this is not an instance of what Sigmund Freud called the "narcissism of small differences." Indeed, the contrasts are so great that it is not illegitimate to speak of a "British school" of IPE, in contrast to the U.S. version.

The distinction is not strictly geographic, of course. There are Britons or others around the world who have happily adopted the U.S. style, just as there are those in the United States whose intellectual preferences lie more with the British tradition. The distinction, rather, is between two separate branches of a common research community—two factions whose main adherents happen to be located, respectively, on opposite sides of the Atlantic. The two groups may all be part of the same "invisible college," to adopt the term of Susan Strange (1988b, ix), patron saint of the British school. But between them lie deep ontological and epistemological differences.

To underscore the diversity of the field, contrasts between the American and British schools will be explicitly drawn in the chapters that follow. My main point is a simple one. Each style has its strengths—but also its weaknesses. Neither may lay claim to comprehensive insight or exclusive truth. To complete the construction of IPE, it is not enough to build bridges between economics and politics. Bridges must be built between the field's disparate schools, too.

Intellectual Entrepreneurs

Students today take for granted the elaborate edifice of concepts and theories that has been erected to help sort out the mysteries of international political economy. It's there in the textbooks; therefore, it must always have been there. But it wasn't. Someone had to do the heavy lifting. IPE did not spring forth full-blown, like Athena from Zeus's forehead. It was quite the opposite, in fact. The construction of the field demanded time and a not inconsiderable amount of creative energy. No great tower of ideas stood hidden in the mists, just waiting to be discovered. IPE's architecture had to be put together laboriously, piece by piece, step by step. Indeed, the edifice is still being constructed.

How did it happen? As in all academic constructions, the achievement was ultimately a collective one—the product of many minds, each making its own contribution. Yet as every student of collective action knows, leadership is also vital to getting a complex project on track. Critical to the construction of IPE were some extraordinary individuals: a generation of pioneering researchers inspired to raise their sights and look beyond the horizon—beyond the traditional disciplines in which they had been trained—to see the politics and economics of international relations in a new, more illuminating light. Call them *intellectual entrepreneurs*, eager to undertake a new scholarly enterprise.

To stress the catalytic role of intellectual entrepreneurs is not to subscribe to a Great Man (or Woman) theory of history. I do not mean to caricature how knowledge is constructed. Ralph Waldo Emerson surely exaggerated when he declared, "There is properly no history, only biography." Yet individuals do matter. Every academic endeavor owes much to the determined efforts of a few especially creative master builders. "If I have seen further," the great Isaac Newton once wrote, "it is by standing on the shoulders of giants." We in IPE may say much the same. If today we can see beyond the horizon, it is because we too are able to stand on the shoulders of giants.

The intellectual entrepreneurs of IPE were economists, political scientists, and historians. Some were lifelong academics; others came to university research only after careers in other fields. Some collaborated actively; others cogitated in relative isolation. Some offered broad visions; others strove more to fill in the details. They didn't always concur. Indeed, disagreements among them were rife. Nor were they always right. But through their arguments and disputes—through the give-and-take of their enthusiastic debates—a new academic field gradually, if fitfully, emerged.

Time does take its toll, however, as inevitably it must. The ranks of the pioneer generation are thinning. Regrettably, a couple of old friends have already passed on; others have opted for blissful retirement. Among those remaining I modestly include myself. Originally trained in economics, I began my own foray into IPE in 1970 when, at the invitation of the New York publishing house Basic Books, I agreed to commission and edit a series of original treatises on international political economy—the first such project ever conceived. Ultimately, five books were published in the Political Economy of International Relations Series, including Robert Gilpin's classic *U.S. Power and the Multinational Corporation* (1975) as well as two volumes of my own, *The Question of Imperialism* (1973) and *Organizing the World's Money* (1977). The rest, as they say, is history.

More than a third of a century later I remain actively engaged in the field, which I have long regarded as my natural home. One source describes me as "one of the rare cases of an economist who came in from the cold" (Underhill 2000, 811). Almost all of my work has been in the general area of international money and finance, where by now, for good or ill, I have attained something of the aura of senior scholar status. "Godfather of the monetary mafia" is the way one younger colleague recently characterized me in a private correspondence. I like to think he meant it as a compliment.

Overall, I may not be the most qualified person to write on the construction of IPE. But neither am I entirely without credentials. I have been there from the start; I have been associated, directly or indirectly, with some of the most notable advances in the field; and I have been personally acquainted with almost everyone involved. Above all, I have no ax to grind, and so hopefully can remain reasonably objective in what I have to say here.

AGENCY AND CONTINGENCY

Throughout this book, two leitmotifs predominate. One involves *agency*—the indispensable role of individual action. Ideas may be in the air, but it takes determined initiative to grasp and wrestle them to the ground. Intellectual entrepreneurs were needed. The field's pioneers contributed to the construction of IPE in all kinds of ways—by their own writing and ideas, by mentoring students, by animating the work of colleagues, by editing, or simply by inspiration. Without their diverse efforts, the bridges between international economics and IR might never have been built.

The other leitmotif involves *contingency*—the unavoidable influence of chance. A new edifice was erected, but there was nothing inevitable about its specific shape or features, as the contrasts between the American and British schools amply reveal. Social and historical contexts matter. A different cast of characters, with other personalities or experiences, might have come up with a rather different style of architecture. Scholars are the product of many individual influences—geographic location, family upbringing, educational opportunities, disciplinary training, thesis advisers, work history, professional successes and failures, and more—all of which may have an effect on how each person responds to the same kinds of stimuli. Entrepreneurship is driven not only by inner convictions by also by external opportunities and constraints (otherwise known as serendipity). The same questions might have been asked. But with another choice of graduate school, another mentor, or some other network of friends and colleagues, the answers and emphases might have turned out quite differently.

Likewise, other historical circumstances might well have resulted in other shared understandings about how the world works. Without the cold war, which encouraged unprecedented generosity by the United States toward its former allies and adversaries, there might have been a different understanding of how power is used in the global economy. Without new multilateral organizations like the General Agreement on Tariffs and Trade (GATT) and International Monetary Fund (IMF), we might well have thought differently about the governance of international markets. Without the memory of the Great Depression, different assumptions might have emerged about the prospects for interstate cooperation or the relationship between economics and national security.

Admittedly, these two leitmotifs, agency and contingency, are not especially novel in the study of intellectual history. Indeed, specialists in the sociology of knowledge, following the seminal work of Peter Berger and Thomas Luckmann (1966), take for granted the central role of individual action, rooted in a specific time and place, in shaping perceptions of the world. "Reality is socially defined," wrote Berger and Luckmann. "But the definitions are always *embodied*, that is, concrete individuals and groups of individuals serve as the definers of reality . . . living individuals who have concrete social locations. . . . No 'history of ideas' takes place in isolation from the blood and sweat of general history" (107, 117). In more contemporary sociology, the people I call intellectual entrepreneurs have been labeled "knowledge specialists" (Swidler and Arditi 1994).

But even if not novel, the two leitmotifs deserve to receive more attention than they have from students of IPE. Too many scholars in the field fail to recognize the degree to which their view of reality has been shaped by influential individuals working in distant times. The great economist John Maynard Keynes wrote in his *General Theory* that "madmen in authority, who hear voices in the air, are distilling their frenzy from some academic scribbler of a few years back" (1936, 383). Today's specialists in IPE may not be frenzied, and few, I suspect, are mad. Yet in the way we approach the field, to some extent we are all responding to the voices of older scribblers. In the ongoing story of IPE, the themes of agency and contingency are particularly apt.

THE HALL OF FAME

Who were these intellectual entrepreneurs? No two observers, knowledgeable about IPE, might answer the question in quite the same way. It's one thing to say, "Round up the usual suspects"; it's quite another to agree on who the suspects are. One person's idea of a creative genius may be another's model of a hack. One person's conception of a core contribution may seem to others to be peripheral or—the worst academic insult possible—merely derivative. Any attempt to establish a definitive list of names, an IPE Hall of Fame, is bound to generate dissent.

It is with no little trepidation, therefore, that I spell out my own nominees in the following pages. They are (in alphabetical order) Robert Cox, Robert Gilpin, Peter Katzenstein, Robert Keohane, Charles Kindleberger, Stephen Krasner, and Susan Strange. For me, these are the people who most influenced the construction of the field in its early years—the Hall of Fame's first team All-Stars, as it were. With a nod to the cinema, we might call them the Magnificent Seven.

A more diverse group could hardly be imagined. At first glance, my nominees would appear to share little in common. They include one Briton (Strange), one Canadian (Cox), one naturalized U.S. citizen (Katzenstein), and four native-born Americans. They include two individuals trained in economics (Kindleberger and Strange) and one in history (Cox) as well as four political scientists. They include just five who received a PhD (Gilpin, Katzenstein, Keohane, Kindleberger, and Krasner) and just one whose earliest work evinced a particular interest in political economy (Krasner). Three had lengthy careers outside academia before committing to a life of scholarship (Cox, Kindleberger, and Strange). And their birth dates ranged from as early as 1910 (Kindleberger) to as late as 1945 (Katzenstein).

Yet on a deeper, more personal level, it is as if they all came from the same mold. With all of them, three indispensable attributes stand out. One is a *broad intellectual curiosity*, which led each of the seven to look for connections between diverse literatures and intellectual traditions. These were people who preferred to build bridges across disciplinary boundaries, not find a secure academic niche in which to specialize for a lifetime. Second is a *contrarian cast of mind*, in some instances verging on outright iconoclasm, which made them all quite comfortable challenging conventional wisdom. The Magnificent Seven were not inclined to accept the status quo as gospel. And third is an *acute sensitivity to experience*, which inspired them to question ideas and theories that seemed at variance with the evidence before their own eyes. For them, the value of scholarship could be measured not by the sophistication of a model or the elegance of a technique but rather by how much it added to an understanding of the real world. They may have differed greatly in nationality, training, or career, but in essential qualities of mind and personality they are as one.

Most important, they are all united by the *durability* of their contributions. Their early work may no longer be cited regularly; some of the specific subjects they addressed, such as international "regimes" or so-called hegemonic stability theory (HST), may today be considered quite passé. But even a casual glance at the contemporary literature reveals a continuing debt to their insight and creativity, as I hope to demonstrate in the chapters to follow. The influence of the Magnificent Seven, particularly in terms of ontology, is pervasive. Their pioneering constructions were decisive in establishing the basic language of the field. More than anyone else, they shaped the way we now think about IPE.

CONSENSUS

Some readers will say that in limiting myself to just seven nominees, I've left out a key name or two. Others will question why so-and-so is included. And still others, certainly, can be expected to challenge the relative significance I attribute to one individual or another. No one familiar with the field is apt to be entirely satisfied with my judgments here. My only defense lies in the modesty of my ambition. This book aims to provide no more than *an* intellectual history of IPE, not *the* definitive treatment. No claim is being made that mine could possibly be considered the last word on the subject.

But neither could anyone accuse this book of being especially far outside the mainstream. While personal, my selections may plausibly be defended as neither unreasonable nor idiosyncratic. Specialists might disagree over lesser luminaries. Nevertheless, across the field as a whole, there is actually a good deal of consensus about whose stars shine the most. How do I know? Quite simply, I asked.

Shortly after the idea for this book was hatched, I conducted a private survey of some sixty-seven acquaintances, all acknowledged experts in IPE. Each person was asked to identify up to six scholars who might be thought to have been the most influential in shaping the evolution of the field. Some forty-five responses were received from a wide range of individuals around the world—junior academics as well as senior, non-Americans as well as U.S. citizens, radicals and neo-Marxists as well as more orthodox centrists or conservatives. Although my unstructured poll could hardly be regarded as scientific, the results are highly suggestive. In all, some fifty-two names were cited at least once. Overall, however, votes were clearly skewed toward a much smaller handful of popular favorites.

The top vote getter was Keohane, whose name appeared on every single return—a notable achievement. Rounding out the roster of favorites (with votes in parentheses) were Gilpin (twenty-eight), Katzenstein (twenty), Krasner (eighteen), Strange (thirteen), and Kindleberger (thirteen), all on my own All-Star list. The only name missing was Cox, who received just four votes in my survey. Cox's absence is probably explained by the fact that the majority of my respondents were Americans, who know little of his work. But I nonetheless include him in this book because his lifetime of scholarship has had an indelible impact on generations of scholars in the British school of IPE.

Indirect support for my selections was also provided by a recent, more formal survey of IR faculty at U.S. colleges and universities (Peterson, Tierney, and Maliniak 2005). Some 1,084 academics, all political scientists, listed the four scholars they felt had made the greatest impact on the study of IR in the previous twenty years (encompassing all aspects of IR, not just IPE). Among the top twenty vote getters were five of the Magnificent Seven—Keohane (again the overall favorite, with votes from 56 percent of the respondents), Gilpin (ranked tenth), Katzenstein (eleventh), Krasner (twelfth), and Cox (eighteenth). Only Kindleberger, an economist, and Strange, the Briton, were nowhere to be found in the ranking.

Each of the Magnificent Seven will be featured in the chapters to come. To fill out the story, so will a variety of other scholars who may be less familiar or more controversial. Some played key supporting roles; others were little more than walk-ons. But all deserve mention if the story is to be anywhere near complete. The choices of who to include as well as the evaluations offered are of course my responsibility alone.

SUMMARY

The goal of this book, in short, is to tell the story of the modern field of IPE. This is not a textbook; we already have enough of those. Nor do I mean to offer a comprehensive survey of all the relevant literature in the field; that would demand far more space than can be provided in a single slim volume. Rather, my intention here is best understood as an exercise in interpretative analysis, selective in both its coverage and emphasis. Explanations are offered;

judgments are made. But there is no pretense that my discussion will meet the fullest standards of empirical proof.

The focus here is on contributions to *theory*—the abstract concepts, principles, propositions, and conjectures that together have shaped the common language of IPE. Purely empirical research or applied policy studies are addressed only to the extent that they are informed by theory, adding to the mental constructs that help us think about the world. My principal aim is to highlight the central role of ideas as such: the vital part that theorizing and theory building have played in the construction of the IPE field.

The intended audience for the book is first and foremost the invisible college itself—the population of scholars and students dedicated to furthering our understanding of the nexus of economics and politics in global affairs. All specialists in the field can benefit from a refresher course on IPE's origins and development. Beginners will gain a greater appreciation of the effort and energy that went into building the first bridges between international economics and IR. Even seasoned veterans are likely to find new discoveries in old, seemingly familiar material.

Beyond the inner circle, researchers in related disciplines—certainly in international economics and IR, and perhaps also in other areas of inquiry—might gain fresh insight into the foundations and construction of their own academic specialties. Students of the sociology of knowledge or intellectual history should find the case of IPE instructive, possibly even illuminating. And with luck, the book might even appeal to more general readers with a particular taste for the interplay of ideas, personalities, and events.

With all these audiences in mind, the style of the book is designed to be as reader friendly as possible. Wherever feasible, jargon is shunned; where specialized language cannot be avoided, every effort is made to define or explain the terms clearly and succinctly. In hopes of sustaining readers' interest, the text departs frequently from a purely abstract analysis of ideas and theories to weave in pertinent historical context, biographical sketches of the Magnificent Seven, and even from time to time a bit of personal memoir. And above all I do not hesitate on occasion to inject humor into the mix, to liven what otherwise could easily become a somber, even drab read. I have never doubted that even the heaviest subjects can be addressed with a light touch.

In the end, the book seeks to make a plausible case for three general arguments.

First, as I noted earlier, there is the critical role of what I call intellectual entrepreneurs—pioneers like the Magnificent Seven who are prepared, even eager, to think outside the box. Though ultimately the creation and cultivation of an academic field is a collective effort—involving many hardworking scholars, not just a few whose names we still remember—there is no question that leadership is essential to provide the necessary catalyst. The agency of intellectual entrepreneurs, I contend, is indispensable.

Second, there is the equally crucial role of contingency, as also mentioned above. That does not mean that all is arbitrary. Even with different personalities or historical circumstances, the broad contours of the field might have turned out pretty much the same. But it does mean that within the natural limits set by past experience and tradition, little is predetermined. The details of content and emphasis can vary considerably, depending on little more than chance. The influence of contingency must not be underappreciated.

And third, there is the issue of diversity and what to do about it. Differences between factions, such as exist between the American and British schools, are not necessarily to be deplored. Contestation between contrasting perspectives is often the richest source of intellectual growth. But the key is engagement. To promote new knowledge, factions must expose themselves to fruitful, honest debate. The American and British schools are in many ways complementary, and have much to learn from one another. Yet they have to try. The concluding argument of the book, spelled out most clearly in the final chapter, is that much can be gained from building new bridges between scholars on the two sides of the Atlantic.

ORGANIZATION OF THE BOOK

The book is organized into seven chapters: two chapters on the birth and development of IPE in the United States and Britain, three on broad overarching themes that in my opinion have been most central to the field's construction, and two appraising present accomplishments and future prospects. Throughout, subjects are placed in historical context in order to tie intellectual developments to their roots in the real world. Most important, the text emphasizes the contributions of key members of IPE's pioneer generation—the intellectual entrepreneurs whose initiatives proved most influential in shaping the field as we know it today.

Chapter 1 begins with the birth of IPE in the United States, stressing the critical roles played by Keohane (together with his colleague Joseph Nye) and Gilpin. What accounted for the emergence of the U.S. version of the field in the early 1970s, and why did its development take the course that it did? Crucial here was the relationship between the two disciplines from which the American school drew its main inspiration: economics and politics. Although a few mainstream economists played a vital role in the first years, the school's research agenda was soon seized by political scientists. Had the economics profession been more proactive at the start, IPE in the United States might well have evolved in a quite different direction. Yet in the end, ironically, economics has reclaimed a share of "ownership" of the field, at least in terms of epistemology. More and more, the predominant methodologies of the American school—how things are studied—have come to mimic the research techniques of the economics discipline—a trend that I describe as a kind of "creeping economism."

Chapter 2 traces the parallel development of IPE in Britain, dating back to a seminal paper published by Strange in 1970 titled "International Economics and International Relations: A Case of Mutual Neglect." Her clarion call for a "modern study of international political economy," a virtual manifesto, served as a source of inspiration for successive generations of scholars in Britain and other English-speaking countries, giving rise to what today is recognized as the British school of IPE. The main distinguishing characteristics of the British school are a ready acceptance of links to disciplines other than political science and economics along with a vital interest in a wide range of normative issues. These features stand in sharp contrast to the way that IPE has developed in the United States, where positivism and empiricism rule. The result of this divergence is a new case of mutual neglect that is nearly as profound as the void Strange deplored back in 1970.

In chapter 3, I take up the Really Big Question of systemic transformation, which not surprisingly was among the first issues to be addressed by the infant field. In the United States, thinking about systemic transformation was most fashionable in IPE's early years, when the horizons of inquiry seemed virtually unlimited. The main focus of debate, following the lead of Kindleberger, was HST. But in more recent years, interest in the grand theme of systemic change has largely faded in U.S. academic circles. Remarkably, this comes despite claims by many observers that today, more than ever, we may indeed be living through a truly historical transition—what has come to be known as the age of globalization. Only in the British school, owing especially to the influence of Cox, is there still much interest in the Really Big Question. Nothing better defines the differences between the American and British schools than their respective discourses on systemic transformation. From the start, each tradition constructed its own distinctive approach to the topic.

Chapter 4, in turn, addresses the issue of system governance—the widening "control gap" between state aspirations and state capabilities created by the growth of global economic interdependence. If national governments were losing control, who then would make the rules for the global system, and how would compliance with those rules be assured? For the American school the answer lies in international institutions, broadly conceived as forms of patterned cooperation among states. This discourse was set on track first by Krasner, who popularized the new concept of international regimes, and then by Keohane, who later broadened the inquiry into a more general study of institutional arrangements among governments. For the British school, by contrast, the answer is more complex, going beyond states alone to encompass a much wider array of authoritative actors. On the subject of the Control Gap, as on the Really Big Question of systemic transformation, each tradition has constructed its own distinctive approach.

In chapter 5, we come to the Mystery of the State. Most of the many differences between the American and British schools boil down to their contrasting
attitudes concerning a single issue: the place of the state in formal analysis. Is
the sovereign state the basic unit of interest or just one agent among many? Is
public policy the main concern of IPE, or is there more to the story? Both
schools acknowledge that the state is a key actor. But is the state the *most
important* actor—the only really interesting focal point for analysis? That is
the mystery. Scholars working in the U.S. tradition take for granted that IPE
is first and foremost about states and their interactions. That does not mean
traditional realism—the billiard ball model of rational, unitary states, conceived as closed "black boxes" driven solely by calculations of national interest
and power. States are at the center of analysis, but they are by no means the
sole actors. From early on, thanks in particular to the efforts of Katzenstein,
the black box was opened to admit a much wider range of relevant actors and
influences. Katzenstein's signal contribution was to encourage the addition of
domestic and, later, ideational factors to the mix. As seen from the British
perspective, however, a preoccupation with the state betrays the American
school's early capture by political scientists like Keohane, Gilpin, and Krasner.
Scholars in the British tradition prefer to follow the lead of Strange and Cox,
resisting any attempt to subordinate IPE to the study of IR.

Chapter 6, reprising the field's construction, asks the question: After all
these efforts, what have we learned? What do we know now that we didn't
know before? If knowledge is measured by our ability to make definitive statements—to generalize without fear of dispute—the field's success may be rated
as negligible at best. Many theories have been developed, from HST onward.
But none is universally accepted, and disagreement persists over even the most
basic issues of process and structure. On the other hand, if knowledge is measured by our ability to define the research agenda—to ask the right questions,
even if we don't yet know the answers—progress has been a bit more significant, though here too the diversity of the field is well illustrated by the contrasts
to be found between IPE's American and British versions. Students in the two
traditions are taught to ask distinctly different sets of questions. Whereas the
state-centric U.S. style is most concerned with the causes and consequences
of public policy, the more inclusive British approach is inclined to encompass
a rather broader range of social issues and concerns. Both schools may legitimately claim to have contributed significantly to our understanding. Yet since
their agendas are so divergent, so too is what we have learned from each. The
body of knowledge that has been created is large, but it is hardly tidy.

Chapter 7, finally, asks: What next? Where should the field go from here?
The construction of IPE is unquestionably a major accomplishment. An elaborate edifice of concepts and theories has been put together. But the edifice is
hardly complete. Though much has been learned, serious gaps remain in our

understanding. Arguably, new bridges need to be built in three critical areas: between the past and the present; between rationalist and cognitive analysis; and perhaps most important, between the American and British versions of the field. For all of IPE's accomplishments to date, there is still considerable room for a new generation of intellectual entrepreneurs to follow in the footsteps of the Magnificent Seven.

Chapter 1

THE AMERICAN SCHOOL

We live in an era of interdependence.
—Robert Keohane and Joseph Nye

Politics determines the framework of economic activity.
—Robert Gilpin

IPE, AS GILPIN ONCE FAMOUSLY suggested (1975b, 43), may be defined as "the reciprocal and dynamic interaction in international relations of the pursuit of wealth and the pursuit of power." By the pursuit of wealth, Gilpin had in mind the realm of economics: the role of markets and material incentives, which are among the central concerns of mainstream economists. By the pursuit of power, he had in mind the realm of politics: the role of the state and the management of conflict, which are among the central concerns of political scientists. IPE was to be understood as a marriage of two disciplines, integrating market studies and political analysis into a single field of inquiry. To a remarkable degree, that is precisely what IPE has come to mean today for most specialists—the common denominator even for critics who would prefer some alternative approach to the subject. IPE at its most fundamental, in short, is about the complex interrelationship of economic and political activity at the level of international affairs.

This chapter explores the origins of the dominant version of IPE that I have referred to as the American school. The notion of a "school" here is used loosely, by no means implying any sort of common goal or unified agenda. Scholars in the United States, as elsewhere, differ greatly on matters of substance as well as emphasis; in terms of theory, consensus is often lacking on even the most basic causal relationships. Yet at the level of ontology and epistemology, there does tend to be a shared understanding that distinguishes most inquiry in the United States from the way IPE is typically studied in many other places. The mainstream of U.S. scholarship can be considered a school because of its overarching worldview—a broadly accepted, if typically unacknowledged, sense of how things work and how they should be studied.

What accounts for the birth of IPE in the United States, and why did its early development take the path that it did? The story is vital, since the decisions taken early largely determined how the field was later constructed. Gilpin is a key part of the story, as we shall see. But most central are two familiar names: Gilpin's fellow political scientists Keohane and Nye, a pair of intellectual entrepreneurs par excellence. More than anyone, Keohane and Nye may take credit for setting the study of IPE in the United States on its present course. They were not the earliest on the scene. Others preceded them in seeking to marry international economics and politics. Nor were they alone in midwifing the new field's birth. Others, too, recognized the potential for fresh insights and understandings. But no one came close to matching them for the speed and ingenuity with which they acted to convert potential into reality. Keohane and Nye were uniquely instrumental in nurturing the infant in its earliest years, shaping its growth in ways that today are simply taken for granted.

Birth

Though we date the modern study of IPE only from the 1970s, the field's roots go much further back. What I call the pioneer generation was not the first in history to think of connecting the economics and politics of international relations. Others in earlier generations had also tried. But never before had such efforts, however determined, managed to make it into the scholarly mainstream. The pioneers of the 1970s and beyond were the first to succeed in making IPE a recognized and respected academic specialty. That is their accomplishment, their real claim to fame. On the scale of human achievement, the resulting construction may not rank up there with the taming of fire or the start of organized farming. Yet it was certainly something more than a mere reinvented wheel. A true intellectual breakthrough, the new field's birth was a product of both individual initiative and historical circumstances—agency as well as contingency.

Dialogue of the Deaf

In terms of intellectual antecedents, IPE may be said to have a long and distinguished lineage, going back to the liberal Enlightenment that spread across Europe in the seventeenth and eighteenth centuries. Even before there were the separate disciplines of economics and political science, there was political economy—the label given to the study of the economic aspects of public policy. In a work published in 1671, the English administrative reformer Sir William Petty first spoke of "Political Oeconomies." The term soon stuck. The classical economists of the eighteenth and nineteenth centuries, from the French physiocrats and Adam Smith onward, all understood their subject to be something called political economy, a unified social science closely linked to the study of moral philosophy. The earliest university departments teaching the subject were all designated departments of political economy. John Stuart Mill's monumental summary of all economic knowledge in the mid-nineteenth century was titled *Principles of Political Economy*. Oscar Wilde, as we have seen, was still using the term at the dawn of the twentieth century.

Not long after Mill, though, a split occurred, fragmenting the social sciences. Like an amoeba, classical political economy subdivided. In place of the earlier conception of a unified economic and political order, two separate realms were envisioned, representing two distinct spheres of human activity. One was "society," the private sector, based on contracts and decentralized market activity, and concerned largely with issues of production and distribution. The other was the "state," the public sector, based on coercive authority, and concerned with power, centralized decision making, and the resolution of conflict. University departments were systematically reorganized to address the divergent agendas of the two realms.

The immediate cause of the split was an increasing formalization of economic study and a growing abstraction of its more advanced theoretical ideas. A "neoclassical" school emerged, inspired by the so-called marginalist revolution of the 1870s, when differential calculus first began to be used to explore the effects of small ("marginal") changes in price or quantity. The aim was to develop a pure science, well removed from the minutia and distracting complications of everyday life. Gradually the discipline of economics, as it now came to be known, distanced itself from many of the practical policy and normative concerns that had previously motivated practitioners. So scholars with a more direct interest in institutions or issues of governance gravitated elsewhere, mostly toward the new discipline of political science with its central focus on the workings of political systems. In 1890, Alfred Marshall's *Principles of Economics* supplanted Mill's *Principles of Political Economy* as the English-speaking world's leading font of economic wisdom. By the start of the twentieth century, the divorce of political science from economics was largely complete, with few points of intellectual contact or communication remaining between them. As one source puts it, "Both disciplines grew increasingly introspective" (Lake 2006, 758).

The gap was never absolute, of course. Even after academic economics and political science went their separate ways, a few hardy souls continued to stress connections between the pursuit of wealth and the pursuit of power. This was especially true at the radical fringes—in Marxist or neo-Marxist circles on the Left, where the superstructure of politics was unquestioningly assumed to rest on a foundation defined by the prevailing modes of production; or among laissez-faire liberals or libertarians on the Right, determined to preserve capitalism against the oppressive power of the state. There were also some notable exceptions in the mainstream, such as John Maynard Keynes, who cared deeply about the relationship between markets and politics, or Herbert Feis, whose study of the politics of pre–World War I global finance remains an early classic (1930). Many would also include Karl Polanyi, whose classic treatise on the social foundations of markets, *The Great Transformation* (1944), has proved a lasting source of inspiration for later generations of scholars. For the most part, however, the void only grew deeper with time. References to political economy soon disappeared from polite conversation.

By the mid-twentieth century, the relationship between the two disciplines could best be described as nonexistent, a dialogue of the deaf. Radical perspectives were not entirely extinguished. Especially on the Left, the tradition was preserved in polemics over the allegedly inequitable relations between rich and poor economies. Earlier in the century the issue was framed in terms of "economic imperialism," stirred by the writings of John Hobson, a radical liberal, and such Marxists as Rosa Luxemburg and Rudolph Hilferding—culminating in Vladimir Ilyich Lenin's still widely quoted *Imperialism: The Highest Stage of Capitalism* (1917). Later, following the great wave of decolonization after World War II, debate was recast in various versions of dependency theory, stressing the political underpinnings of economic "underdevelopment" in newly independent states. Though divided on details, dependency theory's many variants were united by the idea that the prospects for development in poor countries (the periphery) were conditioned by a global economy dominated by the rich (the core). Across mainstream academia, though, the frontier dividing economics and political science had become firm and impassable. Scholars working in the separate specialties of international economics and IR simply did not speak to each other.

My own experience as a university student half a century ago was typical. In my one IR course, taken while still an undergraduate, the emphasis was all on the "high politics" of conflict and national security in a dangerous, anarchic world. The policy agenda was preoccupied, not to say obsessed, with the cold war and the threat of nuclear weapons. Foreign economic relations were relegated to the realm of "low politics," not really deserving of serious attention. Conversely, in the several courses on international economics that I sat through, first as an undergraduate and later in pursuit of a PhD, the spotlight was on issues of efficiency and stabilization, with public policy evaluated solely in terms of its implications for consumer welfare. No account was taken of the influence of differing institutional contexts or the political underpinnings of economic relations. The only dimension of power acknowledged was market power, stripped of any connection to interstate politics or issues of war and peace.

The dichotomy was summarized acutely in a seminal article published in 1970 by Strange, a British citizen and one of the most familiar—and beloved—names in IPE. We will hear more about Strange in the next chapter. Her article, as mentioned earlier, was provocatively titled "International Economics and International Relations: A Case of Mutual Neglect," and provocation was what she had in mind. The void between international economics and IR had endured for too long, she declared, leading scholars from both traditions to neglect fundamental changes in the world economy. The dialogue of the deaf should not be allowed to persist. A more modern approach to the study of international economic relations was needed—a new effort at "bridge building" to spotlight the crucial "middle ground" between economic and political analysis. Here, for the first time, was a full and compelling case laid out for a new field of study, a clarion call expressed in the fierce and uncompromising manner that came to be Strange's trademark. The article was for all intents and purposes a manifesto.

To a degree, Strange was pushing against an open door. The impassable frontier between the disciplines had never been without its critics, even in the mainstream of the academic world. In the 1940s, political scientist Klaus Knorr (1947) had lamented the lack of economics in mainstream IR courses, suggesting that new efforts were needed to acquaint students of IR with the chief concepts and methods of inquiry used by economists. Discontent with the dialogue of the deaf was already brewing by the time that Strange spoke out. Here and there, scholars were groping their way toward reconnecting the two realms of inquiry, "reintegrating what had been somewhat arbitrarily split up" (Underhill 2000, 808).

Interestingly, most of these scholars were economists rather than political scientists. An early example was Jacob Viner, who had once been one of Knorr's professors (and obviously left a mark on the younger man's thinking). In a historical study, Viner (1948) sought to explore the relationship between "power" and "plenty" as objectives of foreign policy—a choice of terms foreshadowing Gilpin's "pursuit of wealth" and "pursuit of power." Viner's focus was on the early doctrine of "mercantilism," which dominated European economic thought for much of the seventeenth and eighteenth centuries. Mercantilism, in principle, called for the subordination of economics to the demands of politics. But as Viner demonstrated, how this might actually translate into practice was no simple matter. The relationship between power and plenty was in fact quite complex, and subject to change over time.

Twenty years later Richard Cooper published *The Economics of Interdependence* (1968), highlighting the political challenges posed by the growing interdependence of national economies. Establishing a theme that has echoed through the IPE literature ever since, Cooper drew attention to the inevitable tensions generated by market liberalization in a system of sovereign states. In 1970, the same year as Strange's article, there was *Power and Money*, a short book by Kindleberger (1970). Kindleberger's theme, too, was the growing tension between economic and political activity in an increasingly interdependent world. Basic Books, that same year, also began the Political Economy of International Relations Series, with myself as general editor. And 1971 saw the publication of economist Raymond Vernon's memorable *Sovereignty at Bay*, which heralded the arrival of the multinational corporation as a key political actor on the world's stage.

The period also saw the reissue of a long-neglected study by Albert Hirschman, *National Power and the Structure of Foreign Trade* (1945/1969), now rightly regarded as a classic. Written during World War II, the book highlighted the hidden politics of international trade: how relations of dominance and dependence among states may arise naturally from the asymmetries of foreign commerce, and how import and export policies may be used opportunistically by governments to exert political pressure and leverage. Hirschman's themes too have echoed through the IPE literature ever since.

In a sense, therefore, the new integrated approach that Strange was calling for had already begun to coalesce. Can we date the infant's arrival precisely? Unfortunately, scholarly fields of study don't come equipped with an official birth certificate, listing the time and place of origin. Articles or books start to appear, such as those by Viner and Cooper. At first a scattered few, the contributions eventually multiply until—eureka—we all realize that something new has been discovered. Only in retrospect do we become aware that a birth has taken place. Today all we can say is that by 1970, it was already becoming evident that there was something new under the sun (the pessimism of the Old Testament Ecclesiastes notwithstanding).

Nonetheless, Strange's manifesto deserves a special place in the annals of IPE. Her summons to battle was by no means the sole spark to ignite a renewed interest in the political economy of IR; indeed, appearing in a British journal, the article may not even have been seen at the time by many on the U.S. side of the Atlantic. Yet looking back, we can now appreciate how significant it was. Its publication marked something of a turning point. Never before had the brewing discontent among specialists been so effectively distilled and bottled. Nowhere else had the issue been posed in such concise and focused terms. As such, it is as good a candidate as any to mark the moment of the new field's birth.

A Changing World

What triggered the discontent that Strange captured so effectively? The birth of a new field does not take place in a vacuum. Particularly in the social sciences, intellectual developments tend to be tied to a historical context—to new events and trends that make old ways of thinking inadequate. And so it was with IPE. Fundamental changes were occurring in the world—the "real" world, as we social scientists like to call it (mostly without any sense of irony). Both the politics and economics of global affairs were mutating, calling for new understandings of how thing work and how they might be studied.

Most striking was the remarkable recovery of the European and Japanese economies after the devastation of World War II. By the 1960s, a decisive shift seemed to be taking place in the balance of economic power among industrialized nations. At midcentury, the United States bestrode the world economy like a colossus. But with its growth rate slowing and its balance of payments mired in deficits, the country now looked to be on the brink of decline. Continental Europe and Japan, meanwhile, were roaring back, once again forces to be reckoned with. America's moment of economic dominance—of "hegemony"—appeared just about over (mistakenly, as it turned out, but that's another story). Meanwhile, postwar decolonization had brought new attention to the challenges and dilemmas of economic development. Pressures were mounting for a New International Economic Order that would fundamentally transform the rules governing relations between the wealthy "North" and the poverty-stricken "South."

Behind these changes was a growing interdependence of national economies, as noted by Cooper and Kindleberger, among others. At the end of the Second World War, following years of depression and conflict, links between national economies had reached a nadir. Trade and capital movements were tightly controlled. Insularity was the rule. But then came a gradual liberalization of barriers, particularly among the industrialized democracies, promoted by the liberal policies of the United States and shepherded by the newly created GATT and IMF. Slowly, then with more speed, insularity was replaced by competition, as tariffs declined and currency convertibility was restored. Year by year world trade grew more rapidly than output, bringing greater openness and mutual dependence. And soon financial flows began to accelerate as well with the growth of offshore currency markets—the so-called Eurocurrency markets—from the late 1950s onward. By the end of the 1960s, it was evident that the expansion of international economic networks had reached a critical point. Power now seemed to be slipping from states, limiting their ability to attain critical goals. For governments, markets were becoming a distinct threat, whatever their material benefits.

Following the disastrous experience of the 1930s, when economic warfare was rife, the victorious Allied powers had sought to "depoliticize" international economic relations. The aim had been to control the "mercantilist" temptation to use trade or financial controls to promote national interest at the expense of others. To the extent possible, protectionism—interventionist measures designed to protect national economies from the vicissitudes of international competition—were to be firmly suppressed.

Politics could not be eliminated entirely, of course—certainly not so long as the cold war persisted. How else, for example, could we explain Washington's support of the construction of the Common Market in Europe despite its discrimination against U.S. exports? But the hope was to hold political considerations to an absolute minimum. GATT and the IMF were created to ensure that disputes among states would center largely on technical issues, not broader security concerns. Although trade or monetary negotiations might be tough, even bitter, they would remain at the level of detail. Outside the Soviet bloc, the shared commitment was to a vision of a peaceful and prosperous world economy based on liberal market principles.

In the immediate postwar period, the strategy had worked. Despite challenges, the underlying structure of the system had seemed sound, even immutable. By the 1960s, though, with state power now being threatened, economic peace was becoming increasingly difficult to sustain. Tensions were once again on the rise. By the 1970s they were to multiply exponentially, following the first oil shock in 1973 and the collapse of the Bretton Woods system of pegged exchange rates. A new era of slower growth and higher inflation—"stagflation"—appeared to be upon us. Protectionism, once again, seemed to be on the rise. The world economy could be depoliticized no longer.

The threat to state power, as Cooper insightfully pointed out, was actually threefold. First, growing interdependence was increasing the number and magnitude of potential shocks to national economies—what we could call a *disturbance* effect. Second, interdependence was retarding the achievement of diverse policy objectives, political as well as economic—a *hindrance* effect. And third, it was increasing the risk of mutually damaging competition between national authorities—a *competitive* effect. Such challenges could hardly be dismissed as merely technical, especially not when matters of vital state interest were at stake. Clearly, the salience of international economic relations was rising. No longer, it seemed, could the pursuit of wealth be casually relegated to the realm of low politics.

Conversely, the salience of national security concerns now appeared in abeyance. This was because of a growing détente between the United States and the Soviet Union, the two nuclear superpowers. The cold war had for years held center stage, reaching a dramatic peak in the brinkmanship of the 1962 Cuban missile crisis. But by the late 1960s, despite the distractions of the protracted Vietnam conflict, the competing Western and Soviet blocs seemed to be entering a new era of decreased tensions. Détente did not mean that the high politics of war and peace had suddenly lost all relevance; indeed, in the 1980s the cold war was to intensify once again, as Ronald Reagan declared battle on the "Evil Empire." But for the time being at least, it meant that students of world politics could now safely divert some of their attention elsewhere—for example, to IPE.

INFANCY

Enter Keohane and Nye—two individuals, in the words of their former professor Stanley Hoffmann (1989, 275), "whose character matches their intellectual gifts." Few scholars moved as quickly or effectively to nurture the newborn field in its infancy. Their impact was felt in three ways: through the force of their ideas, through their encouragement of the work of others, and through their role in providing a powerful vehicle, the journal *International Organiza-tion* (IO), to help drive the field's development. In all three respects, the fruits of their early entrepreneurship have proved remarkably durable. Their legacy lives on.

A Collaboration Begins

Consider first their ideas. Neither Keohane nor Nye went into political science with a special interest in political economy; that came later. Nor did they begin to work together as a team until as late as 1969, just prior to the appearance of Strange's manifesto. But their collaboration over the next decade, culminat-ing in the first edition of their landmark volume, *Power and Interdependence* (Keohane and Nye 1977), can fairly be described as foundational. Later, though they remained close and still joined forces on occasion, their careers took divergent paths. Yet the general worldview they articulated in those early years, while still working partners, has endured and remains basic to the dis-course of IPE.

Nye, the older of the two (by four years), entered the PhD program at Har-vard University in 1960 still somewhat unsure of a career direction. After graduating with high honors from Princeton University in 1958, followed by two years at Oxford as a Rhodes Scholar, he arrived in Cambridge, Massachu-setts, thinking that he might perhaps specialize in comparative political devel-opment. His doctoral dissertation, which he completed in 1964, was about regional integration in East Africa. Nye then accepted a junior faculty position at Harvard, which has remained his professional home ever since, apart from the occasional visiting professorship elsewhere along with two extended stints of government service during the presidencies of Jimmy Carter and Bill Clin-ton. It was only after he started teaching that he began to study IR seriously.

In the 1980s, following two years as a deputy to the undersecretary for security assistance, science, and technology in President Carter's Department of State, he and Keohane went their separate ways. Nye's interests gravitated more toward applied policy, where he has made a mark as a public intellectual with such books as *Bound to Lead* (1990), *The Paradox of American Power* (2002), and *Soft Power* (2004b). During the Clinton presidency he returned to Washington, first as chair of the National Intelligence Council and then as the assistant secretary of defense for international security affairs. For each of his three posts in Washington he received distinguished service awards from the U.S. government. Coolly cerebral, yet comfortable in the corridors of power, Nye was once asked why he kept returning to academia after occupying posi-tions of high authority in the nation's capital. "Because I want to understand how policy is made," he replied. The pace of government life, he has written, does "not permit wide reading or detailed contemplation" (Nye 1989, 206). A scholar-statesman needs time and the perspective of distance in order to see things with sufficient clarity.

Keohane, by contrast, preferred to remain firmly planted in the groves of academe after receiving his PhD from Harvard in 1966. His first teaching post was at Swarthmore College, a well-known liberal arts school in Pennsylvania, where he remained until 1973. It was there that he had his first systematic exposure to political economy, in a course that he taught with economist Van Doorn Ooms. Since 1973, Keohane has held faculty positions at some of the highest-ranked universities in the United States, including Duke, Harvard, Princeton, and Stanford. An outstanding scholar of remarkably broad erudition, he has the universal respect of his peers (witness the unanimous vote he received in the private survey reported in my introduction). He has been elected president of both the American Political Science Association (APSA) and the International Studies Association (ISA). Over a career spanning more than a third of a century, Keohane has remained a major force in the ongoing construction of IPE. His contributions are multiple, as will be evident in subsequent chapters.

Twice, Keohane gave up prestigious professorships, once at Stanford and once at Harvard, so that his wife, Nannerl Keohane, could accept attractive academic appointments—first as president of Wellesley College, and later as president of Duke University—while keeping their family together. In that selflessness, some might see an homage to his mother, a public school teacher and political activist whose "moral energy," as Keohane puts it (1989b, 404), made a lasting impression on his personal value system. Others might see a form of tribute to the political theorist Judith Shklar, who Keohane has described as his strongest intellectual mentor during his years of graduate study (Institute of International Studies 2004, 1). Though Shklar was, according to him, the most powerful mind in Harvard's Government Department at the time, she could win no more than an untenured lecturer's position because of discrimination against her as a woman. Today, Keohane is well-known for having mentored some of the most prominent women in IPE, including Lisa Martin, Helen Milner, and Beth Simmons, among others. In 1997, he received the first Mentorship Award from the Society for Women in International Political Economy.

Though not insensitive to the feelings of others, Keohane is a person of strong convictions, which he does not mind sharing openly or even bluntly. Once, a colleague at a conference made an offhand remark that while intended to be humorous, could have been interpreted as a bit sexist. Keohane dressed him down in a manner that left the rest of the conference participants, including myself, temporarily speechless. Another time, I witnessed him serve as a discussant for a research paper presented by a young woman just out of graduate school. Not impressed by her scholarship, Keohane tore her work to shreds, questioning her understanding of basic IR theory. I left the room thinking that

Figure 1.1. Robert Keohane. Photograph by Jon Roemer

the young woman's career was over before it had begun. She had the memorable name of Condoleezza Rice.

Keohane does have a sense of humor. But like the man himself, his wit is refined and just a bit remote. Nothing illustrates that more than the cover of a collection of essays he published not long ago titled *Power and Governance in a Partially Globalized World* (Keohane 2002). Pictured on the cover is a sculpture called *Capricorn* by Max Ernst, featuring a seated king and queen rendered in a Dadaist style not unlike that of early Pablo Picasso when he was most influenced by the primitive art of Africa. The king, a version of the sea god Capricorn, sits imperiously on his throne, holding aloft a scepter; his queen, portrayed as a mermaid, sits demurely at his side. What did this odd regal couple have to do with Keohane's sophisticated ruminations on interdependence and institutions? I wondered when I first picked up the book. But it was not long before I grasped the relevance. Capricorn and his consort were in fact the embodiment of power and governance in a world still far from fully globalized. Keohane had come across the sculpture in a museum in Houston, Texas, while putting the final touches on his essay collection, and had immediately decided to make it the centerpiece of the book's cover. Like a good *New Yorker* cartoon, the joke was calculated, and not obvious. It could hardly have been more clever.

Though Nye and Keohane overlapped as graduate students at Harvard, they did not meet until 1967. Their active collaboration began two years later when they began planning a conference, held in 1970, on new forces in world politics. The resulting collection of papers, which they jointly edited, appeared as a special issue of IO in 1971 and was soon published as an edited volume under the title *Transnational Relations and World Politics* (Keohane and Nye 1972). In their introductory and concluding essays for the collection, as well as in subsequent publications, they began to work out a new conception of the dynamics of international economic relations. A few years onward, these efforts culminated in *Power and Interdependence*, widely hailed as a milestone in the construction of modern IPE. In *Power and Interdependence* they laid out a vision of the world that remains influential to the present day. They even gave their vision a name: "complex interdependence" (Keohane and Nye 1977).

Complex Interdependence

Complex interdependence was defined by three main characteristics: multiple channels of communications, an absence of hierarchy among issues, and a diminished role for military force. The vision was posed as a challenge to the classic state-centric paradigm of world politics that had long dominated the study of IR in the United States. For decades, students of IR theory like themselves had been taught to think as "realists." States were seen as the only significant actors in world politics, conceived for analytic purposes as purposive, rational, and unitary actors. Moreover, states were assumed to be motivated largely by issues of power and security, and to be preoccupied above all with the danger of military conflict. In U.S. scholarly circles, realism ruled.

For Keohane and Nye, the realist paradigm had now become dated. World politics was being transformed. Just look around, they suggested. Who could fail to notice the seeming breakdown of order in the global economy? The government-controlled system of pegged exchange rates established at Bretton Woods had collapsed following America's abandonment of the convertibility of the dollar into gold in 1971. The 1973 oil shock had sharply raised energy prices, bringing stagflation and uncertainty in their wake. Disputes and tensions were on the rise; arguments over everything from tariff policy to the management of the oceans were becoming more and more politicized. For Keohane and Nye, writing in the mid-1970s, the radical change of atmosphere was pivotal. The safe certainties of the earlier postwar period had seemingly vanished into thin air.

The key, they contended, lay in the increasing fragmentation and diffusion of power in economic affairs, stemming from the growing interconnectedness of national economies. As Keohane and Nye said in the opening line of *Power and Interdependence* (1977, 3), "We live in an era of interdependence." States might still be central actors in international affairs, but with the expansion of the global marketplace they could no longer claim sole authority to determine outcomes. The liberalization of trade and finance was widening the range of "transnational" relations, adding new cross-border contacts, coalitions, and interactions beyond those controlled by the foreign policy organs of government. Economic interdependence was spawning a growing swarm of transnational actors—individuals and entities whose control of resources and access to channels of communication enabled them, too, to participate meaningfully in political relationships across state lines. Hence, Keohane and Nye maintained, a new way of thinking was needed: a broader paradigm that would explicitly admit the full panoply of relevant actors. Governments could no longer monopolize analysis. If we really wanted to understand how things work, scholarship would have to catch up with the facts.

The transformation of world politics was not universal, of course. Keohane and Nye did not offer complex interdependence as a fully accurate characterization of the new era of world politics. Rather, it was best understood as an "ideal type" that could be compared with the realist state-centric paradigm in order to highlight what realism had overlooked. The idea was analytic, not descriptive. Much of the real world still exhibited elements emphasized by realist theory. Between the two superpower blocs, for example, security issues continued to dominate the policy agenda despite an evident lessening of tensions after the late 1960s; even in a period of détente, direct economic contacts remained "thin." Nor had the salience of military force declined all that much in a number of other hot spots around the globe, including especially the Middle East as well as parts of Africa and Asia. But at least among the advanced industrial nations of Western Europe, North America, and Japan—encompassing the world's dominant economies—the facts clearly had changed. Economic relations were growing exponentially; the threat of war seemed increasingly remote; and transnational actors were posing an ever-greater challenge to government. Here it was certainly legitimate to speak more of a "zone of complex interdependence," as Keohane later described it (1989a, 9).

The pair's timing was exquisite. According to Harry Johnson (1971), the most important requirement for successful propagation of a new, revolutionary set of ideas is the existence of an established orthodoxy that has clearly grown inconsistent with reality—a dominant paradigm no longer able to account for increasingly recurrent anomalies. For Johnson, once known as "the economist's economist," the orthodoxy he had in mind was Keynesianism, which was then in the process of being dethroned by the monetarism of Milton Friedman and his disciples at the University of Chicago. For Keohane and Nye, the political scientists, the orthodoxy at issue was realism. In a world of accelerating interdependence, the state-centric paradigm was indeed vulnerable to challenge, demonstrably in growing conflict with the facts of everyday experience. At least among the industrial nations, realism had become unrealistic. It also helps, Johnson went on, if the new ideas are genuinely novel yet absorb as much as possible of the valid (or at least not readily disputable) components of existing orthodoxy. This Keohane and Nye accomplished by conceding the still-central role of states even while insisting that governmental authority was being eroded.

Where did their ideas come from? Keohane insists that "in the genealogy of the idea of complex interdependence, Joe should certainly be given top billing. . . . At this time (1972–74), Joe was going to meetings, networking, and picking up impressions. His sense of the contradictions between realism as taught at Harvard then and the complex world of multiple actors and issues that he dealt with in these meetings generated the impetus for our reflections on complex interdependence." But of course it was their *joint* reflections, mostly the result of long conversations at Nye's home in nearby Lexington, that ultimately translated one partner's sense of contradictions into a revolutionary new paradigm. Their collaboration was facilitated by a visiting fellowship that Nye arranged for Keohane at Harvard's Center for International Affairs (CFIA) in 1972. The well-endowed CFIA, thanks to Nye's efforts, had also funded the 1970 conference that resulted in *Transnational Relations and World Politics*.

According to a later recollection (Katzenstein, Keohane, and Krasner 1999b, 15), the transnational paradigm was first inspired by contact with Raymond Vernon, whose *Sovereignty at Bay* was then in its final stages of preparation. Vernon was a colleague of Nye's at the CFIA and was instrumental in encouraging the pair to organize their 1970 conference (Nye 1989, 203). The institutional connection between the two political scientists and the economist was critical. "Without that connection," Keohane suggests, "I am not sure we would have gone down the IPE route." More than a third of the publications cited in the introduction to *Transnational Relations and World Politics* have to do with multinational corporations.

Equally influential was the pioneering work on regional integration by political scientists Karl Deutsch (1957) and Ernst Haas (1958), inspired by developments in postwar Europe that highlighted the role of voluntary agreements among states and the possibility of multiple actors in world politics. An extrapolation from integration studies to the notion of interdependence came quite easily for Nye, whose dissertation on East African integration had been published in 1965. As Nye wrote later (1989, 203), "I felt that many of the insights from regional integration theory were applicable to the broader dimensions of international economic interdependence that were becoming more prominent." His and Keohane's debt to Deutsch and Haas was explicitly acknowledged in a paper published in 1975 (Keohane and Nye 1975).

Major debts were also owed to the economists Cooper and Hirschman. Following Cooper's lead, Keohane and Nye stressed the tightening constraints that interdependence was imposing on the policy autonomy of states—the widening "control gap," as they put it, between state aspirations and state capabilities. Following Hirschman, they laid emphasis as well on the concept of asymmetrical interdependence as a basic power resource.

Looking back later, Keohane and Nye (1987) expressed a degree of modesty over what they had wrought. Their goal, they claimed, simply had been to provide an alternative "ideal type" for analytic purposes. Their intent was not to discredit realism but rather to supplement it. In their words, "We regarded the two as necessary complements to one another. . . . The key point was not that interdependence made power obsolete—far from it—but that patterns of interdependence and patterns of potential power resources in a given issue-area are closely related—indeed, two sides of a single coin" (728, 730). The concept of complex interdependence itself, they insisted, was "underdeveloped" (733). "We did not pursue complex interdependence as a theory, but as a thought experiment about what politics might look like if the basic assumptions of realism were reversed. We therefore did not draw upon . . . theory as fully as we might have" (737).

Their modesty, however, is misplaced. It is true that realism was not discredited. Complex interdependence was indeed best conceived as a complement to realism, not a substitute. It is also true that the new paradigm failed to make the grade as a formal theory. A theory is best defined as a set of general statements combining the features of logical truth and predictive accuracy. Logical truth means that some of the statements (the assumptions or premises) logically imply the other statements (the theorems). Predictive accuracy means that the statements can be cast in the form of falsifiable predictive statements about the real world. Clearly, complex interdependence did neither. It could not be used directly to explain state behavior or bargaining outcomes.

Yet the accomplishment was undeniable. In ontological terms, the idea broke new ground. Here was a wholly different alternative to IR's then-prevailing paradigm—a fresh vision of the world that contrasted sharply with the realist model of unitary states single-mindedly preoccupied with the high politics of war and peace. Here was real value added. Keohane and Nye made us look at the world anew. In so doing, they facilitated the birth of a new field of study.

Today we take for granted that interdependence in the world economy can be analyzed in political terms, not just as an economic phenomenon. We also take for granted that we can examine patterns of interdependence by separate issue areas. We do so because, implicitly or explicitly, we all now share the ontology bequeathed to us by Keohane and Nye—a sense that the three characteristics of complex interdependence define the essential nature of the present-day international system. Without this intersubjective understanding, systematic study of the low politics of trade and finance would have been more difficult, if not impossible. With it, we have a whole new insight into how things work. The term complex interdependence itself may no longer be particularly fashionable in the IPE literature. Many scholars have forgotten it completely. But the weltanschauung it represents is now undeniably a part of the collective unconscious of the field.

Three Models of the Future

Keohane and Nye also made a lasting impact through their encouragement of the work of other scholars, largely via collective research projects that they were instrumental in organizing. Their first such undertaking was, of course, *Transnational Relations and World Politics.* A second special issue of IO came four years later, following two conferences of authors in Massachusetts and Washington, DC (in which I was privileged to participate as a discussant). That special issue, too, was subsequently published in book form, under the title *World Politics and International Economics* (Bergsten and Krause 1975). Keohane and Nye helped to conceive the second project and served, together with the issue's coeditors, on an informal steering group charged with bringing it to fruition. Together with one of the coeditors, the pair also wrote the project's introductory chapter laying out a basic framework for analysis. Even after he and Nye subsequently went their separate ways, Keohane for his part continued to play a major role in yet more such joint efforts, some of which (as we shall see) have achieved landmark status of their own in the field's history.

One great advantage of collective efforts of this kind is the part they can play in framing a program for research. Certainly that was the case with those two projects in the 1970s, which between them provided a compelling set of signposts for the next generation of scholars. The first project, *Transnational Relations and World Politics*, was subsequently described as "chiefly a pointing exercise that made clear how much interesting activity had escaped the attention of analysts" (Katzenstein, Keohane, and Krasner 1999b, 16). The second, according to Keohane, "put political economy on the agenda" (Institute of International Studies 2004, 3).

Another great advantage is the debate such efforts can stimulate among the participants, which in turn aids in identifying critical problems and clarifying issues. That too was the case with those two projects in the 1970s. Most notable was a running debate through both projects between Keohane and Nye, on the one side, and their good friend Gilpin, on the other—a debate that did much to refine thinking about interdependence and its consequences. Keohane and Nye promoted their new vision of complex interdependence. Gilpin became the chief defender of the older realist tradition—"the dean of realist international political economy in the United States," as one source puts it (Murphy 2000, 798).

Realism came easily to Gilpin, who served four years as an officer in the U.S. Navy before going on to complete a doctorate at the University of California at Berkeley in 1960. Gilpin's earliest scholarly publications (1962, 1968), on nuclear weapons policy, were focused entirely on the high politics of conflict and national security. At Princeton University's Woodrow Wilson School of Public and International Affairs, where he taught from 1962 until his retirement in 1998, Gilpin says he was considered "the last of the Cold Warriors" (*International Relations* 2005, 368). But his was not a doctrinaire realism, rigidly closed to alternative perspectives. For him, realism represented a philosophical view of society and politics—one way, among many, of looking at the world—not a definitive portrayal of reality. His own preferred label was "soft realist" (361). Though Gilpin took a certain amount of pride in being the sole Republican on the Woodrow Wilson School faculty, he was always quick to add that he was a "Vermont Republican," not the more doctrinaire Goldwater-Reagan type.

At the outset of his scholarly career, Gilpin had no more interest in political economy than did Keohane or Nye when they were getting started. Yet like his two friends, he couldn't help but notice the seeming breakdown of order in economic affairs, which appeared to challenge inherited presumptions. For him, too, the radical change of atmosphere was pivotal. His early work on nuclear weapons policy, which had highlighted the links between technological development and world politics, provided a natural segue into a new set of issues.

Driven by an intense curiosity, Gilpin began to read the work of Cooper, Strange, and Vernon, all of whom, he acknowledges, were major influences on his thinking (*International Relations* 2005, 367). He also began to teach himself the low politics of economics in order to better understand the implications of interdependence. In this pursuit, he showed all the best characteristics of a true intellectual: an open mind, a keen devotion to learning, and an admirable dedication to craft. Throughout his career, Gilpin had little interest in seeking fame and fortune as an academic superstar, though that might well have been within his grasp. A modest person, self-effacing and even a bit shy, he just wanted to *understand*.

Gilpin had no hesitation in seeking help from his colleagues. Until 1971, I taught alongside him at the Woodrow Wilson School and can remember many an occasion when he would wander into my office to ask a question about some fine point of economic analysis. Usually the question had been scribbled down on a small notepad that he carried with him to record thoughts in situ. Even after I moved on to another university, our private seminars continued at

Figure 1.2. Robert Gilpin. Courtesy of Princeton University Press

long distance, as Gilpin he noted (1975b), with characteristic graciousness, in the preface to *U.S. Power and the Multinational Corporation*. It wasn't long before he was ready to take on the issues raised in *Transnational Relations and World Politics*.

The emergence of transnationalism, he acknowledged, could not be denied. But that didn't mean that realist theory had thus become obsolete; quite the contrary, in fact. In insisting that a transformation was occurring in world politics, Gilpin argued, Keohane and Nye were guilty of hyperbole. Transnationalism could only be understood within the context of the traditional state system, dating back to the Peace of Westphalia of 1648. For the former naval officer, states were still the primary actors on the world stage and security interests remained the key determinants of economic relations. In Gilpin's words (1972, 54), "Politics determines the framework of economic activity and channels it in directions which tend to serve . . . political objectives." Where Keohane and Nye went astray, he felt, was in failing to recognize the extent to which transnational actors and processes ultimately remain fundamentally dependent on the pattern of interstate relations. "Bob was crucial in pointing out that markets rest on political decisions," a colleague has written me about Gilpin. "Others have made this point about domestic markets, but Bob said it best about the international economy."

At issue was the nature of the underlying connection between economic and political activity, an age-old question that had long divided scholars of political economy. Does economics drive politics, or vice versa? Three schools of thought could be identified, Gilpin suggested, all drawn from traditional IR theory—liberalism, Marxism, and realism—each offering students of IPE its own distinct "model of the future." Liberals and Marxists shared a belief that economics was bound to dominate politics, though of course they differed enormously on whether this was a good or bad thing. By contrast, realists retained faith in the power of political relations to shape economic systems. Keohane and Nye, with their paradigm of complex interdependence, could be understood as the latest heirs of liberalism; their approach, widely seen as a new variation on an old theme, was soon given the label "neoliberal institutionalism." Emphasizing the pair's early Harvard connections, one source called it simply the "Harvard school of liberal international theory" (Long 1995). I will have more to say about neoliberal institutionalism in chapter 4. Gilpin himself, of course, was a barely reconstructed realist.

In *World Politics and International Economics* as well as *U.S. Power and the Multinational Corporation*, published the same year (Gilpin 1975a, 1975b), he sought to respond to the new concept of transnationalism by carefully spelling out the strengths and weaknesses of each of the three approaches. Gilpin's aim was to facilitate clearer and more consistent theorizing about the implications of interdependence. But in so doing, he also happened to provide a convenient template for future scholarship—an "intellectual edifice," as one friend describes it in private correspondence—that stands as perhaps his most lasting contribution to the construction of the infant field.

In IPE textbooks today, Gilpin's three "models"—also referred to as paradigms or perspectives—are still regarded as the logical starting point for most serious discussion, even if then amended or combined in various ways. Few sources even bother any more to credit Gilpin for the taxonomy. Like the notion of complex interdependence, this classification has simply become an unexamined part of every specialist's toolkit. Even fewer sources credit Keohane and Nye for their role in animating the projects that prompted Gilpin's creative thinking.

International Organization

Finally, Keohane and Nye deserve recognition for their leadership in building a solid launching pad for the new field. That was the journal IO, which has long been recognized as the premier platform for the publication of IPE scholarship in the United States. The U.S. version of the field, as one source observes, "has been centered in IO since 1971" (Katzenstein, Keohane, and Krasner 1999b, 5). According to another, the American school might just as well be called the "IO school" (Murphy and Nelson 2001). Keohane and Nye played a critical role in establishing IO as a core venue for IPE's pioneer generation.

Disseminating innovative ideas in the academic world is not easy, given the importance of peer review in determining what gets into print and what does not. Editorial boards instinctively tend to favor submissions that run along familiar lines. Anything out of the ordinary—such as an effort to marry traditionally separate disciplines—is bound to encounter skepticism, if not outright hostility. Back in the early 1970s, therefore, there was no guarantee that any of this newfangled hybrid work, no matter how well packaged, would ever see the light of day. A publishing outlet was needed, and that is what IO provided. Without the journal, the infant field in the United States might well have ended up stillborn.

Not that nursing an infant field of study was IO's original intent. The journal was founded in 1947 by the World Peace Foundation, a Boston-based philanthropic institution that itself dated back to 1910. The journal's first mandate was implied by its name—to focus on the new international organizations that had been set up at the end of World War II. These included the full range of agencies established under the aegis of the United Nations, not just economic institutions like the IMF and GATT. The idea was to promote a comparative study of international organizations and how they worked in practical terms. For more than two decades, that is just what the journal did. Most articles published in IO in the 1950s and 1960s emphasized applied policy analysis or commentary; substantial space was also devoted to detailed summaries of the activities of various UN bodies. Little of the work was informed by general social science theory. In the words of a later survey, there was no "theoretical hook . . . no conceptual framework that could tie these insights together" (Martin and Simmons 1999, 92–93).

But then the journal was effectively taken over by Keohane and Nye, who along with several other younger scholars were invited to join the board of editors in 1968. It might have been, as Nye avers (1989, 202), a "serendipitous event." Yet it was also a turning point. As Keohane has written (1989b, 408), "The established members of that board may well have been dismayed by the consequences of their decision, because their new colleagues proceeded within five or six years totally to reconstitute the board." By 1972, Nye had become chair of the board; by 1974, Keohane had become the journal's editor, a position he was to hold for six years.

Almost immediately, the pair engineered a shift of emphasis in editorial policy. Attending a conference in early 1969 on U.S. foreign policy and international organizations, which was intended for a special issue of IO (Finkelstein 1969), the two were appalled by the atheoretical content of most of the papers—"old thinking par excellence," in Keohane's biting words. The journal's traditional approach, they argued, needed a new orientation: toward the study of world politics in general and a more systematic analysis of political behavior in particular. When invited to demonstrate what they meant, they responded with the collective project that became *Transnational Relations and World Politics*, soon to be followed by other initiatives. The intent of their first special issue, Nye later explained, was to escape from the journal's "dull" preoccupation with roll call votes and other institutional trivia. The idea was to "put the horse back in front of the wagon by first describing patterns of interaction in world politics and then asking what role international institutions do or should play" (Nye 1989, 202).

Keohane was especially cognizant of the opportunity that IO presented. As he later remarked in an interview (Institute of International Studies 2004, 3):

> The advantage of being a journal editor is that you're at the center of the process. You see it and you can shape it, to some extent. In my first issue I wrote an editor's essay called "*International Organization* and the Crisis of Interdependence," where I made a claim (and this was in 1974 or 1975, right after the oil crisis) that there was a crisis going on of interdependence, that growth had slowed down or stopped in the West. There was a general sense that we had to restructure the system after Bretton Woods collapsed, and so it was a moment when it was clear that people needed to think politically about the world economy, because it wasn't automatically taking care of itself. I was in the right place at the right time.

By the mid-1970s, IO was firmly established as the flagship of the growing fleet of IPE scholars in the United States. In the years since, it has been consistently ranked as among the most influential of political science journals (Crewe and Norris 1991; Nisonger 1993; Garand and Giles 2003). A survey of U.S. political scientists in 2003 placed IO fifth among all journals in the discipline and, by a wide margin, first among specialists in IR (Garand and Giles 2003). Researchers in the U.S. tradition still look to IO first for the latest developments in IPE scholarship.

CUSTODY

Against the odds, then, the newborn field not only survived but flourished, as the healthy offspring of a marriage of two disciplines. But the liaison was a limited one, a narrow *mariage de convenance* of the two subspecialties of international economics and IR. On a broader scale, the two parent disciplines remained divorced—still firmly separated in terms of orientation and formal academic organization. So who would take custody?

In principle, both parents might have played a role in shaping the infant interdiscipline's development. In practice, however, economists effectively abdicated after the baby's birth, leaving custody to the political scientists. Despite the fact that much of the earliest work in the field was actually done by economists—the likes of Hirschman, Viner, Cooper, and Kindleberger—IPE to this day remains a peripheral interest in most economics departments.

While in the minority, some economists do pursue something that they call political economy, applying the tools of economic analysis to the study of public policy. Many, such as Thomas Willett (1988; Willett and Vaubel 1991), follow the early lead of the Swiss economist Bruno Frey (1984), emphasizing so-called public choice theory. But little of this work makes a serious attempt to incorporate the insights or intuitions of political science. With its methodological individualism, focusing on the individual as the basic unit of analysis, along with its stress on formal modeling, the oeuvre of most economists amounts to little more than an application of traditional economic theory to decision making in the political arena. It might best be labeled the microeconomics of IR. It can hardly be described as a genuine merger of disciplines.

As IPE has grown in the United States, political science, rather than economics, clearly has been the major influence. In no small measure, this was due to the determined entrepreneurship of Keohane and Nye. From the start these two, along with Gilpin and others, moved to claim "ownership" of IPE, raising the newborn as a branch of their own discipline. IPE, even while absorbing elements of economics theory and methodology, seemed a natural extension of IR. As one colleague privately suggested to me, Keohane and Nye "opened the door for scholars with an IR framework to think systematically about international economic relations."

Soon every self-respecting political science department began to reserve a faculty slot or two for specialists. Every political science curriculum began to feature one, if not several, IPE courses. Textbooks in the field—once a trickle, now a veritable flood—were targeted directly at students of political science. By the turn of the twenty-first century, in the words of Helen Milner (2002b, 207), IPE had become "an established part of international relations." Echoing this, Lisa Martin notes (2002, 245), IPE's "questions, methods, and theories were drawn from the study of international relations, not from economics. . . . IPE was seen as fitting into the mold defined by IR."

Why didn't economists fight harder for custody? Had they done so, the field might have followed a different trajectory—addressing different questions, and offering different answers. The basics might have been defined in another manner altogether. But despite the dramatic changes then occurring in the international environment, the mainstream of the economics profession remained largely indifferent. The reasons were threefold: ideological, ontological, and epistemological.

First, there was the chilling effect of postwar anticommunism. Political economy tended to be equated unthinkingly with Marxism or other unacceptable leftist doctrines. By the late 1960s détente was melting the ice of the cold war, reducing tensions between the nuclear superpowers. Even so, the battle to defend the market system went on—a battle in which economists inevitably found themselves on the front lines. Political scientists might be called on to defend the virtues of democracy, but not capitalism. Economists, on the other hand, could not avoid being drawn into the ongoing contest between Marxism and market liberalism. Few U.S. economists at the time had much taste for ideas or arguments that might smack of an anticapitalist sentiment. In any attempt to reunify the economic and political orders, most of the profession saw ideological bias.

The impression was understandable. Marxists, after all, had been among the most prominent of the hardy souls who continued to promote political economy after the split between economics and political science in the nineteenth century. In the United States, during the first decades after World War II, almost all work on international political economy had come from leftist economists associated with the Marxist journal *Monthly Review* and its book publishing arm, Monthly Review Press. Most focused on dependency theory, emphasizing the uneven development and inequalities of the world capitalist system. A prime example was Harry Magdoff's *The Age of Imperialism* (1969), which claimed to find in America's postwar economic hegemony a new form of empire: an updated version of classic colonial imperialism, driven by the imperatives of capitalism and the interests of multinational corporations. Other examples included Andre Gunder Frank's *Capitalism and Underdevelopment in Latin America* (1967), which popularized the notion of the "development of underdevelopment," and Arghiri Emmanuel's *Unequal Exchange* (1972; first published in France in 1969), which turned traditional trade theory on its head, claiming to find capitalist exploitation where others saw mutual gain. The very idea of political economy seemed tainted by socialist sympathies.

That didn't stop a vocal group of younger economists, who in 1968 formed the new Union for Radical Political Economics (URPE). URPE's origins lay in the New Left politics of the turbulent 1960s, driven especially by a revulsion with the war in Vietnam, which many felt simply confirmed the imperialist

nature of U.S. foreign policy. The group's aim was to promote a new interdisciplinary approach to political economy, a fresh look at the connections between
economics and politics. Like Keohane and Nye, URPE even provided a publishing outlet, the *Review of Radical Political Economics*, to showcase its members'
work. But in tying its aspirations to the social movements of the day, URPE
merely served to reinforce the impression of ideological bias. According to the
group's Web site (www.urpe.org), URPE "presents constructive critical analyses of the capitalist system and supports debate and discussion on alternative
left visions of a socialist society." At the time, rhetoric like that was more than
enough to persuade mainstream U.S. economists to keep a safe distance.

Second was a kind of intellectual myopia in the prevailing ontology of economics. The new discipline that emerged after the marginalist revolution of
the 1870s preferred to concentrate on the private sphere, mainly addressing
considerations of technical efficiency and economic welfare. Economists were
simply not trained to think in terms of the public sphere—the issues of authority and conflict that are inherent in processes of governmental decision making.
Nor were they comfortable when confronted with the very political question
of distribution—how the economic pie gets divvied up.

This created two blind spots. First, the importance of institutions was discounted. In the "timeless" analytic framework favored by the mainstream of
the profession, political structures, if considered at all, were introduced only
as a constraint on economic activity, with underlying power relationships being
taken more or less for granted. Neoclassical economics discouraged any interest in questions concerning how rules or norms are created, or how over time
they might support or undermine different patterns of economic activity. Second, attention was directed to the outcomes of policy rather than to its inputs.
The aim of theory was to *evaluate* policy, not *explain* its origins in the give-
and-take of distributional conflict. An old adage has it that politics is like
sausage making: you really don't want to know what goes into it. Neoclassical
economics took that advice seriously.

There have always been exceptions, of course. For example, in an earlier
era the study of institutions actually enjoyed a place of some prominence in
the economics discipline, promoted by the likes of Thorstein Veblen and
John Rogers Commons. A high point was reached with the publication in 1934
of Commons's *Institutional Economics*. But by the 1960s, the mainstream of
the profession had taken a quite different tack, preferring instead to focus
narrowly on the direct links between opportunities and behavior, leaving
little room for the influence of alternative institutional settings. It was only in
the 1980s—with the work of inter alia Douglass North (1981), Ronald
Coase (1984), and Oliver Williamson (1985)—that economists once again
began to think seriously about the significance of organizational variety and
path-dependent historical processes on actor behavior. Known as the "New
Institutional Economics" or the "New Institutionalism," the movement stressed

the role of institutions as devices to lower transactions costs and protect property rights.

By contrast, resistance to looking into the process of sausage making has always been strong. To this day, few mainstream economists show much interest in seriously exploring the connection of policy to the dirty game of politics. John Odell, who edited IO from 1992 to1996, tells a story about a conference paper he once presented analyzing why, at the time of the breakdown of the Bretton Woods currency system in the early 1970s, there had been no negotiated agreement to restore pegged exchange rates. Included in the paper was some counterfactual reasoning about how such an agreement might have been attained and how it might have worked. For this approach he was sharply criticized by his paper's discussant, an economist, who devoted his time to explaining why floating exchange rates were actually to be preferred to a pegged-rate regime. Continues Odell: "In the room was one Bob Keohane, who complained impatiently that the discussant was not reading carefully, that Odell was not engaging in that debate but trying to *explain* a political outcome." When IPE was getting started, mainstream economists naturally resisted modes of thought that might sully pure analysis with the stain of scruffy bargaining or political compromise.

Finally, there was resistance to IPE on epistemological grounds. Mainstream economists also were understandably hesitant to take up issues that could not be addressed comfortably using the standard toolkit of neoclassical economics. For a century, especially in the United States, the discipline had been growing increasingly abstract, relying ever more on deductive logic and parsimonious theoretical models to pare messy reality down to its bare essentials. The style was reductionist. The aim was to uncover core relationships—"to predict something large from something small," as Johnson put it (1971, 9).

In the postwar period, Paul Samuelson, one of the first Nobel laureates in economics, set the standard. With his seminal *Foundations of Economic Analysis* (1947), Samuelson sparked a new emphasis on the use of high-powered mathematics in economic analysis. A few lone voices held out for more inclusive approaches that might more closely approximate the complexities of life as it was actually lived. Perhaps most prominent was Harvard's John Kenneth Galbraith, who deplored what he called the "willful denial of the presence of power and political interests" (quoted in *Economist* 2006). But Galbraith and his like were drowned out by the clamor for ever-greater numeracy and abstraction in the formulation of economic theory.

Theorists of every stripe face a fundamental trade-off between parsimony and detail—between the deductive simplicity required for theoretical generalization and the inductive description required to assure external validity. Mainstream economists favor deductive simplicity, showing little interest in Galbraithian-style complexity. Galbraith himself published more than forty books during his lifetime, making him one of the most widely read authors in the history of economics. He held a variety of public offices and was consulted frequently by national leaders (Parker 2005). Yet for all his professional achievements, he is barely remembered today by any economist born since World War II. In the words of the *Economist* (2006), noting his death in April 2006 at the age of ninety-seven, Galbraith's "contributions to economics are underappreciated by a profession obsessed with mathematical formulae."

In effect, mainstream economics presumes that social phenomena are amenable to scientific explanation in essentially the same manner as are natural phenomena. Hence, the same principles of positivism and empiricism that are employed to isolate causal mechanisms in the physical sciences can be applied to the study of social relations as well. Universal truths are out there, just waiting to be discovered. Galbraith labeled the approach "imitative scientism"—a replication of the methods of the natural sciences that "is carried further in economics than in any other [social science] discipline" (1970, 8). The highest rank in what Galbraith called the "prestige system of economics" goes to those who best mimic the reductionist epistemology of the physical sciences.

To achieve deductive simplicity, strong assumptions must be tolerated or even encouraged as an integral part of reasoning. Parsimony demands that the largest range of phenomena be explained with the smallest number of premises. The more "heroic" the assumptions, the better. This may make economists the butt of humor, such as in the old joke about a can opener. (A case of canned goods washes up on a desert island, where the survivors of a shipwreck are stranded. They wonder how to open the cans. "No problem," says the economist. "Assume a can opener.") But it has also enabled them to derive theorems and predictions that are scrupulously fine-tuned. Imprecision, to the extent possible, is banished from discourse.

In this context, political economy seemed to fit like a square peg in a round hole. How was formal analysis to account for the uncertainties of the political process? How could theory model the exigencies of war and peace? How could existing empirical methods cope with seemingly vague notions like power or dependency? Questions like these ran against the grain of the discipline's methodological standards. Thus mainstream economists could be excused for demurring. As one economist colleague said to me back when IPE was first getting started, "If I can't quantify it, I'm not interested." His remark was only partially in jest.

AN IRONY

Yet in the end, who is to say which of the parent disciplines has really taken custody of IPE in the United States? There is a deeper irony here. As the epistemology of the American school has become increasingly standardized, it has come to resemble nothing so much as the methodology of neoclassical economics, featuring the same penchant for positivist analysis, formal modeling, and where possible, the systematic collection and evaluation of empirical data. More and more, what gets published features the same sorts of mathematical and statistical techniques that we have come to expect in economics journals.

Why is this? Puzzling over the trend, which has been evident for years, the economist Vernon once suggested that it might have something to do with the deceptive accessibility of a reductionist style. "The ideas that appear to travel most easily between the social sciences are the simpler, more inclusive ideas; and when gauged by the criteria of simplicity and inclusiveness, neoclassical propositions have had a decisive edge" (Vernon 1989, 443). But there may also be an element of envy involved. Political scientists have an inferiority complex when it comes to economics. Even such notables as Katzenstein, Keohane, and Krasner—three of the Magnificent Seven—bow their heads, describing economics as "the reigning king of the social sciences" (1999b, 23). Whether the title is deserved or not, it is certainly true that the "imitative scientism" of economics now appears to set the standard for what passes for professionalism among social scientists in the United States. If today the most highly rated work in the American school tends to mimic the economist's demanding hard science model, it may simply be to demonstrate that the still-young field, for all the uncertainties of the political process, is no less capable of formal rigor. Specialists in IPE want respect too.

The trend is easily observable. For illustrative purposes, we may consider how much change has occurred in the pages of IO since the Keohane-Nye takeover in the early 1970s. Among the total of some 170 articles that appeared in 1975–1979, less than 10 percent (9.4 percent) emphasized formal modeling or econometrics. During the next half decade, 1980–1984, the percentage was even lower, at 7.4 percent. By the second half of the 1990s, by contrast, in 1995–1999, the percentage was up to nearly 26 percent, and in the first five years of the new millennium, 2000–2004, it was almost half (47.5 percent). A simple Pearson correlation shows the trend over the entire thirty-year period to be statistically significant at the 1 percent level—a result that can hardly be dismissed as chance.

In fact, the trend may be considered official editorial policy. In 1998, a special issue of IO was published to celebrate the journal's fiftieth anniversary, appearing a year later in book form (Katzenstein, Keohane, and Krasner 1999a). Although all but one of the collection's seventeen authors were political scientists, the final word was given to a respected economist, Barry Eichengreen, who seized the occasion to celebrate the superiority of economic methodology. "The strength of economics," Eichengreen argued (1999, 354), "is the complementary and mutually supporting character of theoretical and empirical work." IPE could only benefit by going the same route. As he concluded enthusiastically in the collection's last pages, "The field needs to move in the direction of formulating parsimonious models and clearly refutable null hypotheses, and toward developing empirical techniques that will allow these hypotheses to be more directly confirmed by the data" (372).

An enthusiasm for the methodology of economics is understandable, offering as it does both technical sophistication and intellectual elegance. Who wouldn't like to be able to predict something large from something small? But it is also undeniable that reductionism comes at a price in terms of descriptive reality and practical credibility. On the one hand, the full flavor of life is sacrificed for what one critic calls a "tasteless pottage of mathematical models" (DeLong 2005, 128), often wholly unintelligible to a wider public. On the other hand, the true character of life is often caricatured by the implausible assumptions that parsimony demands. The increasing standardization of IPE methods in the United States is by no means costless.

Once upon a time, it was possible to joke about the epistemological differences between economics and political science. A political scientist, one quip had it, was someone who thought that the plural for anecdote was data. The economist, by contrast, was someone who might not be able to remember your phone number but was willing to estimate it for you. Today, however, it is clear those differences between the disciplines are rapidly disappearing. Political scientists may feel they still own IPE, and so they do in terms of the research agenda. But in terms of methodology—*how* things are studied—in practice the dominant role seems to be circling back to economics, along the lines urged by Eichengreen. The trend might be described as a kind of "creeping economism." Economists, it would appear, may have the last laugh.

Chapter 2

THE BRITISH SCHOOL

Question authority.
—Susan Strange

THERE WAS NOTHING inevitable about the way that IPE was constructed in the United States. Had economists fought harder for custody, the infant field might have developed a different sense of priorities. Had Nye and Keohane not produced their vision of complex interdependence, others might have seized the moment to promote another paradigm altogether. The ontology and epistemology that the American school takes for granted are the product of a particular confluence of place and personality, historical circumstance and individual action. Given a different cast of characters or a different location, the outcome might have been something else entirely. For a case in point, consider the British school.

In Britain as well as elsewhere in the former British Empire, the field has diverged sharply from the U.S. model, giving rise to what has been dubbed the British school (Murphy and Nelson 2001). Here too as in the previous chapter, the notion of a school is used loosely to denote a shared understanding of broad basics rather than a narrower agreement on specific goals or agenda. In the British style, scholars work from a distinctively different vision of how the world works and how it should be evaluated. The study of IPE generally tends to be more multidisciplinary in scope and more normative in ambition, more critical of established orthodoxies and more engaged with social issues, more impatient with the status quo and more eager to change attitudes or practices. The British school's worldview is anything but dispassionate. Likewise, its methods are anything but reductionist. As compared with the U.S. style, scholarship tends to be more qualitative than quantitative, attaching less importance to the systematic analysis of hard empirical evidence. Work is typically more interpretative in tone, and harking back to the traditions of classical political economy, more institutional and historical in nature. Scientific method is valued less. A broad comprehension of "society"—the social context of IPE—is valued more.

Many factors help to account for these differences. Above all looms the towering figure of Strange, another intellectual entrepreneur par excellence. Among American school scholars, Strange's influence has been limited. But in her own country her impact was immense. What Keohane and Nye managed to do to get the field started in the United States, Strange did in Britain, shaping an approach that quickly became as distinctive in style as in substance. Her legacy also has proved incredibly durable. In the words of one obituary published after her untimely death in 1998, it was "a remarkable legacy that few can match. . . . Her impact is hard to overestimate" (Sen 1998).

GETTING STARTED

It all began with her memorable manifesto, "International Economics and International Relations: A Case of Mutual Neglect" (Strange 1970). Characteristically, Strange did not just sit back to wait for others to heed her call to arms. If a more modern approach was needed, she might as well get it started. So that is precisely what she proceeded to do. Over the next three decades she went on to produce a series of IPE classics, from *Sterling and British Policy* (1971) and *Casino Capitalism* (1986) to her final two works before her death, *The Retreat of the State* (1996) and *Mad Money* (1998a). Like Keohane and Nye across the Atlantic—on the other side of the pond, as the saying goes— she also made an impact through her encouragement of the work of others and her role in providing a vehicle to help drive the field's development. The study of IPE in Britain today clearly bears the stamp of her powerful personality.

"I Never Meant to Be an Academic"

"I never meant to be an academic," Strange once confessed (1989, 429). "If I had had the chance . . . I would have dearly liked to be an independent newspaper columnist." The admission is telling. When we think of a newspaper columnist, we think of someone who is both perceptive and articulate: whose interests are practical rather than abstract; whose style is informal, not formal; and whose ideas are eclectic, unbounded by the limits of established disciplines. We read columnists for their opinions, not for weighty analysis. We value them for their insight, not their methodology. In short, we look for a shrewd observer, not a disciplined theoretician. Even in her most serious work, Strange exhibited all the best traits of a columnist—and those traits, in turn, became a standard for all who followed her.

Her formal university education was limited, terminating with an undergraduate degree in economics from the London School of Economics (LSE) in 1943. With a war on and a newborn baby to care for, graduate school seemed out of the question. So she opted instead for journalism, taking a job with the *Economist* and later with the *Observer* as the youngest White House correspondent of her time. This of course helps to explain her ambition, which was never realized, to don the mantle of a columnist. It also explains the distinctive style

Figure 2.1. Susan Strange. Courtesy of The London School of Economics and Political Science

of her writing, which was always direct, clear, and admirably free of jargon. She knew how to communicate.

Strange's first academic position did not come until 1949, when she began lecturing on IR at University College London. Her intention, Strange later related (1989, 432), was to "stick to it for a couple of years and use it as a learning device to broaden my reading and deepen my understanding." But she ended up staying for a decade and a half, attracted by the opportunities that academia offered to speak her own mind. "I was increasingly impatient of The Establishment and all it stood for. . . . Academic life at least gave the freedom to teach and write independently" (432). A university position also made it easier for her to raise the two children from her first marriage and then four more from her second.

Political economy began to enter the picture in 1964 when Strange moved to the Royal Institute of International Affairs, commonly called Chatham House (after the building in central London where the institute is housed). Appointed a research fellow, she was asked to write something on the travails of the pound sterling, Britain's crisis-ridden currency—a project that culminated seven years later with her landmark *Sterling and British Policy*, which firmly established the political sources and consequences of international currency use. "The connections between power, influence, the reserve currency role, and the national economy were an enticing subject," she recalled, "and there was very little that was political written about it" (433). The politics of international monetary relations soon became her specialty and remained at the heart of her intellectual interests even after her return in 1978 to her alma mater, LSE, as a tenured professor.

Once started on her project at Chatham House, she adopted the cause of IPE with a missionary zeal. I received my personal baptism in 1968, when I arrived in London intending to write a book of my own on sterling (Cohen 1971). If you're going to research the pound, I was told, you should meet Strange. So I sought her out. When we got together, I dutifully told her about my plan to do a strictly economic cost-benefit analysis of sterling's role as an international currency. "Oh, Jerry," she replied, squinting at me through hooded eyes, "you can't possibly write about the pound without talking about the politics, too"— a remonstration that she would subsequently repeat on every possible occasion. At the time I resisted, with a stubbornness born of my orthodox economics training. The loss was mine: her book turned out to be far more interesting. But ultimately her message did get through. By the time I got back to the United States, I was determined—thanks in good part to her—to dip my toe into this new current of IPE.

Taking Action

Strange's first initiative, following her "Mutual Neglect" manifesto, was to create an institutional vehicle to help promote the more modern approach she was calling for. In her case the vehicle was not a journal, though she did later have a hand in the genesis of the *Review of International Political Economy* (RIPE). The first issue of RIPE appeared in 1994. For the British school, RIPE quickly became as indispensable an outlet for IPE scholarship as IO had long been for the American school. Strange's first contribution, however, was an organized research network, the International Political Economy Group (IPEG), which she set up under the auspices of Chatham House in 1971.

The aim of IPEG was to bring together scholars, journalists, and policymakers for regular discussions of issues concerning the world economy. For adherents of the British school, choosing to ignore parallel developments then occurring on the other side of the Atlantic, this truly was the moment of IPE's birth. Declares one source flatly, "Today's field of international political economy can be traced back to 1971, when Susan Strange . . . founded the International Political Economy Group" (Murphy and Nelson 2001, 393). IPEG still exists as a research group within the British International Studies Association (BISA), which Strange was also instrumental in founding in 1974. It is symptomatic of the differences between the American and British schools that while the preeminent showcase for IPE scholarship in the United States is the annual meeting of the American Political Science Association, in Britain it is BISA, a more multidisciplinary organization.

Getting these vehicles under way was no easy task given the limited financial resources available in Britain at the time. "We did not have the resources available to Nye and Keohane in America," Strange later noted ruefully (1989, 434), but "we too were convinced that this was the coming new wave in international relations." For the conference that led to *Transnational Relations and World Politics*, their first collaborative effort, Keohane and Nye had the support of Harvard's Center for International Affairs. For their second project, *World Politics and International Economics*, they received generous financing from two foundations and the Brookings Institution in Washington, DC. And for *Power and Interdependence*, they got help from inter alia the Rockefeller Foundation and a university consortium for world order studies. By contrast, Strange had to scrounge shillings and pence wherever she could. For IPEG, she was able to obtain a minimal amount of funding from the British Economic and Social Research Council. To get BISA off the ground, she wrote to every university vice chancellor in the country, asking for the derisory amount of two pounds each for start-up money.

She had more success in gaining support for another early initiative—the memorable Cumberland Lodge Conference of July 1972 (Brown 1973). Her "Mutual Neglect" manifesto had thrown down the gauntlet: Could international economics and IR be successfully merged? So she decided to respond to her own challenge by inviting a gaggle of scholars together to try. The funding was obtained from Chatham House and two British foundations. For ten days, some forty economists and political scientists sought ways to overcome the long-standing gap between their respective (if not always mutually respectful) disciplines. It is rare for an academic field of study to be able to boast of what amounts to a constitutional convention, where the foundations are laid for future growth and development. But to a large degree that is precisely what the Cumberland Lodge Conference did for the British school of IPE.

Not that the conference was without its difficulties. On many points, not surprisingly, discord reigned. Political scientists accused the economists of being essentially one-dimensional in their preoccupation with the pursuit of wealth, focusing on just a single aspect of human behavior. Economists, in turn, were critical of the political scientists for their seeming lack of methodological rigor or theoretical sophistication. On the fundamental trade-off between parsimony and detail—between the pursuit of eternal truths and the imperative of external validity—the void remained as deep as ever.

Yet there were also key points of consensus, which encouraged participants to persist in their efforts to nurture the infant field, following Strange's lead. More important, they all agreed on the need to keep trying. In the words of one of those in attendance, "There was general agreement that the gap between, on the one hand, the changing nature of the real world and, on the other, the conventional divisions of academic study has increased, is increasing, and should be decreased . . . general agreement about those trends and tendencies in the world which were making the isolated study of politics or economics untenable" (Brown 1973, 52). They also agreed that an integration of political and economic analysis into a viable field of study would not be easy. But after ten days they returned home energized, determined to find ways to bridge the gap between the two disciplines that would not discount the multiple dimensions involved. As a final report of the meeting concluded (Brown 1973, 60)

> The conference revealed serious disagreements over methods and a discouraging degree of ignorance of each other's disciplines. At the same time, it confirmed the participants' belief in the importance of not rigidly confining the study of social problems within the conventional boundaries and strengthened their resolve to overcome the difficulties involved in putting the study of international political economy on a proper footing.

In ensuing years, Strange continued to labor to put the new field "on a proper footing." Like Keohane and Nye (and later Keohane and others), she promoted collective research projects that might push thinking forward in new and innovative directions. One notable example was *Paths to International Political Economy* (Strange 1984a), a collection of essays that she commissioned and edited at the invitation of the British Political Studies Association. Another was *Transcending the State-Global Divide*, edited by two colleagues (Palan and Gills 1994), which developed from a seminar that Strange organized at the European University Institute in Florence, Italy. Volumes like these have been decisive in defining how the British school understands the world.

And then, of course, there was her role as a mentor of students. Strange's aim in returning to the LSE in 1978 was to build Britain's first IPE graduate program, which she ultimately managed to do despite resistance from more traditional faculty colleagues. At first, she wasn't even permitted to use the term IPE. Economics department faculty, arguing that what they taught was international political economy, did not want to give up the label. So Strange's program instead had to be branded Politics of the World Economy, only later changed to IPE. Similar programs soon began to spring up elsewhere as well, including at the universities of Leeds, Manchester, Newcastle, Sheffield, and Warwick.

Strange's blunt style as a teacher could be demanding, even intimidating. Yet she is best remembered for her warmth and the graciousness of her critical encouragement. Her first PhD student at the LSE recalls that Strange "was a good-humored and fun person, willing to listen and cross swords good-naturedly with colleagues and students over a beer, never resorting to intellectual terrorism by wielding her authority. If she thought she had encountered an interesting idea she would yield with enthusiasm" (Sen 1998). Even after reaching the formal age of retirement, she persisted in offering support to aspiring young scholars, first at the European University Institute and then, lastly, at Warwick, where she aided in putting together that university's new IPE program.

It is perhaps a measure of the widespread affection and respect Strange inspired that her career prompted the publication of no fewer than three substantial volumes of essays written in her honor (Morgan et al. 1993; Lawton, Rosenau, and Verdun 2000; Lorentzen and de Cecco 2002) as well as a posthumous edited collection of many of her own writings (Tooze and May 2002). To all those she encountered, including myself, she was a lovable character, tough but tender. A friend at the LSE, Fred Halliday, perhaps put it best when he wrote (1998), "Her ideas were pioneering, robust and convincing. It was, however, as much as anything her personality—the smiling eyes and the exigent criticism—that her colleagues and former students will treasure." Wouldn't we all like to be recalled so fondly?

Founding a School

Strange may never have meant to be an academic, but she became one. According to a sympathetic source, she never meant to found a school either (Murphy and Nelson 2001, 398–99). Yet she did that too. In the words of Barry Gills, one of the founding editors of RIPE, "She founded IPE as we know it here in Britain and she left a great hole in it when she left." Ronen Palan, an admirer, calls her "an empire builder" (2003, 117). Intentionally or not, the substance and style of the British school came to be constructed very much in her image.

In purely intellectual terms, Strange's contributions were limited. She was, by her own admission, no theoretician. Indeed, she always had a suspicion of grand theory. Gills remembers that "she told me and others in confidence that 'I do not consider myself a theorist' but rather someone who was primarily empirical and analytical." Her aim, according to two colleagues, was not "to develop a full theory of IPE, but a way of thinking, a framework for thinking" (Tooze and May 2002, 15). Her long-term impact is measured less by her own ideas than by the critical entrepreneurial role she played in stimulating the ideas of others.

Strange did have ideas of her own, of course—lots, in fact—but she rarely took the time to develop them in a systematic fashion. In the United States, Strange's lack of formal rigor was considered a distinct liability. She was admired for her daring—her willingness, even eagerness, to defy conventional wisdom. As one U.S. scholar wrote to me, she "was never swayed by fashion [and was] always ahead of the curve." But for most Americans in the field, the erstwhile journalist was more pundit than profound, more agent provocateur than savant. Her work, in general, was not thought to be particularly compelling. Yet in Britain her writings took on the aura of gospel, inspiring devotion and emulation.

Illustrative was her approach to the issue of power, which has been described as her "most significant contribution towards IPE" (Tooze and May 2002, 8). Power, for Strange, was central to any explanation of the character and dynamics of the global economy. Her views were best spelled out in her textbook *States and Markets* (1988b). Traditional studies of world politics, which she criticized as narrow and old-fashioned, had mostly tended to identify power with tangible resources of one kind or another: territory, population, armed forces, and the like. But in economic affairs, Strange perceptively argued, what mattered most was not physical endowments but rather structures and relationships—who depends on whom, and for what. Hence power could be understood to operate on two levels: structural and relational. *Relational power*, echoing more conventional treatments in the IR literature, is the familiar "power of A to get B to do something they would not otherwise do" (24). *Structural power*, by contrast, is "the power to shape and determine the structures of the global political economy . . . the power to decide how things will be done, the power to shape frameworks within which states relate to each other" (24–25). Four key structures were identified: security, production, finance, and knowledge.

Strange's distinction between relational and structural power was not entirely new. Keohane and Nye in *Power and Interdependence*, echoing Hirschman's long-neglected *National Power and the Structure of Foreign Trade*, had already stressed the role of asymmetrical interdependence as a source of power in economic affairs, highlighting the twin dimensions of sensitivity and vulnerability at the relational level. And in a study that I published the same year as *Power and Interdependence* (Cohen 1977)—a book that Strange reviewed (1979), not unkindly—I had tried to make the same distinction that Strange did later, labeling the two levels as "process power" and "structure power." Nor could Strange's insight be genuinely described as theory. Her approach was essentially descriptive. Though her discussion in *States and Markets* offered a rich array of illustrations and a historical narrative, it lacked any kind of formal analysis of either the sources of power or the determinants of its use. Strange's "famous four structures," acknowledges Palan (2003, 121), were really no more than "a mere organising framework, a heuristic typology in place of a theory." Nonetheless, her layered conception of power in IPE quickly became a core theme of the British school.

Much the same can also be said of other of Strange's ideas. Keohane (2000), in an appreciative retrospective, lists five major themes in her scholarship: her emphasis on structural power; a focus on agency and the behavior of self-interested actors; a pervasive skepticism about international organizations and regimes; an emphasis on competition among authorities within different sectors of the world economy; and a profound ambivalence about the role of the United States. Though none of these themes was developed by Strange with the kind of attention to causal relationships or predictive accuracy that American school scholars would have preferred, they remain central to the study of IPE in Britain.

Promoting a School

It is easy to understand why one might think Strange never meant to found a school. She was tireless in her crusade for a new field of IPE. But she was also indefatigable in arguing for as much openness of inquiry as possible. Scholarly ecumenism was a persistent refrain in her writing. "International political economy is still unfenced, still open to all comers," she declared (1984b, ix). "It ought . . . to remain so." In her opinion, "the study of international political economy would do well to stay as an open range, like the old Wild West, accessible . . . to literate people of all walks of life" (1991, 33). She firmly abhorred any artificial constraints on inquiry. Leading by example, she freely crossed academic boundaries in pursuit of her scholarly interests.

For Strange, an open range meant eclecticism. It meant resisting the disciplinary compartmentalization of the social sciences that had prevailed since the nineteenth century—what she jokingly referred to, with a nod to earlier British history, as the enclosure movement. And it especially meant transcending the cliquish jargon of narrow specialties that retarded fruitful dialogue. "One of the fatal weaknesses of social science during the enclosure movement," she wrote (1984b, ix), "has been the tendency of each specialism to become a closed shop, a self-perpetuating secret society of the initiated." The fences that had grown up between disciplines misdirected choices and resulted in bad theory, she insisted.

The message was clearly conveyed to her students. Typical was a pair of questions included in the 1988 exam for the core IPE course that she offered in what was then still called the Politics of the World Economy program at the LSE. Students were directed to explain and discuss one of the following: "The eclecticism of international political economy prevents the drawing of boundaries which would define it as a discrete field of study"; or "the international political economist, by definition, must take note of work done in other social sciences." Intellectual ecumenism was simply a given.

The problem was the dialogue of the deaf. The solution, for Strange (1984b, ix), was to remain "alertly attuned to a variety of special insights and concerns"—in other words, to remain *multidisciplinary.* "It would be fatal," she concluded (ix), if IPE "were ever to become the exclusive preserve of economics, of international relations, or of political science." As matters turned out, a school was indeed founded, based on that very principle of openness.

The contrast with the American school could not have been greater. For Strange, allowing custody of IPE to go to the political scientists, as happened in the United States, would be a serious error. IR should be viewed as a subset of IPE, Strange felt (1994, 218), and not the other way around:

> The whole point of studying international political economy rather than international relations is to extend more widely the conventional limits of the study of politics, and the conventional concepts of who engages in politics, and of how and by whom power is exercised to influence outcomes. Far from being a subdiscipline of international relations, IPE should claim that international relations are a subdiscipline of IPE.

In short, a more heterodox approach was needed. As first articulated in her "Mutual Neglect" manifesto, this meant integrating two specialties—a "middle ground" between political and economic analysis (Strange 1970, 307). By the time that Strange edited *Paths to International Political Economy* (1984a), it had come to mean much more—an inquiry open to the perspectives and concerns of an even broader range of disciplines, from sociology and history to psychology, anthropology, and even gender studies. The essays that Strange commissioned for *Paths to International Political Economy* were deliberately designed to highlight what could be learned from tearing down fences. Contributors came from a wide variety of backgrounds, including fields as diverse as population studies, ecology, and the law. Each one, separately, was invited to explain the insights that might be offered by their particular specialty. (Strikingly, there were no women among the authors.) Collectively, the purpose was to emphasize the value that could be added to the study of IPE by following different paths.

Others quickly took up the theme of eclecticism, which soon coalesced to become a hallmark of the British school. Scholars were motivated, wrote one young lecturer, by a "growing realization that many of the world's problems . . . cannot be understood within the conventional framework of knowledge whereby historically defined academic disciplines each have their own exclusive area of inquiry" (Tooze 1984, 2). In effect, the aim to was to resurrect the broader, more inclusive perspective of classical political economy as it had existed before the amoeba subdivided in the nineteenth century. "The classical political economists were polymaths who wrote on a variety of subjects," an analyst has written (Watson 2005, 18). "They did not study 'the economy' as an enclosed and self-contained entity." IPE was about human experience; nothing should be left out.

By the 1990s it was clear from comparative surveys of British and U.S. university curricula that "inclusiveness" had become the key factor distinguishing IPE in Britain from the American version (O'Brien 1995; Denemark and O'Brien 1997). Inclusiveness meant transcending all traditional disciplinary boundaries, broadening the focus of analysis to open up new, exciting areas of inquiry. Bridges were to be built not just between international economics and IR but between them and other disciplines as well. Some in the British school have even promoted a different name for the field—Global Political Economy (GPE), rather than IPE—to affirm the school's more holistic approach (Gill and Law 1988; Palan 2000a; Tétreault et al. 2003). Others are content to retain the label IPE, but insist on the need to "globalize" the field's range of study (Phillips 2005).

When the first issue of RIPE appeared in 1994, the commitment to an open range was, in effect, codified by the editors. "RIPE's raison d'être," they announced, "is to bring together these exciting new attempts to understand contemporary social change by facilitating dialogue and debate across existing academic divides. . . . The journal will inevitably be 'multidisciplinary' in scope and 'interdisciplinary' in spirit" (Editors 1994, 2). Inclusiveness has marked the journal from the start. Of the four founding editors, two—Gills and Palan—were trained in IR and two—Ash Amin and Peter Taylor—were geographers. In subsequent years, several Americans played a critical editorial role, including Jeffry Frieden and Helen Milner. And most recently, the editorial board has included inter alia both a geographer and a development economist.

Similarly, when RIPE was joined two years later by *New Political Economy*—now widely seen as RIPE's biggest rival for IPE scholarship in the British style—the new journal called for "a readiness to tear down intellectual barriers and bring together many approaches, methods and disciplines. . . . We want to encourage conversations and exchanges of ideas and experiences across boundaries which in the past have often been unnecessarily fixed" (Gamble et al. 1996, 5, 11). The theme of eclecticism had by now become official.

Eclecticism did not mean a relaxation of scholarly standards. Tearing down intellectual barriers would not require the abandonment of analytic rigor or nuance. In fact, British school scholars on the whole are every bit as committed to the careful, systematic use of theory and theoretical paradigms as are their U.S. counterparts. But a more open range plainly was antithetical to the sort of reductionist epistemology that is characteristic of a hard science model. With greater inclusiveness came a lessened emphasis on formal empirical inquiry. A breadth of vision was not to be sacrificed on the altar of standard social science methodology.

Perhaps that is why economics, the only discipline that Strange ever studied formally, became her particular bête noire. The "imperialism of economics" was to be fought at all costs. "Always attack the economists," she would tell her colleagues. Their methods were narrow and in her opinion often downright wrong. It was no accident that economists were excluded from *Paths to International Political Economy*. "If there are would-be 'enclosers' lurking about," Strange declared (1984b, x), "they are more likely to be found in departments of economics than elsewhere." The economics profession's commitment to "imitative scientism" (Galbraith 1970, 8) was, for her, "phoney science, not social science" (Strange 1994, 217).

Strange's antipathy for reductionist epistemology quickly came to be widely shared by others, including the editors of RIPE. By way of comparison with the trend in the pages of IO that I noted in the previous chapter, we can look at the kinds of articles published in RIPE during its first decade. Among the total of 161 articles published in the British journal's first five years, 1994–1998, only six (3.7 percent) emphasized formal modeling or hypothesis testing. Similarly, in the next half decade, 1999–2003, the numbers were 8 of 144 (5.6 percent), showing little change. It is obvious that the methods of economics hold much less sway in RIPE than they do in IO. No creeping economism here.

Today, the British school is owned by no one academic specialty. Rather, discourse ranges widely, resisting the forms and norms of any single tradition. A mix of ingredients from different perspectives is welcomed, even celebrated. As Craig Murphy and Douglas Nelson, two U.S. social scientists (the first a political scientist, and the second an economist), conclude in a comparative survey (2001, 404), "The British School is clearly heterodox relative to American social science in general and the IO school in particular." All this, in no small measure, may be attributed to Strange's unusual powers of persuasion.

Imprinting a School

Other contrasts with the U.S. version of IPE are also attributable to Strange's influence. The British school tends to be more normative in ambition, more critical in inclination, and more passionate in tone. All these, too, were traits of Strange's personality that she succeeded in imprinting on the infant field.

For example, no one could miss Strange's intense engagement with social issues. Indeed, for the would-be newspaper columnist, the whole point of intellectual inquiry was to find ways to right the wrongs of the world. In this, Palan (2003) sees a commitment to the social philosophy of pragmatism as it emerged in the late nineteenth century in the work of, among others, William James and John Dewey. Theory, for the pragmatists, could only be judged by its usefulness. Asks Palan: "Does philosophical pragmatism hold the key to

Susan Strange's brand of IPE? I think so" (123). Distributional considerations in particular were always on her mind, whether speaking of the pursuit of wealth or the pursuit of power. The key question was always: *Cui bono?* For whose good?

Nor did she shy away from judgments about matters of ethics or equity. For her, scholarship was inseparable from values. She loved to remind everyone of the link that had long existed between classical political economy and the study of moral philosophy prior to the fragmentation of the social sciences in the nineteenth century (Strange 1985, 14). That link, she felt, needed to be revived. IPE should be "about justice, as well as efficiency: about order and national identity and cohesion, even self-respect, as well as about cost and price" (Strange 1984b, x). True to her beliefs, she continually dared colleagues to make moral judgments.

Strange had no illusions that sweetness and light would ultimately prevail; she was too worldly for that. As one longtime acquaintance remarked, "She belonged to a pedigree that echoed the Manchester School liberals, believing in the pragmatic possibilities of human improvement, although she had fewer ideological illusions" (Sen 1998). She was determined to give it her best shot, though, and thought others should try as well. As Strange once reminisced (1989, 436), "I have tried to teach both students and children not to expect justice in life—but to try hard to get it." The broad range of practical issues addressed by the British school, in the pages of RIPE and elsewhere, attest to the fact that many of her students did indeed take her teaching seriously.

Nor could anyone miss her impatience with "The Establishment," as she put it, which led her to adopt a skeptical attitude toward orthodoxy of any kind. She was an iconoclast and radical, recalls one former student. "She was no revolutionary, but she questioned prevailing nostrums with ill-concealed glee" (Sen 1998). Strange herself attributed her irreverence to her late start as a full-time academic. "By that time, I suppose I felt there was no point in being too conformist. To make any kind of mark, I had to develop ideas on my own" (Strange 1995, 295). But there can be no doubt that her disdain for "the barons and the top brass" (295) was also rooted in her personal experience as a woman trying to make her way in a man's world. Another lesson she sought to teach students was "to question authority, whether political or academic" (Strange 1989, 436). And here, too, those who followed her took her teaching seriously. A thread running through much of the British school today is a strong distaste for anything that might be regarded as mainstream thinking.

Finally, there was Strange's passion, which suffused everything she undertook. This was not a woman who could do things halfway. Passion was evident in the initiatives she took to organize IPEG and the Cumberland Lodge Conference. It could be seen in the wide range of issues she chose to take on, from the decline of sterling to the rise of globalization. It could be found in her confrontational, in-your-face approach to academic debate and teaching. To be a serious scholar, she told her students, you must have "fire in the belly." And most of all, it was manifest in her prose, which made even the dreariest subjects come vividly alive. What might seem grimmer, for instance, than a book titled *States and Markets*? But who could fail to be enticed by Strange's witty prologue—beginning with the cliché "It was a dark and stormy night"—that establishes its basic argument through an allegory about a disastrous shipwreck and three groups of survivors on a desert island? Passion is not a word normally associated with the kind of parsimonious, positivist analysis encouraged by the American school. Even after Strange's passing, however, passion remains a central hallmark of the contrasting British approach to IPE.

The Contrast

Nowhere have I seen the contrast between the two schools drawn more clearly than in an anecdote related to me by a young friend of mine, a U.S.-trained political scientist who, with his freshly minted PhD, not long ago accepted a faculty position at the LSE, Strange's old home. "Our department requires PhD students," he wrote me, "to be questioned on their dissertation chapters by a panel of faculty each year. On one panel on which I served, I encouraged the student to clarify the 'puzzle' or 'gap' that his approach was addressing or filling. On hearing my advice, one of my colleagues suggested that while such advice was appropriate, it tended to reflect an American concern with positivist social science. On the other side of the pond, he suggested, we don't necessarily do things that way."

In my own experience, the contrast was best brought home by a 1991 paper coauthored by the U.S. political scientist Craig Murphy and Roger Tooze, a once-prominent member of the British school. The paper commented on a survey article that I had written a year earlier for IO reviewing five new books on the political economy of international trade (Cohen 1990). Describing my piece as "authoritative [and] representative of orthodoxy" (that is, the American school), Murphy and Tooze took me to task on both ontological and epistemological grounds. Together, their objections defined the key differences between the American and British schools.

On ontological grounds, they criticized me for what they called a preoccupation with "interstate material relationships." At the outset of my survey, I suggested that the research agenda of the then newly emergent field of IPE "focuses largely on two broad sets of questions. One set has to do with *actor behavior*—meaning, in particular, government behavior, since the fundamental unit of authority in the international system still remains the sovereign nation-state. What motivates government behavior in foreign economic relations, and how is it best explained and analyzed? The other has to do with *system management*—coping with the consequences of economic interdependence. How do state actors manage (or fail to manage) their conflicts, and what determines whether they cooperate or fail to cooperate to achieve common objectives?" (Cohen 1990, 264).

Today, of course, the latter set of questions would be labeled system *governance* rather than system management, in keeping with the standard language of political science. But whatever the language used, for Murphy and Tooze this was all far too state-centric—too reminiscent of the traditional agenda of IR theory. It was also too concerned with strictly material considerations, discounting matters of culture, identity, and the like. The focus, Murphy and Tooze argued (1991, 16), was too narrow, "a fundamental ontological weakness."

To some extent, the objection was misplaced. Murphy and Tooze appeared to equate the agenda I outlined with nothing more than traditional realism, which treats the state as a rational and unitary actor. "The state is important," they conceded (15–16), but "it is essential [also] to consider a large number of other nonstate social and economic actors . . . through analysis that disaggregates the state and encompasses a broad understanding of society." In fact, that is precisely what I had in mind, as I tried to make clear in my discussion of the five books under review. The paradigm I was working from was not realism but complex interdependence, which does indeed encompass a much wider range of relevant actors. Their reproof was telling nonetheless. In raising the issue, Murphy and Tooze highlighted the British school's determined resistance to disciplinary compartmentalization in general and any subordination to IR in particular.

On epistemological grounds, they criticized me for a preoccupation with "scientific" method. They acknowledged that I had not insisted on the superiority of any single methodology. Indeed, I wrote that the methods of IPE vary, "depending both on the disciplinary training of the individual scholar and on the nature of the specific issue-area under consideration" (Cohen 1990, 264). But not even this formulation left sufficient latitude, according to the pair. To consider just these two factors as determining methodology, Murphy and Tooze contended (1991, 16), "is to adopt a relatively narrow and particularist conception of methodology as scientific technique, along with a wholly positivist conception of the possibility and desirability of objective analysis." As a card-carrying member of the American school, I will not deny my allegiance to the principles of positivist social science, which seem to me to be essential for valid cumulative research. Murphy and Tooze, by contrast, clearly preferred to leave more room for normative concerns and value judgments—another hallmark of the British school.

Ultimately, the issue comes down to the basics: what understanding is shared about how things work and how they may be studied. Murphy and Tooze attacked my "authoritative" article as representative of a specific *culture* of orthodoxy—"a particular view of what and who . . . constitute the legitimate study of IPE" (16–17). The British school manifestly has a different culture—a different intersubjective understanding, as Murphy and Tooze demonstrated. Each school, in the end, is the product of a different construction.

FOLLOW THE LEADER

But why did the constructions turn out so differently? Why did the British school ultimately diverge so sharply from the American model? Strange's powerful personality was certainly part of the explanation. With her determined entrepreneurship and persuasive style, she opened the door wide to an alternative understanding of the way the world works. Yet to gain acceptance for her distinctively different vision, she also needed a receptive audience—a critical mass of scholars prepared to follow her lead rather than that of Keohane and Nye, Gilpin, or others across the Atlantic. I have said that there was nothing inevitable about the way that IPE was constructed in the United States. There was nothing inevitable about the way IPE was constructed in Britain, either.

In fact, the audience for Strange's ideas turned out to be remarkably broad. An old slogan for an American bread product proclaimed, "You don't have to be Jewish to love Levy's Jewish rye." In Britain, you didn't have to be British to be in the British school; indeed, you didn't even have to reside in Britain. Though rooted in geography, the distinction is as much intellectual as territorial. The school of course has included many Britons, such as R. J. Barry Jones and Tooze. But it has also included the likes of Philip Cerny (American), Gills (dual U.S-British citizenship), Richard Higgott (dual Britain-Australia citizenship), Palan (Israeli and British passports), and Timothy Sinclair (from New Zealand). It includes Geoffrey Underhill, who decamped to the University of Amsterdam, and John Ravenhill, who has spent much of his career at the Australian National University. And it even includes a fair number of U.S.-based scholars, such as Murphy and Nelson.

The audience also includes many Canadians, still receptive to British intellectual influence despite Canada's close proximity to the United States. True to the old cliché about Canadian moderation (Question: Why does a Canadian cross the road? Answer: To get to the middle), many of that country's best-known IPE specialists have tried to keep a foot in each camp, respecting the American school's emphasis on scientific positivism and empiricism even while hearkening to Strange's message of multidisciplinary eclecticism and inclusiveness. Scholars like Eric Helleiner and Louis Pauly (an American based in Canada) in effect seek to build bridges between the two versions of the field. But Canada is also the home of some of the best-known members of the British school, such as Stephen Gill and most notably Cox. We will hear more about Cox in the next chapter.

Why was the audience for Strange's ideas so receptive? Standard explanations point to a basic difference in intellectual culture—broadly, the way international studies traditionally had been approached in British universities as compared with the United States. On the U.S. side of the Atlantic, links with political science had always dominated. International studies grew up in an environment framed by the norms of conventional social science, with a particular emphasis on training in quantitative methods. Once IPE was born, it seemed natural for U.S. scholars to channel the infant field's development along similar lines.

In Britain, by contrast, international studies had roots that were spread much more widely into a variety of other disciplines such as sociology, philosophy, religion, and law. Direct links with political science were weaker, with most universities maintaining a strong institutional separation between IR faculty and others. At Cambridge, international studies was for a long time located in the history faculty. At the LSE and some other schools, IR had a department of its own, quite distinct from other disciplines. British academics were already conditioned to think about the international realm in multidisciplinary and normative terms.

Particularly influential was the so-called English school of IR, which stressed the existence of a global society that could be studied only in the broadest social and historical terms—an idea rooted in the classical legal tradition whose origins could be traced as far back as Hugo Grotius. Built on foundations laid by inter alia Hedley Bull (1977), the English school was "skeptical of the possibility of a scientific study of International Relations," as one sympathetic history puts it (Dunne 1998, 7). Indeed, resistance to any kind of hard science model was actually a point of some pride among its adherents. As another survey summarizes it, "The epistemological status and methodological principles of English school arguments are left rather obscure" (Linklater and Suganami 2006, 114). Hence, it was no surprise that in Britain IPE might develop in the same open manner. Formal methodology was de-emphasized. Instead, the milieu encouraged what Tooze labeled a "historical-relativist paradigm . . . drawn from an eclectic mix of factors" (1985, 121).

Historical circumstances also differed sharply on the two sides of the Atlantic. In contrast to the United States, the new top dog in the global economy, Britain seemed a spent force—a nation mired in a long, painful decline. Once the country had been the proud center of an empire on which the sun never set. Now it feared becoming little more than a collection of sad offshore islands, overshadowed by the newly prosperous economies of the Continent and prone to a seemingly endless streak of financial crises. U.S. scholars understandably accepted the new world order as natural or even desirable. British scholars, on the other hand, could be excused for adopting a more jaundiced view of the status quo and a greater openness to alternative perspectives.

But these broad differences were hardly the whole story. There were also other, more specific factors at work to build an audience for Strange's ideas. First was a latent anti-Americanism often found in British universities, which helped encourage scholars to define their efforts more in opposition to, rather than in imitation of, U.S. trends of thought. In the jargon of IR theory, British academics were more inclined to balance than bandwagon. Second was a more relaxed attitude toward Marxism or other leftist doctrines, which reinforced a critical disposition toward markets and their consequences. And third was the less formal approach to economic studies in Britain, as compared with the United States, which reduced pressures to conform to a demanding set of methodological standards.

Anti-Americanism in British universities, where it existed, involved two intertwined strands. One was geopolitical, concerning the emergence of the United States after World War II as leader of the Western world. In Britain, now eclipsed as a global power, this rankled. The resentment of U.S. dominance at some level was natural or perhaps even inevitable. (Remember the old wartime line about the Americans: overfed, overpaid, oversexed, and over here.) Britons, like their counterparts in the antiwar movement in the United States, were particularly revolted by America's seemingly imperialist war in Vietnam. The other strand was intellectual, concerning the rise of U.S. universities after 1945 to the peak of the world's academic hierarchy, eclipsing the likes of Cambridge and Oxford. U.S. scholars were seen as privileged by their access to the resources of a much wealthier economy. They were also thought to be unduly influenced by the foreign policy concerns of a hegemonic power.

These strands came together to encourage resistance to any new scholarly fashion emanating from the other side of the pond. Strange, with her marked ambivalence about the United States, helped to set the pattern. In some ways, Strange truly admired the United States—the only country, she once noted, where you can buy a T-shirt emblazoned with her favorite slogan, "Question Authority" (1995, 295). As Keohane has accurately observed (2000, xiv), "She loved the openness and irreverence of American society. . . . In a sense, she was by instinct and temperament a woman of the American West." Yet this did not stop her from being offended by what she perceived as the selfishness of U.S. power and the arrogance of American academics, whom she attacked with unrestrained vigor. In one famous essay, Strange (1983) compared her U.S. counterparts to those medieval scholastics who, in their superstitious ignorance, imagined dragons lurking beyond Europe's western horizon. In another piece, Strange (1994) publicly challenged a respected U.S. professor to "wake up" and face the facts.

Jibes like these found a ready audience among British academics, many of whom were understandably eager to create an alternative to what Murphy and Tooze describe as the "self-identified U.S. 'supremacy' in the scholarly fields of international relations and IPE" (1991, 17). As one admiring source puts it,

Strange's "stinging criticism of U.S. intellectual trends provided room for British scholars and students to ask different types of questions and use different methodologies from their US counterparts" (O'Brien and Williams 2004, 28). Typical was a broadside published in the second issue of RIPE, when the journal was just beginning its campaign for a more open range. The U.S. version of IPE, proclaimed Peter Burnham (1994, 221–22), is "a vulgar, fraudulent discipline . . . a crude amalgam of neoclassical economics, pluralist domestic political science, and realist international relations theory. . . . We can only wonder why the tradition of classical political economy is passed over in such haste. . . . [The Americans] fail to grasp the complex organic set of social relations which is the global political economy." A more "scientific" political economy was needed to supplant the American school's "unsatisfactory eclectic mixture of analytical methods and theoretical perspectives," Burnham concluded (222).

It may be an exaggeration to suggest that the British school defined itself simply by its opposition to U.S. thinking. But that would not be entirely inaccurate, either. Even for its sympathizers, the British school's hostile attitude toward scholarship on the other side of the Atlantic has long been one of its chief sources of inspiration. In the words of Murphy and Nelson (2001, 405), "The success of British school IPE is relatively easy to explain. American hegemony and the hegemony of IO school IPE created opportunities for those who opposed either or both projects."

Attitudes toward Marxism or other leftist doctrines, by contrast, were far more relaxed than in the United States, where most academics were wary of anything that might seem tainted by socialist sympathies. Hence, there was less inclination in Britain to resist a new field of study that could possibly smack of anticapitalist sentiment; quite the contrary, in fact. Skepticism regarding markets and their consequences was much more acceptable there than in the United States. After all, wasn't Britain where many fashionable leftist doctrines, such as Fabianism, had first developed? Wasn't one of the country's two biggest political parties at the time avowedly socialist in intent? Criticism of the allegedly oppressive nature of markets came easy—especially markets as they were allowed to operate in the United States. Scholars needed little prodding to look for the politics in economic relations; nor did they find it difficult to heed Strange's call to make fundamentally moral judgments on matters of public concern.

Least of all did British academics require any encouragement to question authority. So-called critical theory, challenging orthodoxies of all kinds, has long found a comfortable home in the country's universities. Given its many variants, critical theory is not easily characterized. A "broad church" is how one practitioner calls it (Mittelman 1998, 64). Encompassed by the term are varieties of Marxian analysis, some forms of feminism, and other radical schools of thought. One sympathetic source suggests that a more adequate label would be "ideologically oriented inquiry" (Griffiths 1999, 114).

Yet there is a common denominator—what one observer, himself a critical theorist, calls an "oppositional frame of mind" (Brown 2001, 192). Though divided over issues of ontology and epistemology, most versions of critical theory converge on a revisionist critique of modern capitalism, a heretical disposition that many scholars found easy to carry over into the new field of IPE. Cox, as we shall see in the next chapter, was among the first to go down this road; others soon followed, making an oppositional frame of mind a key element of British school discourse. Indeed, many in the school, one source suggests, might actually prefer to see their field called simply Critical IPE (Murphy and Nelson 2001, 394). Another source, using a biological metaphor, amusingly defines the "diverse critical species that comprise the genus" of the British school as *Querimonia*, in contrast to the rationalist species *Ratiosaurus rex* that we know as the American school (Dickins 2006, 480).

Finally, there was the difference in the British approach to economic studies, which was far less abstract than in the United States. British economists may have considered themselves more intellectually uncompromising than their political science brethren, as they argued at the Cumberland Lodge Conference, for example. But as compared with the way the economics discipline was developing in the United States, there was still much less emphasis on reductionism in Britain and certainly less reliance on numeracy. British economists still wrote with words. (Jokes a U.S. economist, "That's what we call ambiguity.") Typically they also remained more inclusive in their analysis, sensitive to the role of institutions and history; many British universities, including the LSE, even had a separate economic history department, counting among their faculty some of the best-known economists in the land. Thus as the infant field of IPE developed, there was correspondingly less pressure to conform to a highly demanding positivist or empiricist epistemology. One's professional status did not require sacrificing detail for parsimony. Scholarship could be every bit as heterodox as Strange was suggesting.

ANOTHER IRONY

None of this is meant to imply that one of the two schools is somehow better or worse than the other. Any such comparison would obviously be invidious. The relationship between the two constructions is more akin to Akira Kurosawa's 1950 film *Rashomon*, where separate narrators recalled the same basic story in vastly different ways. Here the story is the interaction of economics and politics in international relations. The American school has one way of telling the story, and the British school has another. Despite what many on either side of the Atlantic might contend, neither is inherently superior.

Quite the contrary, in fact. In practice, the two schools complement each other neatly, the strengths of one largely balancing weaknesses of the other. The American school may take justifiable pride in its allegiance to the demanding principles of positivism and empiricism. But arguably it may also be reproached for its narrow preoccupation with scientific method and disdain for normative work. Scholars in the U.S. style, absorbed with midlevel theory building, are frequently insular in their intellectual interests, and indifferent to matters of equity or justice. Daring new ideas tend to be discouraged by the need to demonstrate careful methodological rigor. History and social context take a backseat to the parsimony of abstract, deductive logic.

Scholars in the British style, by contrast, help to compensate for such shortcomings with their intellectual ecumenism and critical attitude toward orthodoxy. The British school may be fairly criticized for its less rigorous approach to theory building and testing, thereby making generalization difficult and the cumulation of knowledge virtually impossible. But the British school may also legitimately claim to make a useful contribution by opening discourse to a wider range of insights and highlighting the normative element in scholarly inquiry. The more open range for research, as we shall see in subsequent chapters, permits consideration of grander issues of social transformation and historical change. Each school adds value in its own way.

But here too there is a deeper irony. When Strange began her campaign for a more modern approach, her aim was to end a dialogue of the deaf—the mutual neglect of two self-contained academic traditions. That battle is now won. IPE has become a recognized field of study. Yet the new school that was born in Britain has not only evolved in a manner quite different from that of its U.S. counterpart; it has also grown apart. In effect, a new dialogue of the deaf has emerged—a new case of mutual neglect of two academic traditions. In the words of one keen observer, "US-based and British school IPE have . . . evolved largely separately from each other, identified little with one another as parts of the same enterprise, and spoken largely to their own audiences rather than to each other" (Phillips 2005, 12). As the Murphy and Tooze critique of my 1990 essay suggests, the two schools have diverged on even the most basic questions of ontology and epistemology.

Each school has its own showcase for scholarship: respectively, BISA and APSA. Each also has what amounts to its own house journal: RIPE versus IO. Whereas RIPE proudly promotes the work of the British school, IO retains a distinctly American flavor. About nine of every ten articles published in IO are authored by scholars of U.S. nationality or affiliation (Aydinli and Mathews 2000; Breuning, Bredehoft, and Walton 2005). And the divergence is reflected in reading habits as well. Surveys have shown little correlation between the journals read on either side of the pond (Crewe and Norris 1991; Norris and Crewe 1993), nor is there much overlap in the authors favored by British and U.S. scholars (Murphy and Nelson 2001). The point was well illustrated in a comment to me by a good friend (and leading member of the American school) who consented to read an earlier draft of this book. Referring to RIPE, my friend wrote that "it is hard to think of a journal that was first published in 1994 as having a big impact on the field. I see few cites to this journal in the stuff I read." I was tempted to respond simply, "Your Honor, I rest my case."

Divergences like these are not entirely surprising. Across the discipline of political science as a whole, it has long been known that U.S. and British scholars tend to tread separate paths—reading different literatures, taking part in different debates, and following different agendas (Norris 1997). Why should the subset of specialists in IPE be any different? Moreover, given their separate starting points, it was to some degree inevitable that over time their mutual insularity would be reinforced by divergent patterns of socialization. Winston Churchill, echoing an earlier thought of George Bernard Shaw, said that the United States and Britain are two nations divided by a common language. In similar fashion, the American and British schools of IPE have come to be two factions divided by a common subject.

This sort of phenomenon is hardly unfamiliar in academic life. Disciplines and specialties often fragment as researchers seek out the comfort of others who share the same perspective. As Margaret Hermann has observed (1998, 606), "Our identities become intertwined with the perspectives and points of view of the theoretical cohort to which we perceive ourselves belonging. And we tend to distance ourselves from those we do not understand or whose ideas seem discordant with our group's theoretical outlook." The process is a natural one and tends to be self-reinforcing. Once begun, its momentum is hard to overcome.

A new dialogue of the deaf was surely not what Strange had in mind. Her own inclination, true to her convictions about U.S. academia, was to blame it all on the Americans. Three years before her death, she suggested that U.S. scholars needed a hearing aid. Americans, in Strange's words (1995, 290), are "deaf and blind to anything that's not published in the U.S.A." Unfortunately, there is some truth to that, as a recent survey of IPE curricula in U.S. universities testifies. The survey concludes that "frankly, American international political economy could benefit from becoming a little less American and a little more international" (Paul 2006, 733). But that is hardly the whole truth. Arguably, Strange too might be said to bear a good part of the responsibility, owing to the vigor of her entrepreneurial efforts and the sheer strength of her personality. Just as she never meant to be an academic, she may not have meant to create a new case of mutual neglect. Nonetheless, that is the result.

Chapter 3

A REALLY BIG QUESTION

For the world economy to be stabilized, there has
to be a stabilizer, one stabilizer.
—Charles Kindleberger

Theory is always *for* someone and *for* some purpose.
—Robert Cox

IPE'S BIRTH was sparked by the growing interdependence of national economies after World War II. But why did the international environment change?
What were the implications? And what could be expected in the future? Not
surprisingly, questions like these were among the first to be addressed by the
infant field. After all, what could be more fascinating than the grand theme of
systemic transformation? It was what old-time television host Ed Sullivan
might have called a Really Big Question. Every generation is tempted to believe that it is in the midst of an unprecedented historical transition. That may
be something of a conceit. As I remind my students, probably the best definition of a transition is that interval of time between two periods of transition.
The degree of change in any given era may be easily exaggerated. Exaggerated
or not, however, thinking about systemic transformation has contributed richly
to the intellectual development of the field.

In the United States, thinking about systemic transformation was most fashionable in IPE's early years, when the horizons of inquiry seemed unlimited.
In more recent years, interest in the grand theme of change has largely faded
among U.S. specialists, despite evidence that this time, it might actually be
true that we are living through a historical transition—what has come to be
known as the age of globalization. Only in the British school is there still
much interest in the Really Big Question. Indeed, nothing better defines the
differences between the American and British schools than their respective
discourses on systemic transformation. From the start, each tradition constructed its own distinctive approach to the subject.

Yet for all their differences, one element was shared in common. In both
traditions, thinking about the Really Big Question was largely shaped by individuals with a particular passion for history. In the United States it was an
economist, Kindleberger, whose first love by his own admission was always
economic history. For the British school it was the Canadian Cox, whose for-

mal training was in the history discipline. Both Kindleberger and Cox led by the force of their ideas. Coincidentally, both also spent years in public service before beginning academic careers. Perhaps there is something about earning a living in the real world that encourages a broad perspective on global events.

HEGEMONIC STABILITY

Central to the Really Big Question is of course the underlying connection between economic and political activities. Does economics drive politics in transforming the global system, or vice versa? In the United States, where political scientists early on captured the infant field, it seemed natural to think first about politics and the role of the sovereign state. Even for liberals like Keohane and Nye, the state remained the central actor. The system was defined in terms of the pattern of interstate relations; the pattern of interstate relations, in turn, was understood to be above all a function of the distribution of state capabilities. Hence for U.S. scholars, the key variable was *power*, particularly as exercised by dominant states.

In the first years after World War II, power in the world economy was obviously concentrated in the United States. "Gulliver among the Lilliputians" was the way Keohane described it (1979, 95). Postwar America represented a textbook case of hegemony—an overwhelming preponderance of power. By the time IPE was getting its start, however, America's hegemony appeared to be going into decline. Gulliver was shrinking. Thus, in U.S. academic circles it seemed natural to focus on hegemony as the central driver of change. A historical transition did seem in progress. Systemic transformation was equated with hegemonic decline.

Did hegemonic decline presage a new era of insecurity and peril? Discussion centered on what came to be known as HST—the controversial idea that global economic health was somehow dependent on the presence of a single dominant power. For two decades, HST remained atop the agenda of IPE in the United States before fading into obscurity.

HST has been described as IPE's first genuine theory. (Cynics would say that it was the field's *only* claim to theory.) Two questions dominated. The first was empirical. Was the theory's premise accurate? Was U.S. hegemony really in decline? The second was ontological. Whether the premise was accurate or not, was the theory's logic plausible? Was hegemony really the key to systemic stability? Opinions, not surprisingly, varied widely.

For many in the British school, HST was a little more than a distraction—a sideshow orchestrated by U.S. academics overly preoccupied with their own nation's place in the world. And we now know that the skeptics were not entirely wrong. The theory's premise, it is now acknowledged, was always something of a canard. The distribution of state power had not changed nearly as much as HST assumed. In empirical terms, the debate turned out to have been over a nonissue.

But that does not mean that all the time devoted to the theory was wasted. In ontological terms, the debate proved highly instructive. Efforts to explore the logical truth and predictive accuracy of HST added greatly to the infant field's understanding of a range of critical issues—including, not least, the issue of system governance, which I will take up in the next chapter. The theory itself may have died a natural death, but its legacy lives on.

Rise of a Theory

HST got its name from Keohane, who first coined the phrase in a paper published in 1980. As Keohane summarized it (132), HST argues that "hegemonic structures of power, dominated by a single country, are most conducive to the development of strong international regimes whose rules are relatively precise and well obeyed." Keohane was not the source of the theory; in fact, he didn't even agree with it, as we shall see. The credit for originating HST actually goes to three other key members of IPE's pioneer generation: above all to the economist Kindleberger, together with political scientists Gilpin and Krasner, two prominent realists. All three wrote within years of the collapse of the Bretton Woods system, which many interpreted as the beginning of the end of America's hegemony. The fear, as Keohane put it (132), was that "the decline of hegemonic structures of power can be expected to presage a decline in the strength of corresponding international economic regimes."

Pride of place here goes to Kindleberger. Charlie, as he was known to his friends, was the oldest of the Magnificent Seven. Born in 1910, he received his PhD from Columbia University in 1937. During World War II he worked for the Office of Strategic Services, selecting Allied bombing targets, and then after the war's conclusion, while at the Department of State, played a major role in initiating the Marshall Plan. His academic career began in 1948 when he moved to the Massachusetts Institute of Technology (MIT), where he taught international economics and economic history for some thirty-three years. Even after formal retirement, he remained active as a scholar, published an autobiography at the age of eighty-one (Kindleberger 1991), and was still writing articles and reviewing manuscripts at the time of his death in 2003, at the age of ninety-two. He always reminded me of a Nobel Prize–winning professor I once knew who at his retirement dinner exclaimed, "Just think, here I am retiring, and until a couple of years ago I still thought of myself as a promising young scholar." One could easily imagine the ever-youthful Charlie saying much the same. In his autobiography he expressed the hope that even after "shuffling off this mortal coil" (209), his papers would continue to come out for a reasonable period of time.

Figure 3.1. Charles Kindleberger. Courtesy of MIT Museum

One of Kindleberger's best friends was Galbraith, who wrote the foreword to his autobiography. Like Galbraith, who had also worked outside academia before becoming a university professor, Kindleberger had little patience for the economics profession's growing love affair with mathematics, as promoted by his MIT colleague Paul Samuelson, among others. His distaste for high-powered math may have been a product of his early professional experience;

molded by the twin disasters of depression and war, he put a premium on practical solutions, not elegant model building. It may also have been due to the fact that he just didn't care all that much about numbers. His passion was for the big picture, not the details. Students affectionately recall the many arithmetic errors he would make in his class lectures. Kindleberger mentored some of the most accomplished international economists of the day, including Robert Mundell, a Nobel Prize winner. When asked how that could be, despite his apparent lack of ease with math, one of his protégés quipped that it was because they could all sharpen their skills correcting his mistakes. Adds Jagdish Bhagwati, "You learned technique from others. What you learned from Charlie were ideas" (quoted in Stein 2003).

For Kindleberger, as for Galbraith, what mattered most was to keep an open mind, not relying unduly on parsimonious models or inherited theory. "I remember him for his kindness," notes another former student, who applied to study at MIT in 1957. "With some trepidation, I said that, as a physics major, I had taken only two semesters of economics. With a smile he said, 'that's all right, you won't have to unlearn anything' " (Synnott 2003).

Among his friends, Kindleberger was well-known for a wicked sense of humor. For evidence, one need only consult his autobiography, which contains more than enough wry commentary to persuade readers that an economist need not be dull. (An old joke has it that an economist is someone who wanted to be an actuary but didn't have the personality for it.) My own first exposure to Kindleberger's wit came during a break at an economics conference in the early 1970s, at a time when long hair was becoming increasingly fashionable among younger men. One of the other conferees was Cooper, still young but by no means hirsute. "This morning I decisively proved that Dick Cooper is sixty-nine years old," Kindleberger smilingly declared. "How could that be?" I responded. "During the meeting I did a mental calculation," he replied, "correlating age and length of hair around the conference table. Then I plugged in Dick Cooper, and the model says he's sixty-nine."

The joke solidified for me a sense of affinity with someone whose career path had already begun to feel something like a model for my own. Like Kindleberger, I had received my doctorate from Columbia University after studying with inter alia the noted international economist James Angell, who had supervised Charlie's dissertation years before; also like Kindleberger, I had taken my first job after graduate study in the research department of the Federal Reserve Bank of New York, working on problems of international finance, prior to starting an academic career. At the New York Fed they still spoke of Charlie proudly as one of the research department's most illustrious alumni. He set a standard that was not easy to follow.

Over the course of his career Kindleberger wrote more than thirty books, his interests evolving from international economics to development economics to, finally, economic history, which was his real passion. "It was in economic history that he really found his comparative advantage," says Bhagwati (quoted in Stein 2003). And among his many contributions to the study of economic history, none surpasses his classic 1973 study of the Great Depression, *The World in Depression, 1929–1939*, in which he first spelled out the logic of HST (Kindleberger 1973, 28):

> The international economic and monetary system needs leadership, a country which is prepared, consciously or unconsciously, under some system of rules that it has internalized, to set standards of conduct for other countries; and to seek to get others to follow them, to take on an undue share of the burdens of the system, and in particular to take on its support in adversity by accepting its redundant commodities, maintaining a flow of investment capital and discounting its paper.

The logic was straightforward. Looking back over the previous two centuries, a striking correlation appeared to exist between great power dominance and economic stability. This seemed so both in the late nineteenth century, the era of the classical gold standard, and during the Bretton Woods period. The first period was led by Britain (an economic Pax Britannica), and the second by the United States (a Pax Americana). After World War I, by contrast, leadership had been absent. Britain was willing but no longer able to underwrite the global system; the United States was able but for political reasons not yet willing. Should it have been any surprise, therefore, that the system might break down? For Kindleberger it hardly seemed unreasonable to attribute causation to the relationship: "The 1929 depression was so wide, so deep and so long because the international economic system was rendered unstable by British inability and United States unwillingness to assume responsibility for stabilizing it" (1973, 292). Hence his famous aphorism: "For the world economy to be stabilized, there has to be a stabilizer, one stabilizer" (305). HST was born.

The World in Depression stands as a landmark in the construction of IPE—"crushingly influential," as one U.S. scholar put it to me privately. In articulating his argument, Kindleberger was inspired not by theory but by practice—by a close reading of the historical facts and also, no doubt, by his own personal history. He had lived through the chaos of the Great Depression, after all, witnessing firsthand the price to be paid for a lack of leadership. After such a formative experience, should we be surprised that he might have been inclined to concentrate on the need for a powerful stabilizer?

Perhaps even more critical were his years of service in government. Early in 1947, while head of the Department of State's German and Austrian Economic Affairs Section, he and two other young economists prepared a proposal for a European recovery program that ultimately formed the basis for Secretary of State George Marshall's famous commencement address at Harvard—the first outline of what came to be known as the Marshall Plan. Later, Kindleberger was appointed executive secretary of the Department of State's working committee for the plan's implementation, charged with estimating the needs of the sixteen European countries that accepted U.S. aid. Those years undoubtedly impressed on him how much a dominant state can do, when it tries, to tame an unruly world economy. In a sense, HST was simply the Marshall Plan writ large.

Two Versions

As an economist with no formal training in political science, Kindleberger made little effort to connect his state-centric logic to the dirty game of politics. Consistent with the liberal tradition of mainstream economics, his purposes were mainly normative—to describe what he regarded as essential to prevent the breakdown of the global economy. The core of his argument can be understood in terms of the logic of collective action, derived from Mancur Olson's celebrated book of the same name (1965). Systemic stability, Kindleberger contended, should be regarded as a kind of public good since it embodies the two main characteristics of collective goods: nonexcludability and nonrivalry. Nonexcludability means that others can benefit from the good, even if they do not contribute to its provision. Nonrivalry means that the use of the good by one will not seriously diminish the amount available to others. Given these characteristics, Kindleberger reasoned, stability will be underprovided without the leadership of a dominant power.

Three functions, he said, were critical to systemic stability: maintaining a relatively open market for imports, providing contracyclic long-term lending, and supplying short-term financing in the event of a crisis. Since such functions could be costly, the hegemon might have to bear a disproportionate share of the burdens involved, especially if other countries chose to free ride. But for Kindleberger, that was simply the price to be paid for the responsibility of leadership. His version of HST could thus be characterized as benevolent, a benign exercise of power. His approach was subsequently identified with the neoliberal institutionalist tradition in IPE. One source described it as the "collective goods" version of HST (Webb and Krasner 1989).

Political scientists, on the other hand, had no difficulty at all in connecting Kindleberger's logic to politics—in particular, to the possibility that hegemony might be exercised coercively rather than benevolently, seeking to benefit the leader even at the expense of others. Economic power might serve as a means, not an end. For example, markets might be forced open to satisfy the security needs of the hegemon; alternatively, threats might be made to cut off trade or investment flows to compel others to share in the cost of public goods. Several scholars quickly seized on Kindleberger's theme to develop their own ideas about systemic transformation, stressing the self-interest of the dominant power. The result was an alternative version of HST, a "security" version (Webb and Krasner 1989) more in line with the realist tradition of IPE. Realists, typically, have little interest in the theme of change as such. Two notable exceptions were Gilpin and Krasner. We have already encountered Gilpin in chapter 1. We'll hear more about Krasner in the next chapter.

As early as 1972, in his contribution to *Transnational Relations and World Power*, Gilpin had hinted at the logic of HST. Surely, he asserted, there was some connection between the exercise of power in the economic realm and the world of security. Colleagues who disagreed wondered if he might be a Marxist. But says the self-declared Vermont Republican, "I knew I was not a Marxist. . . . I read other things on the interplay of economics and politics, and then I discovered a book on mercantilism and said to myself: 'Ah! That's what I am!' I began to realize that you could have a realist view of world economics without being a Marxist" (*International Relations* 2005, 368). A key influence was Jacob Viner's 1948 study of mercantilist thought and practice, which we already encountered in chapter 1.

Gilpin's ideas were more fully elaborated a few years later in *U.S. Power and the Multinational Corporation*—a book that was to have a lasting impact on a new generation of scholars. It was "the big opening," one younger colleague has written to me. "It opened an intellectual and analytical space in which IPE was to develop in the second half of the 1970s and 1980s."

As in Kindleberger's analysis, Gilpin's perspective was broad, encompassing the full economic system. "A liberal international economy requires a power to manage and stabilize the system," Gilpin declared (1975b, 40), echoing and generously acknowledging Kindleberger's own formulation. But he also added a new twist, a generalization about historical change that went beyond anything Kindleberger himself had suggested. "The modern world economy has evolved through the emergence of great national economies that have successively become dominant. . . . Every economic system rests on a particular political order; its nature cannot be understood aside from politics" (40). Onto a normative proposition about the functions required for stability, Gilpin grafted a new positivist thesis about the nature of systemic transformation. Historical change was driven by the self-interested behavior of powerful states.

Further elaboration came in two later important works: *War and Change in World Politics*, and *The Political Economy of International Relations*. By 1981, in *War and Change in World Politics*, Gilpin's argument had become a full-fledged theory of systemic evolution. A social structure, he contended, is created to advance the interests of its most powerful members. Over time, however, as the distribution of capabilities changes, rising powers will seek to alter the rules of the game in ways that favor their own interests, and will continue to do so as long as the benefits of change exceed the cost. "Thus, a precondition for political change lies in the disjuncture between the existing social system and the redistribution of power toward those actors who would benefit most from a change in the system" (Gilpin 1981, 9). Hegemonic stability will last only so long as there are no challengers waiting in the wings.

By 1987, in his monumental *The Political Economy of International Relations*, Gilpin's theme had become grounds for an intense pessimism about the future of the global economy. America's hegemony in the post–World War II period may have been self-serving, but it had also served the world well, suppressing protectionism and managing financial crisis. But the times, they were a-changin'. "By the 1980s, American hegemonic leadership and the favorable political environment that it had provided for the liberal world economy had greatly eroded. . . . One must ask who or what would replace American leadership of the liberal economic order. Would it be . . . a collapse of the liberal world economy?" (Gilpin 1987, 345, 363). The outlook, he suggested, was exceedingly gloomy.

Krasner's contribution was more narrowly focused on just one dimension of the global system: the structure of international trade. In 1976, he published an oft-cited paper titled "State Power and the Structure of Foreign Trade," deliberately evoking Hirschman's 1945 book *National Power and the Structure of Foreign Trade*. Reviewing a century and a half of commercial history, he found evidence of a systematic relationship between hegemony and openness in the world trading system. Openness, he asserted, "is most likely to occur during periods when a hegemonic state is in its ascendancy. . . . It is the power and the policies of states that create order where there would otherwise be chaos" (Krasner 1976, 323, 343). He called his proposition a "state-power" argument.

Despite its relatively narrow focus, Keohane credits Krasner's paper—even more than the books of Kindleberger or Gilpin—with "setting the terms for more than a decade of work. . . . Krasner defined the agenda for years of scholarship" (1997, 151). As in Gilpin's approach, the exercise of power was assumed to be self-serving. The argument, as Krasner put it (1976, 317), "begins with the assumption that the structure of international trade is determined by the interests and power of states acting to maximize national goals." And here, too, the analysis ended on a pessimistic note. Krasner took the erosion of America's postwar hegemony as a given. We were living through a period, he insisted, "of relative American decline" (341). Could a turn toward closure, then, be far behind?

Both Gilpin and Krasner freely acknowledged their debt to Kindleberger's initial inspiration. Their contribution, as they saw it, was mainly to add a political dimension to the story. As Gilpin recently put it, "Kindleberger was a wonderful man, a liberal economist who saw the United States pursuing cosmopolitan goals. It was not for him a policy driven by interests but an ideological projection of our belief in free markets. Stephen Krasner and I shifted the argument from this being a cosmopolitan goal of the United States to being a goal in the national interest" (*International Relations* 2005, 369). The underlying theme was the same; only the motivation was different.

And so HST had its start. By the time Keohane got around to naming the theory, HST was already a well-developed idea. Indeed, the idea had already subdivided into two separate and distinguishable versions: one more benevolent, in the style of liberalism, and one more coercive, in the realist tradition. In either version, the theory was highly controversial.

The Decline of Hegemony?

Ironically, the controversy turned out to be based on a false premise. HST assumed that U.S. hegemony was in decline. A truly historical transition was purportedly in progress. Today we know better. The international environment was indeed changing. But with the wisdom of hindsight, we can see now that the change was far less dramatic than earlier thought.

At the time, the evidence for hegemonic decline seemed obvious. In 1950, the United States accounted for a remarkable one-third of all world output of goods and services. Twenty-five years later, its share was less than one-quarter. In manufacturing the decline was even steeper, from nearly half the global total at midcentury to less than one-third by the 1970s. Overall, U.S. economic growth in the 1950s and 1960s was significantly below that of continental Europe and Japan. America's share of world trade dropped from some 33 percent in 1948 to less than 24 percent by the mid-1970s. In 1971, persistent balance of payments deficits forced Washington to terminate the convertibility of the dollar into gold, precipitating the collapse of the Bretton Woods system. By the 1970s it was clear that the country, once the world's greatest creditor, was rapidly becoming a net debtor. And where as recently as the 1950s the United States had been a net exporter of oil, it now appeared that the economy's continued access to energy resources had been placed in the unreliable hands of the Organization of Petroleum Exporting Countries (OPEC).

Given such evidence, observers could be forgiven for concluding that the erosion of U.S. hegemony was real. The premise quickly became conventional wisdom, best symbolized by the title of an influential book published by Keohane in 1984. The book was titled simply *After Hegemony.* Henry Luce, fabled editor of *Time* magazine, had called the twentieth century the "American Century." But by 1984, according to Keohane, the American Century was winding down, inexorably and irretrievably: "Hegemonic leadership is unlikely to be revived in this century for the United States" (9). Among other things, the trend raised serious questions about the management of the global economy, to which I will return in the next chapter. The main purpose of Keohane's book, as we shall see in chapter 4, was to assess prospects for system governance after hegemony.

Most specialists at the time took the trend of U.S. decline for granted. That included, I confess, myself. As early as 1974, concurring with Gilpin, I asserted that "the balance of power in economic relations has changed; it is necessary to adjust to the new reality. . . . The United States is no longer the dominant economic power in the world" (Cohen 1974, 129, 133). And a decade later I was still writing of the "historic ebb of power away from the 'imperial' United States" (Cohen 1983b, 109). America, I concluded, was "still pre-eminent but no longer predominant" (109). During this period, such views were not considered particularly fanciful.

Only a few voices dissented. Among the most notable was Strange (1987), who with her characteristic iconoclasm insisted that the idea of America's lost hegemony was nothing more than a "myth." The United States still dominated all the key structures of the global economy, she contended, including in particular the newly emergent technology sector. The dollar still reigned as the world's top international currency. U.S. service industries still accounted for half the world market. The story of decline was overblown, based on a misreading of historical trends. In fact, Strange predicted, "it seems likely that America will enjoy the power to act as hegemon for some time to come" (571). In a similar vein, recalling Mark Twain's reaction to a premature obituary notice, Bruce Russett wrote that "Mark Twain did die eventually, and so will American hegemony. But in both cases early reports of their demise have been greatly exaggerated" (1985, 231).

In retrospect, it is clear that the dissenters had a point. America's unprecedented predominance at midcentury was an aberration, the product of wartime mobilization combined with widespread devastation in other industrial areas. The rest of the globe was bound to start catching up once postwar recovery got under way. By the end of the 1980s, however, most of the downward trends of the 1950s and 1960s had more or less leveled off. Nye called it the "vanishing World War II effect" (1990). Openly splitting with his former partner Keohane, Nye insisted that despite all the changes that had occurred in the international environment, the United States was still "bound to lead."

To his credit, Krasner was among the first to acknowledge the error of his ways. In 1989, in a reassessment written with a younger colleague, he conceded that "the position of the United States . . . has stabilized. . . . In aggregate terms the capabilities of the United States remain formidable" (Webb and Krasner 1989, 183). Eventually even Keohane graciously gave in. Writing after Strange's death, he granted that his 1984 book—or at least its title—might have been premature. Strange "thought that a book properly entitled *After Hegemony* would have to be about the distant future," he said, "and she was right. On this point, I simply concede; I should have listened to her earlier" (2000, xii). Even after the World War II effect had vanished, the United States maintained a substantial lead over other national economies.

Indeed, during the final years of the twentieth century America's lead seemed, if anything, to be widening again, reinforced by the collapse of the Soviet empire, which left the United States as the world's last remaining superpower. Over the course of the 1990s, the U.S. economy enjoyed its longest peacetime expansion in history, avoiding the high unemployment that plagued continental Europe, the stagnation that dragged down Japan after the bursting of its bubble economy, and the financial crises that disrupted emerging markets from East Asia to Latin America. At the dawn of the new millennium, America's economic primacy was once again unquestioned. The twentieth century had been the American Century. Now more than one source was predicting more of the same, perhaps even a "Second American Century" (Zuckerman 1998). If no longer a Gulliver among the Lilliputians, the United States had clearly reclaimed its position as number one. The aging hegemon had gained a new lease on life.

Decline of a Theory

But this does not mean that all the debate about HST was a waste of time. In the real world, the system may not have been transformed as much as first thought. Yet in the minds of scholars, ideas were significantly changed as a result of thinking about the possibility. Some of the most basic elements of IPE, as understood in the United States today, were constructed in the heat of battle over the logical truth and predictive accuracy of HST.

In its crudest form, HST argues that hegemony is both necessary and sufficient to ensure global stability. We should have known from the start that such a simple proposition, however attractive its parsimony, was far too categorical in its implications. Its predictions, it turns out, were supported by neither historical evidence nor theoretical reasoning. Leadership does matter, of course. But the question is how much? In a complex world, we have learned that outcomes depend on much more than a concentration of power alone.

Certainly that would appear to be the lesson of history. The broad correlation noted by Kindleberger and Gilpin, linking great power dominance and economic stability during the Pax Britannica and Pax Americana, looks credible at first glance but fails to stand up well to a detailed analysis, as multiple studies have demonstrated. Even Krasner, in his analysis of trade structures, admitted that the empirical evidence was a good deal less than perfect. His "state power" argument explained only half of the six historical periods he examined, stretching from 1820 to the 1970s (Krasner 1976).

Economist Barry Eichengreen (1989) provides an even more telling example in a historical study of global monetary arrangements. He considered the role of hegemony at each of three distinct stages in the evolution of the international monetary system—genesis, operation, and disintegration—comparing three distinct episodes—the classical gold standard, the interwar period, and Bretton Woods. What Eichengreen found was evidence both for and against HST. The relationship between the market power of the leading economy and the stability of the international monetary system is considerably more complex than suggested by simple variants of hegemonic stability theory" (258). Hegemony seemed neither necessary nor sufficient to explain the rise or fall of past financial orders.

That also appeared to be the message of theoretical reasoning. Keohane spelled out the main flaws of HST in his *After Hegemony*, in what amounted to a devastating critique of the theory's logical underpinnings. Concentrating on the collective goods version of the theory as originated by Kindleberger, Keohane pointed out that there is nothing in the logic of collective action that limits leadership to a single state. In principle, a core of two or more states acting cooperatively can also jointly maintain systemic stability. In *The Logic of Collective Action*, Olson himself spoke of the possibility of a "privileged group"—a core group including one or more states that could expect to enjoy a net benefit from providing a public good even if obliged to absorb all the costs involved. In a parallel fashion, using the reasoning of game theory, Thomas Schelling (1978) developed the notion of a "k-group"—a core of states small enough so that each member's contribution to the public good could be made conditional on the contribution of others. In Olson's framework, the equivalent of a k-group was an "intermediate group." An intermediate group does not have any one member that can expect individual net benefits but is small enough so that all members can see the effect of their own noncooperation.

Given the possible role of such a core, a narrow preoccupation with hegemony would appear to be beside the point. The real issue is not a concentration of power. Rather, it has to do with the conditions that facilitate the production of needed public goods, whether by one state or several. As Duncan Snidal put the point (1985, 612–13), extending Keohane's analysis, "The theory of hegemonic stability is a special case. . . . Since collective action can provide an alternative basis for cooperation, the possibility and requirements for collective action also need to be built into the analysis."

Effectively, the debate over HST was brought to a close by David Lake in a notable paper published in 1993, just about the time when we all began to realize that reports of the demise of America's hegemony had indeed been exaggerated. Reviewing two decades of discourse, Lake offered a useful distinction between two different strands of HST, roughly analogous to the divide between the theory's collective goods and security versions. One was *leadership theory*, building on the logic of collective action and focused on the production of stability, redefined as the "international economic infrastructure." The other was *hegemony theory*, which seeks to explain patterns of international economic openness by focusing on national trade preferences. Both pointed to the salience of the global economy's political foundations—to the critical role that politics can play in overall system governance. Power matters not because it may be concentrated but rather because it is relevant to the management of economic relations. As Lake concluded (485):

The research program skyrocketed to prominence in the 1970s largely on its intuitive appeal. We must resist the equal error of rejecting the theory.... Perhaps more than anything else, the hegemonic stability research program has sensitized the current generation of scholars to the international political underpinnings of the international economy. This insight should be preserved and built upon, not ignored and abandoned.

GLOBALIZATION

Since the end of the HST debate, fascination with the Really Big Question has noticeably waned in U.S. IPE. Specialists in the United States, by and large, appear to have lost interest in the grand theme of systemic change—all of which is a bit of a shame, given where the world would appear to be going today. Yet another irony is evident here. As noted above, it may be the conceit of each generation to believe that it is in the midst of a historical transition. This time it might actually turn out to be true. Arguably, a major systemic transformation may indeed be occurring. The American school, though, is paying little heed.

The difference this time is that it is economics, not politics, that is the central driver of change. Today systemic transformation, if that is what is happening, is equated not with hegemony but with market forces—specifically, with an expanding and intensifying range of linkages among national economies. International economic integration, which Keohane and Nye captured so neatly in their vision of complex interdependence, has now grown so dense that what was once seen as a difference of degree may now be in the process of becoming a difference of kind. Once we could speak of a world made up of separate national markets, connected through flows of trade, investment, and the like, but nonetheless fundamentally distinct. Nowadays that may no longer be possible.

In fact, the feeling is widespread that something truly new is being created: a rearticulated world. National economies, many contend, are swiftly being subsumed into a globalized system of transnational processes and structures. We are entering a genuinely new era: the age of *globalization*. If so, the Really Big Question remains as fascinating as ever.

Globaloony?

What do we mean by globalization? Though there is no standard definition of the term, most sources agree on the essentials. In its economic dimension, globalization is equated with an increasingly close integration of national markets—a fundamental transformation of economic geography. In place of territorially distinct economies, we are said to be moving toward a more unified model, a truly *global* marketplace. Production processes and financial markets are becoming more international, transcending space. Economic networks are spreading without regard for distance or borders. Transactions are speeding up, compressing time, and relations are growing more and more intense, deepening linkages. In short, the term globalization represents a dramatically new spatial organization of economic activity.

But is globalization real? Are we truly entering a new era? In the popular imagination in the United States there seems little doubt, fueled by sensationalist tracts with titles like *The Borderless World* (Ohmae 1990) or *One World, Ready or Not* (Greider 1997). Journalist Thomas Friedman is representative, assuring us that today's transition "will be remembered as one of those fundamental changes—like the rise of the nation-state or the Industrial Revolution" (2005, 45). As a result of the combined forces of technological development and market competition, the global playing field is being leveled. The world, Friedman declares, has now become "flat."

Nor is there much doubt on some of the radical fringes of the U.S. intellectual community, particularly among scholars working in the tradition of historical materialism—the style of historical interpretation derived from Marxist thought that has long been popular among critical theorists of all stripes. The "materialism" in historical materialism means placing economic relations and the social organization of production at the center of analysis. For historical materialists, globalization is simply the latest stage in the evolution of global capitalism. As one source puts it, "Contemporary globalization is distinctive because it is indeed based on a capitalist logic and is, as a consequence, transforming the social organization of production" (Rupert and Solomon 2006, 22). Claims another source: "Globalization represents a new stage in the evolving world capitalist system . . . the near-culmination of a centuries-long process of the spread of capitalist production around the world" (Robinson 2004, 2).

In the mainstream American school, however, there is considerably more skepticism. That something significant is going on is undeniable. But whatever it is, according to many, there may be rather less here than meets the eye. Globalization, it is widely felt, is overhyped, more a buzzword than a breakthrough. Indeed, for some, globalization is just so much "globaloney," or maybe even "globaloony"—no less a myth than the story of America's lost hegemony turned out to be. It was certainly no accident that in the fiftieth anniversary issue of IO (Katzenstein, Keohane, and Krasner 1999a), there was not a single article devoted to the subject of globalization. U.S. IPE today has little appetite for globaloney.

Rationales for the skepticism vary. For scholars of a realist persuasion, such as Gilpin and Krasner, reasoning goes back to the underlying connection between economic and political activity. The notion of globalization assumes that economics is driving politics in transforming the global system. Markets dominate states. But for realists this is far too deterministic, underestimating the continued centrality of the sovereign state in global affairs. As Gilpin has insisted (2001, 363), "No doubt there have been very important changes [but] for better or for worse, this is still a state-dominated world." It also overestimates the consequences of the changes that have in fact occurred. In Krasner's words (1999, 223), "I do not want to claim that globalization has had no impact on state control, but these challenges are not new. Rulers have always operated in a transnational environment."

For others in the American school, reasoning is more empirical. Yes, they concede, there has been an acceleration in the integration of national economies. Interdependence has continued to spread. But no, that does not necessarily mean that a broader systemic transformation is in progress. For the most part, globalization is simply more of the same—a fashionable new label for what specialists have been writing about for years. As Keohane and Nye put it in the latest edition of *Power and Interdependence* (2001, xv), "Globalization refers to an intensification of what we described as interdependence in 1977."

American school scholars have no hesitation in talking about globalization as interdependence. In fact, when understood in that more limited sense, notes Helen Milner (2002b, 215), "the issue of globalization has captured the heart of the field's attention over the last decade." But there is considerable resistance to any grander interpretation, with much effort directed to debunking all those headline-grabbing claims about a borderless world or the latest stage of capitalism—"unraveling the myths of globalization," as one recent tract puts it (Veseth 2005). In general, like the late comedian Rodney Dangerfield, broader notions of globalization "just can't get no respect."

Only a relatively small handful of mainstream U.S. scholars, including most notably Miles Kahler (2002) and Katzenstein (2005), have chosen to take the possibility of systemic transformation seriously. Even then, most analysis tends to address globalization mainly in terms of specific actors or issue areas rather than as a general phenomenon. When Geoffrey Garrett (2000), for example, attempts to explore the causes of globalization, he does so by disaggregating global market integration into three distinct components: trade, multinational production, and finance. Perhaps not surprisingly, he finds the sources of globalization to be unique to each component. The perspective is fragmented rather than holistic. No broad vision emerges from the analysis.

The story is also the same with efforts to study the consequences of globalization. Is the creation of a global marketplace erasing all differences at the state level? One group of scholars responds by focusing on globalization's impact on multinational corporations (Doremus et al. 1998). Their research finds that corporate structures remain deeply embedded in their national institutional and cultural environments, implying durable sources of divergence. Does the new spatial organization of economic activity have uniform effects on political authority? Another group, including myself, examines a collection of narrowly drawn case studies (Kahler and Lake 2003). The result is a potpourri of "variegated and contingent findings" that defy easy generalization. Where my own contribution to the collection, focusing on monetary governance, found some evidence of pressure to delegate authority upward from states to more supranational currency arrangements, others saw tendencies in the reverse direction, devolving authority downward to diverse subnational units or outward toward market actors. Again, no broad vision emerges.

A Loss of Ambition

Skepticism is not necessarily a bad thing. If grand theories about the Really Big Question fail to stand up to rigorous analysis, it is not the critics who should be criticized. But the waning of the American school's interest in systemic transformation is nonetheless striking. Clearly there has been a loss of ambition. In effect, horizons have shrunk.

It is tempting to attribute the retreat to purely personal considerations. Perhaps having put their faith in one dramatic historical scenario, only to be embarrassed by later facts, U.S. scholars are reluctant to risk their reputations again. Once bitten, twice shy. Yet the reality is that more fundamental factors are also involved, reflecting the way the IPE field has been constructed in the United States. Underlying issues of both epistemology and ontology are involved.

At the level of epistemology, the issue is the growing methodological standardization of U.S.-style IPE. In American economics, it has long been evident that the discipline's reductionist methodology has encouraged an increasingly cramped approach to inquiry. Broad theories attempting to explain how the overall economy works are no longer fashionable. Rather, individual studies focus more and more on small insights about economic behavior in specific, narrow contexts. In the words of one prominent economist, Steven Levitt, "We have moved to a much more micro view of the world" (quoted in Uchitelle 2006).

In their pursuit of professional respect, specialists in IPE appear to have gone the same route. In the field's early days, when the basics were still up for grabs, intellectual entrepreneurs like Kindleberger and Gilpin felt free to Think Big—to explore the furthest horizons of inquiry. But as the American school's approach has become increasingly "professionalized," hostage to creeping economism, mainstream scholarship has correspondingly narrowed in scope. If the challenge is to formulate parsimonious models and clearly falsifiable hypotheses, inquiry must be disaggregated in order to make it analytically tractable. The focus must be on determinants of behavior and outcomes in more and more finely defined issue areas. Hence grand themes are out; midlevel theory is in. Little room is left for holistic thinking about the system as a whole.

At the level of ontology, the issue is what Michael Zürn, a noted German political scientist, calls "the analytical shackles of 'methodological nationalism' " (2002, 248). Methodological nationalism "sees national self-determination as ontologically given and as the most important cleavage in the political sphere" (248). For the American school, national governments are still the core actors. The system is still defined in terms of interstate relations. As indicated at the start of this chapter, it was natural for political scientists to think first about politics and the role of the sovereign state when addressing the Really Big Question. Systemic transformation, for them, could not even be conceived apart from a dramatic shift in the distribution of capabilities among states.

That approach is limited, however, since it discounts the importance of a range of emerging and increasingly relevant transnational actors in the global economy. In introducing the notion of complex interdependence, Keohane and Nye made the reasonable argument that studies should incorporate all relevant agents—all individuals and entities whose control of resources and access to channels of communications enabled them to participate meaningfully in political relationships across state frontiers. But in the years since, state actors have continued to hog the analytic stage, even as market processes in the real world have become more and more international. That too has left little scope for thinking holistically about the system as a whole.

Is it any wonder, then, that U.S.-style IPE would show so little interest in a broad interpretation of globalization? Having defined its basic understandings in the way that it has, the American school has in effect washed its hands of the Really Big Question. Loss of ambition does not seem an unkind way to describe the development. One might even call the attitude timid. For more ambitious studies of systemic transformation today, we must look elsewhere.

WORLD ORDERS

One place to look, of course, is to the British school, where the Really Big Question remains high on the research agenda. Strange and her followers have long been motivated by a sense that the world truly is in transition. As indicated, nothing better defines the differences between the American and British schools than their respective discourses on systemic transformation.

Strange got the ball rolling with her "Mutual Neglect" manifesto. "What I have in mind," she wrote (1970, 304–5), "is that the pace of development in the international economic system has accelerated, is still accelerating and will probably continue to accelerate. . . . [Economic interdependence] is outdistancing and outgrowing the rather more static and rigid international political system." And that theme of accelerating change continued to feature prominently in her published work right up to the time of her death. It is no accident that when once asked who her heroes were, she started with Kindleberger—a rare economist who she did not feel the need to attack (Lorentzen 2002, ix).

Once the ball got rolling, however, it was left to others to map out more formal explanations of the causes and consequences of change. Most influential in this respect was Cox, whose views on systemic transformation have shaped a generation or more of scholarship. Cox, though largely ignored in the United States, is revered as second only to Strange in the pantheon of the British school. His ideas continue to reverberate in the contemporary debate over globalization.

A Challenger of Orthodoxies

Like Kindleberger, Cox had a distinguished career in public service before starting his life as an academic. A graduate of McGill University in Montreal, where he received a master's degree in history in 1946, he spent a full quarter century at the International Labor Office (ILO) in Geneva, Switzerland, serving for many years as *chef de cabinet* (executive assistant) for the director general and then as chief of the ILO's Program and Planning Division. After five years at Columbia University, he moved in 1977 to York University, where he remained until his retirement in 1992, often working in collaboration with his late wife, Jessie. Also like Kindleberger, he has stayed active as a scholar even after formal retirement, and still writes and gives occasional lectures.

Modest almost to a fault, Cox abhors pretension and is disinclined to stand on ceremony. One former student recalls a seminar at York, shortly before Cox's retirement, when the now-revered senior scholar entered the room late. Finding no seat, he simply squatted down on the floor for the remainder of the session. Colleagues, it is said, spoke of the incident for years afterward. Others describe him as a person of integrity, generous of spirit and unfailingly caring. Another former student says that his work with Cox "confirmed for me that humane individuals can also make first-class academics" (Germain 1997, xiii).

On the other hand, Cox is hardly averse to the good life. Even after leaving the ILO, he and Jessie retained a comfortable chalet in the Swiss Alps, where they preferred to spend most summers. An admirer reports that "I learned everything I know about Campari and soda from Bob Cox." I am reminded of a Marxist historian who my wife (also a historian) ran into at an upscale restaurant one evening. When joshed about his choice of venue, her friend replied, "Nothing's too good for the working class." One could imagine Cox, with a knowing smile, offering much the same response.

Most notable about Cox is a fierce independence of judgment and a fearless, even eager willingness to challenge established verities. He himself admits to a "disposition to question the dominant attitudes of my milieu" (Cox 1996b, 19), which he attributes to his experience growing up as an Anglo-Canadian

Figure 3.2. Robert Cox. Courtesy of the International Labor Organization

in French (and Catholic) Montreal. "From an early age," he writes, "I was inclined to see the contradictions in the values of my milieu and to challenge its orthodoxies" (19). There are few universal truths, insists Cox. Ideas must be understood as historically contingent, rooted in the particularities of a time and place. He is a relativist through and through.

Cox's early penchant for skepticism carried over to his years at the ILO, where he frequently felt at odds with what he saw as the dominant ideology of the organization. "I found myself in the moral position of the anthropologist—a participant observer of my new tribe. I was in it but could not be entirely of it" (1996b, 22). Cox was happy to help promote the ILO as a defender of worker interests. But he was resistant to bureaucratic pressures to conform to a single mental framework "committed to the universality of some very obviously historically contingent European-American practices in labor-management relations" (22). Industrial relations meant much more than just the institutionalized collective bargaining arrangements characteristic of the advanced industrial economies. What about the mass agricultural populations of the world, he asked, or the many marginal workers in the informal sectors of developing nations? He could never fully reconcile himself to the notion that there was just one way to approach the organization of production.

In the 1960s, he was instrumental in designing and setting up the International Institute for Labor Studies, intended to operate within the ILO as a research and educational center enjoying full intellectual freedom; eventually, he also became the institute's director. But then a new director general was appointed in 1970, whose views of intellectual freedom, Cox says, "were molded by analogy with the imprimatur and *nihil obstat* practice of Catholic orthodoxy (albeit he was no Catholic)." For the Anglo-Canadian from Montreal, this was all too much. When the new chief moved to rein in the institute's independence, Cox decided to move on, first to Columbia University in 1972, and then five years later to York. He simply could not accept the constraints now being imposed on the institute's work. In his letter of resignation from the ILO, Cox wrote (1996b, 36):

> International organizations are passing through a critical period. . . . The first requirement for a constructive transformation of existing international organizations such as would merit renewed support is a healthy spirit of self-criticism and responsiveness to the new demands of social change. An intellectually independent institute could have helped. But if instead of allowing the critical spirit to grow, the Institute is now to be caught up in the old game of bureaucratic politics and to begin to screen out opinions which do not show deference to the canons of official doctrine, it may, I fear, become of little use either to the ILO itself or to social policy thinking in the world at large.

And so he chose to leave the ILO in order to nurture his "critical spirit," and freely pursue his interest in "transformation" and "social change." At last, as an academic, he had license to challenge orthodoxies to his heart's content. In Cox's words (1999, 391), "I felt a kind of liberation."

His earliest scholarly publications, dating from his years at Columbia, appeared mainly in U.S. academic journals and were actually quite conventional in orientation. Not surprisingly, given his career up to that point, his attention then was focused mainly on decision making in international organizations. But as he became more immersed in U.S. academic life, he gradually turned more toward political economy. "I became more interested in the substantive issues—economic and social—that international organizations had to confront," he has written to me. "The issues called for innovative approaches; the institutions were more preoccupied with their own survival and aggrandizement." For a period, Cox was even a member of the board of editors of IO, becoming the board chair in 1979–1980, and one of his first publications as he was leaving the ILO was a chapter in Keohane and Nye's landmark *Transnational Relations and World Politics* (Cox 1972).

By the time he arrived at York, however, his early training in history had begun to reassert itself, leading him to take on much more ambitious themes—ultimately, nothing less than "the structures that underlie the world" (Cox 1999, 390). Increasingly he began to publish in Britain, where the academic audience was far more receptive to a "historical-relativist paradigm." International studies in Britain had long encouraged interpretative historical analysis. In the nascent field of IPE, Strange had already established a precedent with *Sterling and British Policy*, which took a distinctly historical approach to the politics of international money. Cox was completely at home working in the same tradition. His newer writings quickly gained acceptance among British scholars and soon came to be widely taught in British universities.

Historical Structures and Social Forces

The breakout was not long in coming. In 1981, Cox published "Social Forces, States, and World Orders: Beyond International Relations Theory," a paper that has since attained virtually iconic status among British school scholars. Although much more was to come later, including his monumental *Production, Power, and World Order* (Cox 1987), nothing else matched the impact of that early, innovative essay. The changes then occurring in the world economy, he contended, were profound and needed to be seen in their totality. Much more was involved than merely an increase of economic interdependence. At issue was nothing less than the emergence of a new world order, a new historical structure reflecting an expansion and integration of production processes on a transnational scale. And central to it all was a transformative realignment of social forces—a new "global class structure alongside or superimposed on national class structures" (Cox 1981, 147).

Cox's starting point was a distinction between positivist social science—what he called "problem-solving" theory—and critical theory. For Cox, the principal difference between the two had to do with the dimension of time. As he saw it, the perspective of problem-solving theory, by which he meant most of what is done in the American school, is relatively short-term. In effect, Cox said, problem-solving theory timidly assumes that the major components of a system, including above all states, are not subject to fundamental change. Underlying structures are simply parameters, a kind of "continuing present"

(Cox 1981, 129), fixing the limits within which action occurs. The approach is therefore essentially ahistorical. Analysis focuses on the action, not the limits. Solutions are sought within the existing system.

Critical theory, by contrast, deliberately adopts a much lengthier time horizon, measured not in months or years but in decades, even generations. As indicated in the last chapter, critical theory had already been around for some time; an oppositional frame of mind was nothing new. Cox, however, put a particular spin on it. For him, what most distinguished critical theory was that it steps outside the confines of existing relationships to highlight a system's origins and above all its development potential. The approach's main value lies in the fact that it is anything but ahistorical; structures are anything but parameters. As Cox explained it (1981, 129), "Critical theory is theory of history in the sense of being concerned not just with the past but with a continuing process of historical change." Critical theory permits analysis of the relationship between structure and agency. Inquiry can focus on how systems came into being in the past, what changes are presently occurring within them, and how those changes might be shaped in the future. What are the sources of conflict in a system, and what patterns of change are possible? In short, critical theory allows one to think seriously about systemic transformation.

Cox may fairly lay claim to be the first major scholar to apply critical theory to the study of IR (Schechter 2002, 2). In the words of one admirer, Cox "offered a counter-hegemonic alternative to the canon" (Mittelman 1998, 88). In stressing critical theory's advantages over positivist social science, Cox may have been highlighting his own intellectual growth since his days at Columbia. As the same admirer has suggested, "Maybe Cox's distinction between problem-solving theory and critical theory is an auto-critique, a useful way to assess the contributions and limitations of his early work on international organizations" (88). Or maybe, as a trained historian, he just wanted to return to his roots. Either way, Cox clearly broke new ground.

As a practical matter, his take on positivist social science was a bit unfair. What Cox called problem-solving theory could also address the interaction between structure and agency, as we shall see in looking at mainstream institutional theory in the next chapter. But that is a quibble. The real key, for Cox, was the issue of historical change. Critical theory appealed to him because it focused centrally on the potential for systemic development and transformation. Cox's take on critical theory enabled him to project a much longer view of the interactions of global economic and political activities. World politics could be studied as a dialogue between the past and present, offering alternative possibilities for the future.

Critical theory also provided a legitimate outlet for his critical spirit—an opportunity to engage directly with important social issues. Analysis need not be separated from ethics. Like his longtime friend Strange, he firmly believed in the moral purpose of inquiry. As Cox put it in his famous aphorism (1981,

128; 1995, 31), which he is never loath to repeat, "Theory is always *for* someone and *for* some purpose."

A principal advantage of critical theory, for Cox, was that instead of taking prevailing institutions and power relationships for granted, it would question them. Instead of disaggregating issues to make them more analytically tractable, it would keep attention focused on the system as a whole, seeking out sources of contradiction and conflict. In his view, problem-solving theory was conservative since it does not question the underlying interests that are served by a given system. Problem-solving theory, he insisted, was about managing the world as it is, not changing it. Critical theory, by contrast, directly "allows for a normative choice in favor of a social and political order different from the prevailing order" (Cox 1981, 130). For Cox, as for Strange, the key question was: *Cui bono?*

The answer, he felt, was to be found in the concept of "world orders," historical structures that he saw as a function of three broad categories of influences: material capabilities, ideas, and institutions. Material capabilities, as reflected in technological capacities and modes of production, were rapidly becoming integrated across national frontiers; and the accelerating internationalization of production, in turn, was generating new intersubjective understandings of social relations and new innovations in governing institutions. Profound change was occurring, with unmistakable distributional implications.

How would it all turn out? In assessing future world order prospects, Cox rejected the state-centrism of traditional IR theory. The state could not be analyzed in isolation. Historical change had to be thought of in terms of the reciprocal relationship of structures and actors within a much broader conceptualization of IR: the "state-society complex." Outcomes would depend on the response of "social forces," defined as the main collective actors engendered by the relations of production both within and across all spheres of activity. "International production," Cox wrote (1981, 147), "is mobilizing social forces, and it is through these forces that its major political consequences *vis-à-vis* the nature of states and future world orders may be anticipated." The overriding imperative was to support social forces that would "bargain for a better deal within the world economy" (151).

Sources

The sources of Cox's ideas were diverse. As with Kindleberger, personal experience undoubtedly played a role. During his quarter century in Geneva, Cox was witness to massive changes in the world economy—inter alia the miraculous recoveries of continental Europe and Japan, the creation of the European Common Market, and the seeming decline of U.S. hegemony. Since the world order had already evolved so greatly, why not think about where it might go in the future? Likewise, his perch at the ILO made it natural to conceptualize change in terms of social forces, with a particular emphasis on labor. In bureaucratic settings, it is said, where you stand depends on where you sit. After sitting for some twenty-six years in the aptly named ILO, Cox had little difficulty in taking a stand against more conventional state-centric approaches to historical analysis. His stress on the social organization of production clearly reflected his years of work in Geneva on problems of industrial relations.

In intellectual terms the most obvious influence on Cox's thought was Marxism, with its emphasis on class relations and the material forces of production. Marxian terminology runs persistently through his writings. Like Marx, Cox insisted that change could only be understood dialectically, with each successive world order generating the contradictions that bring about its transformation. Of particular importance in his perspective was the work of Antonio Gramsci, the Italian Marxist of the interwar period, who emphasized the power of ideas and knowledge structures, and how they emerged from the material interests of dominant classes. Like Gramsci, Cox saw the hegemonic control of ideas as central to legitimizing and maintaining a particular social order. Cox's debt to Gramsci was freely acknowledged in an oft-cited paper published in 1983.

Another inspiration was Karl Polanyi's *The Great Transformation* (1944), which placed systemic change center stage and was unabashedly normative in its tone. Polanyi, too, stressed the social underpinnings of structural transformation. Central was a dialectical process that he called the "double movement": first market expansion (the "first movement"), and then society's attempt to protect itself against the market's disruptive and destabilizing consequences (the "second movement"). The family resemblance between Polanyi's double movement and the dynamics of Cox's world orders is transparent, as Cox is the first to admit. Here also his debt has been freely acknowledged. As Cox stated (1995, 39), "Polanyi has given us a framework for thinking about . . . the global economy."

A third influence came from the world-systems approach of Immanuel Wallerstein (1984), who sought to reconceptualize the international environment as a broadly integrated political economic system, downplaying the role of interstate politics. And still other influences came from dependency theory and from the long-cycle analysis of George Modelski (1987). Even the term "historical structure" was borrowed, by Cox's own admission, from the French historian Fernand Braudel. In keeping with one of the cardinal principles of the British school, Cox's scholarship was nothing if not eclectic.

But it was also decidedly original, defying easy classification. In good part this is because he was so willing, as a former student has written (not disapprovingly), "to sample from discordant intellectual traditions to create a method" (Sinclair 1996, 9). He himself preferred to place his work in the tradition of historical materialism (Cox 1996c, 58). His focus on the concept of world orders, embodying a succession of historical structures defined by their modes of production, was certainly consistent with the historical materialist approach. In an early essay Cox described himself as a "conservative," which he equated with "historicism." In his words (1979, 258 n1): "My conservatism is in the first place historicism, or the sense that ideas and events are bound together in structural totalities that condition the possibilities of change—what I understand Machiavelli to have meant by *necessità*."

Others, however, have never been quite sure how to categorize him. In his time he has been called everything from a neorealist to a neo-Gramscian. Where one source labels him a "fairly conventional Marxist" (Brown 1992, 202), another accuses him of "bowdlerizing Marxism" (Shaw 2000, 84–85), and a third calls his variant of Marxism "watery" (Adams 1989, 224). Much of the uncertainty about his core orientation appears to relate to his notion of social forces, which is much broader than the classic Marxist concept of class. Strange may have put it best when she called him an "eccentric," though quickly adding "in the best English sense of the word, a loner, a fugitive from intellectual camps" (1988a, 269–70). Cox later returned the compliment, identifying her as a "loner," someone who does not fit into conventional classifications, rather than a "groupie" (1996d, 178–79). For himself, Cox took some measure of pride in what he depicted as "the unconventionality of my intellectual journey" (1996b, 19).

Reception

In the United States Cox has been received coolly, occasionally even with contempt. Not unusual was one U.S. review of *Production, Power, and World Order*: "This book is an ambitious but failed attempt. . . . It fails so completely that there is not even anything interesting about the failure" (Adams 1989, 224). Among British school scholars, on the other hand, his work is held in the highest regard and continues to be influential.

Why has Cox failed to make an impact in the United States? In part, the rejection can be attributed to the American school's waning interest in the Really Big Question since the end of the HST debate. In part also it can be attributed to his underlying ontology, which places modes of production rather than state relations at the heart of the analysis. Cox's emphasis on the state-society complex does not mix well with the "methodological nationalism" of mainstream U.S. scholarship.

Mostly, though, the rejection reflects a frustration with an intellectual approach that is so infuriatingly at variance with contemporary standards of U.S. social science. As Cox himself ruefully conceded (1996b, 29), "An interpretive, hermeneutic, historicist mode of knowledge lends itself to the epithet 'unscientific.' " His grand eclecticism, dense with historical and institutional detail, simply does not fit easily with the reductionist epistemology that is currently favored by U.S. specialists. Because of the high degree of historical contingency in his approach, it is difficult to reduce his insights to a concise set of logical theorems. Because of the lengthy time perspective of his analysis, it is difficult to convert his conclusions into empirically falsifiable propositions. And because of his propensity to mix positivist observation and moral judgments, it is difficult even to assess the fundamental soundness of his reasoning. So rather than engage Cox directly, scholars in the United States have found it easier simply to dismiss or ignore him.

In Britain, on the other hand, as well in other outposts of the British school, Cox's distinctive approach has become a key source of inspiration for younger scholars. "The work of Robert Cox," remarks one observer, "has inspired many students to rethink the way in which we study international political economy, and it is fair to say that [his] historical materialism is perhaps the most important alternative to realist and liberal perspectives in the field today" (Griffiths 1999, 118). Numerous sources cite Cox as the starting point for their own theoretical studies.

Stephen Gill and David Law, for example, in an influential paper published in 1989, explicitly build on Cox's dynamics to explain the development of what they described as the structural power of capitalism. "His analysis of social forces," Gill and Law contend, "points to a more comprehensive and flexible approach to the question of structural change than that provided in various mechanistic 'modes of economism' in the literature" (475–76). Likewise, Ronen Palan and Barry Gills (1994) credit Cox as a central wellspring for their own "neostructuralist" agenda in international relations. Geoffrey Underhill describes the study of the state—"what it is, what it does, and where it fits into Cox's state-society complex"—as *the* problem of international political economy" (2006, 16).

Cox's historical materialism appeals to British-style scholars for several reasons——not least of which is the critical spirit that animates his work, emphasizing the normative dimension of academic research. In promoting a skeptical attitude toward prevailing institutions and power relationships, Cox has pushed against an open door. As Timothy Sinclair remarks, the favorable response to his work in Britain no doubt reflects in good part "the relative openness to critical perspectives in research and teaching in that country" (1996, 13). Strange and others had long encouraged rebellion against "The Establishment." Hence, students in the new field of IPE were already primed to question authority and pass moral judgments. With his insistence that theory is always for someone and some purpose, Cox legitimized a passionate engagement with social issues.

Also important is the eclecticism of his scholarship, which does not hesitate to draw from a wide range of scholarly traditions. Insights are sought from fields as diverse as religion and anthropology, ethnic studies and feminist theory, philosophy and even ecology. His aim has always been, in his words, to clear the ground "for a more integrated knowledge about processes of world order" (Cox 2002, 80). In this respect too the door was open to his influence. Inclusiveness was already a hallmark of the British school.

Above all, Cox provides a framework that permits specialists to keep their eye on the Really Big Question. His emphasis on world orders and social forces may not appeal much to U.S. scholars, who would prefer less transcendental constructs to work with. But for British school scholars, concerned less with scientific method than with informed interpretation, his broad perspective provides just the language needed to uncover long-term trends and universal truths. With Cox as a guide, the grand theme of systemic change need not be abandoned. Scholars can still legitimately look for signs of historical transition.

GLOBALIZATION, AGAIN

All of which brings us back to today's grand theme of globalization. For Cox, the world really is going through a major phase of structural change, reshaping social relations on a global scale. The accelerating integration of national economies, coupled with deregulation and privatization, is giving markets free rein to reinforce the power of privileged classes. The results, predictably, are dismal: "social conflict arising from the growing polarization between rich and poor, recourse to violent forms of protest, the prospect of financial collapse, and the impending threat of biospheric crisis" (Cox 2002, 94). The problem, Cox argues, is "how to manage a radically shifting balance of economic power with an eye to preserving and advancing social equity—an achievement of equity that is being eroded by unregulated markets" (2006, 17). The challenge is to promote a broad-based countermovement, premised on the principles of collective creativity and social justice, that might successfully contain the excesses of "hyper-liberal globalizing capitalism."

Given Cox's influence, it should be no surprise that the idea of globalization would receive more attention from the British school than it does on the U.S. side of the Atlantic. For the American school, the notion may be little more than globaloney. Indeed, how could it be otherwise if theory implicitly assumes a "continuing present"? Genuine transformation would appear to be ruled out by definition. But for British school scholars, with their much greater concern for what Braudel called the *longue durée* of history, globalization is indeed real—not a myth at all. We truly are entering a new era. As Stephen Gill and James Mittelman asserted in the preface to a volume of essays written in Cox's honor, "We are in the throes of structural change in world order" (1997, xvi). The implications, therefore, need to be carefully studied, using elements of Cox's historical materialism where appropriate. In the British style globalization is analyzed holistically, as a general systemic phenomenon, not in bits and pieces. And scholars do not shrink from normative analysis highlighting issues of justice or equity. There's no timidity here.

Representative are three prominent texts prepared for the British academic market in recent years: *Globalisation and Interdependence in the International Political Economy*, a broad survey by R. J. Barry Jones (1995); and two essay collections, *Global Political Economy* edited by John Ravenhill (2005), and *Political Economy and the Changing Global Order* edited by Richard Stubbs and Geoffrey Underhill (2006). In his book, Jones provides a sweeping review of the globalization phenomenon, seen as the dominant trend in today's international system. Throughout the discussion, Jones insists that analysis cannot neglect "the source and role of the basic values and ideas that direct human action and underpin human institutions" (1995, 40). In the Ravenhill volume, fully half the chapters address globalization and its consequences. In the Stubbs and Underhill collection, twenty-three of the thirty-four chapters include some variant of the word globalization in their title. None of these texts evince the least doubt that the broad phenomenon of globalization is both real and important.

Even Strange got into the act before her death, though she didn't care much for the term globalization as such. Strange preferred to speak simply of the "impersonal forces of world markets, integrated over the postwar period," which in her view were "now more powerful than the states to whom ultimate political authority over society and economy is supposed to belong" (1996, 4). The British school, plainly, is eager to talk about globalization. But in a clear demonstration of the dialogue of the deaf that has emerged across the Atlantic, the American school just doesn't seem to be listening. In the United States, minds are elsewhere.

Chapter 4

THE CONTROL GAP

Once regimes are established they assume a life
of their own.
—Stephen Krasner

In a world without centralized government, why
should states comply with obligations that had
become inconvenient?
—Robert Keohane

WHERE ELSE have minds been? One theme that has especially preoccupied the American school is system governance. The growth of economic interdependence after World War II may not have amounted to a grand historical transformation. But even if it was no more than a matter of degree, the change was obviously pivotal and raised serious questions about the management of the world economy. As Keohane and Nye pointed out from the start, complex interdependence implied a widening "control gap" between state aspirations and state capabilities. The essence of governance lies in the authority to define and enforce norms for the allocation of values in a collectivity—to write the rules of the game, as it were. If national governments were losing control, who then would make the rules for the global system, and how would compliance with those rules be assured? In a prime example of their penchant for what Cox called problem-solving theory, specialists in the United States have made the Control Gap a central concern of IPE scholarship.

Along the way, many individuals have contributed to thinking about the Control Gap. Of the pioneer generation, none has been more deeply involved than the familiar Keohane, who over the years has made the study of system governance central to his life's work. In his collaborative projects with Nye in the 1970s, Keohane succeeded in promoting a new interest in the role of institutions in world politics, broadly conceived as forms of patterned cooperation among governments. Given the pair's liberal orientation, it was perhaps inevitable that their new line of thought would soon come to be known by the tongue-twisting sobriquet neoliberal institutionalism, though Keohane himself has more recently expressed a preference for the simple label "institutionalism" without the adjective (Keohane 2002, 3). Even after he and Nye went their separate ways, Keohane continued to exercise major influence over the development of institutional theory, as we shall see.

In first setting the discourse on track, however, no one was more influential than Krasner, the erstwhile realist. Though skeptical about many of the tenets of liberal IR theory, he was nonetheless principally responsible for the new IPE field's first comprehensive exploration of institutions governing global economic relations—what quickly came to be known as regime theory. Keohane and Nye first highlighted the notion of so-called international regimes in *Power and Interdependence*. Following their lead, Krasner engineered a collective research project designed to advance an understanding of both the causes and consequences of this newly recognized form of interstate cooperation. The result of his entrepreneurship, a collection of essays published under the title *International Regimes* (Krasner 1983a), remains to this day a cornerstone for U.S.-style scholarship on system governance.

Again, the contrast with the British school is stark. British scholars have not been indifferent to the issue of system governance. They also stress the loss of control by governments in an increasingly interdependent world economy. But consistent with the greater inclusiveness of the British version of IPE, discourse tends to be less state-centric in its conception of governance. On this subject too, as on the Really Big Question of systemic transformation, each tradition has constructed its own distinctive approach.

FROM ORGANIZATIONS TO REGIMES

For American scholars the question appeared straightforward: How would states be able to manage interactions in the new era of complex interdependence? Much was clearly at risk. No authoritative enforcement agency existed at the level of world politics to promote a degree of order in economic affairs. In formal terms, anarchy prevailed. Hence, some form of cooperation among governments seemingly was required to achieve common objectives. Could increasingly transnationalized markets be managed to preserve mutual benefits? Could economic conflict be successfully resolved or avoided? In short, could there be effective governance without a global government?

Prior to the 1970s, as we saw in chapter 1, most work on system governance had focused narrowly on the details of formal organizations such as the IMF or GATT. One of the accomplishments of Keohane and Nye, after their takeover of IO, was to shift attention to the broader notion of institutions, conceived as "persistent and connected sets of rules (formal and informal) that prescribe behavioral roles, constrain activity, and shape expectations" (Keohane 1989a, 3). International institutions encompass all forms of patterned cooperation among states. World politics may be anarchic, Keohane and Nye noted, but it is not chaotic. Institutions serve to aggregate preferences into policy, and when preferences clash, they provide a mechanism for conflict resolution. They are, in other words, the glue that holds the system together. With *Power and Inter-*

dependence, Keohane and Nye called for the study of regimes as the most representative form of international institution. With his collective project, Krasner sought to build on their insights and extend the logic of their approach. In the process, his edited volume firmly laid the foundation for much of the construction to follow.

Reassessing Realism

Unlike other political scientists in IPE's pioneer generation, such as Keohane or Gilpin, Krasner developed an interest in political economy early on, even before the completion of his doctorate at Harvard University in 1972. A graduate of Cornell University, where he majored in history, he spent two years in the Peace Corps in Nigeria and then earned a master's degree in international studies at Columbia, taking more courses in economics than political science. Pivotal for him, by his own testimony, was a Harvard seminar with Hirschman, which led Krasner to write his PhD dissertation on the international coffee market. "When I began work on my dissertation," Krasner avers (1989, 418), "I had no sense that international political economy would develop as a distinct field. No jobs were offered in international political economy. . . . Had I known more about the risks, I probably would have done something else." But jobs, in fact, did turn out to be available, first at Harvard, then at the University of California at Los Angeles (UCLA), and finally at Stanford University, which has been his home base since 1981.

Born and bred on the island of Manhattan, Krasner has never lost many of the traits typically associated with native New Yorkers, including an intense competitiveness and an almost gleeful pugnacity. Playing tennis with him, especially in his younger days, was a frustrating experience. No matter how skillful an opponent's shot, he never gave up, returning ball after ball until forcing an error on the other side of the net. Once, flashing his infectious grin, he explained to me the secret of how to avoid a mugging on New York's mean streets. Always walk "tough," he said. Look as if you're ready for a fight, and would-be muggers will back off.

A bit of that streetwise combativeness has always been evident in Krasner's approach to academic dialogue. Carl von Clausewitz said that war was politics by other means. Krasner approaches intellectual discourse in much the same spirit. Like a fine Talmudic scholar, he relishes the cut and thrust of debate, and thrives on controversy. "Refreshingly frank" is the way one of his students tactfully describes his style; Krasner "does not pull punches when he goes after flaws in an argument" (Chan 2005).

Yet few scholars are more talented at tempering disputatiousness with a rapier-like wit. There may be a touch of cynicism to his views, as in his characterization of the concept of state sovereignty as little more than "organized hypocrisy" (Krasner 1999). When once asked if the term could be applied to

Figure 4.1. Steven Krasner. Courtesy of the Freeman Spogli Institute for International Studies, Stanford University

international politics more broadly he shot back "Life," suggesting a dim view of all existence, not just politics (Institute of International Studies 2003, 3). But there is often a touch of whimsy as well, implying more *gaieté de coeur* than Krasner himself might be willing to admit. Could a truly unredeemable cynic have written an article on the world energy crisis with such a droll title as "The Great Oil Sheikdown" (Krasner 1973)? Colleagues line up at conferences and professional meetings to hear his latest witticisms, which are all the more amusing for being delivered with an absolutely deadpan mien.

In his early days, Krasner says (1989, 421), he saw himself "as something of a gadfly," and even later continued to enjoy testing the waters with heretical thoughts. He never feared taking on Big Ideas, and with his habitual contentiousness, was always prepared to challenge orthodoxy. In time, however, the erstwhile rebel gradually took on the aspect of an elder statesman. From 1986 to 1991 he served as editor of IO, and in 2005 was named the director for policy planning in the Department of State by his old friend and former Stanford colleague Condoleezza Rice. "It has come as a shock in recent years," he noted ruefully not long ago, "to be treated as part of the conventional wisdom" (421).

Always a convinced realist, Krasner was particularly struck by the work of Gilpin—especially Gilpin's contribution to *Transnational Relations and World Politics*, the early project organized by Keohane and Nye (Gilpin 1972). Gilpin's essay, Krasner said later, "provided me with the intellectual direction that was to inform my work for the next decade" (1989, 420). At last he could see a way to meld his early economics training with his interest in state power. More than a little courage was involved in going this route; it would mean taking on some of his own senior colleagues at Harvard. But for a would-be gadfly, that was probably part of the attraction. The affinity with Gilpin's approach was evident in Krasner's celebrated 1976 paper "State Power and the Structure of International Trade" as well as his first major book, *Defending the National Interest*, which followed two years later (Krasner 1978a). In these efforts and subsequent scholarship, a friend has commented, Krasner demonstrated a "striking ability to think about the relationships between power and economics."

It is perhaps noteworthy that the "State Power" article was written in Krasner's last year at Harvard, just before he moved to UCLA; Keohane calls it his "farewell address" (1997, 167). For Krasner at this stage, as for Gilpin, the allure of a state-centric paradigm of world politics remained strong. States could be treated as unified actors pursuing aims defined in terms of national interest. System governance, in turn, could be understood as a direct function of the distribution of state power. The logic of HST appeared to make a lot of sense.

But what, then, if it were true that U.S. hegemony was in decline? The evidence at the time seemed unmistakable; as I noted in the previous chapter, the erosion of America's power then looked real. Yet for all its troubles, the world economy in the 1970s did not appear rudderless. Protectionism did not increase significantly; the trading system did not take the turn toward closure that Krasner had feared. In fact, trade liberalization under the auspices of GATT continued, culminating in 1979 with the conclusion of the Tokyo Round, which for the first time addressed nontariff barriers as well as more traditional tariff reductions. Nor, despite the collapse of the Bretton Woods system, did global monetary relations unravel. In 1976, after four years of negotiation, amendments were agreed to in the Articles of Agreement of the

IMF designed to restore a degree of cooperation to the collective management of exchange rates. For a realist, the challenge seemed acute. In Krasner's words (1983b, viii), "Although difficulties multiplied, international behavior did not deteriorate to the degree that a straightforward realist analysis would have predicted." A reassessment therefore seemed in order. And who better to organize such a reassessment than Krasner himself? His ego was certainly strong enough to withstand critical scrutiny of his own ideas.

The result, Krasner's most lasting contribution to the construction of IPE, was *International Regimes* (1983a), first published as a special issue of IO in 1982. Krasner wrote the introduction and conclusion, summarizing the project's main issues and findings. Other oft-cited chapters came from Keohane (1983), John Gerard Ruggie (1983), and Oran Young (1983), among others. Strange (1983), playing her accustomed role of iconoclast, joined in with a now-notorious critique challenging the validity of the regime concept and vigorously denying its utility.

Regime Theory

Thus was regime theory born. Though the original initiative for *International Regimes* was Krasner's, much credit also goes to Keohane, who was editor of IO at the time the project was first conceived in 1979. It was at Keohane's urging that Krasner's early ideas were expanded to focus broadly on the new notion of regimes about which Keohane and Nye had just written in *Power and Interdependence*. Having myself been a contributor to the *International Regimes* volume, I can testify from firsthand experience that Keohane also played a leading role at the two meetings of the project's authors. And his own chapter for the collection proved to be of especial value in outlining the basic rationale for the creation of regimes.

Regimes represent a particular form of international institution. Simply put, regimes embody implicit or explicit understandings about the rules of the game that help to sustain mutually beneficial patterns of cooperation. The concept of regime enabled scholars to move beyond the study of formal organizations to a broader understanding of the structure and processes of system governance. Cooperation has been famously defined by Keohane as a mutual adjustment of behavior achieved through a formal or informal process of policy coordination (1984, 51–52). Cooperation becomes institutionalized when coordination becomes an established practice, regularized through law or custom. Regimes may be thought of as one species of institutionalized cooperation.

Borrowed from the language of international law, the term regime quickly entered the lexicon of IPE after publication of *Power and Interdependence*. Keohane and Nye (1987, 732) themselves credit Ruggie (1975) and Cooper (1975) for first employing the notion in the context of the increasingly integrated world economy. I myself made use of the concept in some of my earliest work on international monetary relations (Cohen 1976, 1977). But *Power and Interdependence* was the first treatment to put regimes at the very center of analysis. After the appearance of Krasner's volume, regime theory attained its fullest expression in Keohane's *After Hegemony*, whose main theme was that "nonhegemonic cooperation is possible, and that it can be facilitated by international regimes" (1984, 50).

Power and Interdependence had been vague about the specifics of the regime concept. Like many theoretical exercises, therefore, *International Regimes* began with a definition. It is easy to satirize the scholarly world's preoccupation—some would say obsession—with definitions. If patriotism is the last refuge of the scoundrel, the demand "Define your terms" is the last refuge of the academic, frequently deployed in desperation as a shield against adverse criticism (much as in the *Peanuts* cartoon where Lucy accuses her junk-food-eating brother of getting fat; "Define fat," he replies). Yet could we do otherwise? Definitions are essential if dialogue is to be clear and productive, especially when attempting to wrestle with a new and unfamiliar notion. After some debate, the contributors agreed on a definition of regimes that quickly gained widespread currency in the field as a whole. In Krasner's words (1983d, 2):

> Regimes can be defined as sets of implicit or explicit principles, norms, rules, and decision-making procedures around which actors' expectations converge in a given area of international relations. Principles are beliefs of fact, causation, and rectitude. Norms are standards of behavior defined in terms of rights and obligations. Rules are specific prescriptions or proscriptions for action. Decision-making procedures are prevailing practices for making and implementing collective choice.

Only one contributor dissented. That of course was Strange, in her searing critique. Strange considered the whole idea of regimes unrealistic, little more than an intellectual fad promoted by arrogant U.S. academics. Regime theory ran directly counter to all the themes that she was then promoting among her British colleagues. The approach, Strange argued (1983, 337), was narrow-minded, "rooted in a state-centric paradigm that limits the vision of a wider reality." It was also imprecise, too "woolly" to add anything of significance to our understanding. And worst, with its focus on the establishment and maintenance of order, it embodied a hidden bias, ignoring the "*dynamic* character of the 'who-gets-what' of the international economy" (354). The whole thing was not much more than a figment of the American school's imagination, she declared, conceived out of distress over the seeming decline of U.S. hegemony.

Unfortunately, the alternative that Strange proposed was vulnerable to most of the same criticisms. Anticipating an idea that she was soon to develop at greater length in *States and Markets*, she contended that system governance was best understood as the product of a process of piecemeal bargaining. In lieu of regimes, we should think in terms of "bargaining maps"—networks of interlocking, overlapping bargains that determine the range of choice for all concerned. Her approach was certainly less state-centric than regime theory. The process of bargaining might include multinational corporations and other nonstate actors as well as governments. But the notion of bargaining maps could hardly claim to be any more precise or dynamic than the regime concept; nor was it any less concerned with the underlying issue of order. Indeed, it couldn't even pretend to be novel, since many regimes, too, could be understood as the product of a process of formal or informal negotiation. Yet for all the vulnerabilities of her own approach, Strange's critique continues to resonate with the mainstream of the British school.

For Krasner's other contributors, Strange apart, the existence of regimes was undeniable. Indeed, for some, such as Young, regimes were universal, a pervasive characteristic of the global system. The main question was, Do they matter? That is, do they really "govern"?

The answer, according to the majority, was a resounding yes. Regimes do matter, albeit not under all conditions. The evidence from a variety of cases suggested that state action could indeed be constrained by the convergent expectations fostered by regimes. Even without world government, transnationalized markets could be managed cooperatively to preserve mutual benefits. Summarized Krasner (1983d, 5), regimes "could be conceived of as intervening variables standing between basic causal variables . . . and outcomes and behavior. . . . They are not merely epiphenomenal." More important, regimes could be counted on to continue to matter, for shorter or longer periods, even after the initial circumstances changed. They are not ephemeral either. As Krasner put it: "Once regimes are established they assume a life of their own" (1983c, 358).

This did not mean that regimes were immutable; quite the contrary. In *Power and Interdependence*, Keohane and Nye accepted the idea that regimes could evolve over time, and they devoted much energy to trying to explain why. Four models of change were offered: one emphasizing economic and technological processes, and the remaining three stressing different dimensions of power. Likewise, in *International Regimes* several contributors directly addressed the issue of regime change (not to be confused with the recent use of the same term by the administration of George W. Bush). Regimes were neither epiphenomenal nor ephemeral. But neither should they be regarded as eternal.

Most notable in this respect was the chapter by Ruggie (1983), which made a crucial distinction between two forms of regime change. One was at the level of rules and decision-making procedures, leaving the normative framework of existing regimes intact, which Ruggie called "norm-governed change." The other was at the level of the normative framework itself, something truly transformative, which he called "norm-transforming change." The distinction was critical, he argued, in understanding the recent evolution of the international economic order. The rules of the game that were codified in the IMF and GATT after World War II had aimed explicitly at safeguarding the right of governments to promote domestic stability, while at the same time preserving an open and multilateral market system. In a now-familiar turn of phrase, Ruggie labeled the arrangement the "compromise of embedded liberalism."

Significant changes had occurred in the 1960s and 1970s, he acknowledged. But at the start of the 1980s, in his view, they were still largely within the normative framework of the existing regime, not norm-transforming change. In Ruggie's words (1983, 228), "Norm-governed change accounts for more of the variance than claims of fundamental discontinuity." Following his lead, my own contribution to the volume (Cohen 1983a) stressed the extent to which changes in the balance of payments financing regime that had been established at Bretton Woods were also best understood as norm-governed rather than norm-transforming. Regimes, it appeared, might evolve, but they also had more staying power than generally thought.

A younger Krasner might have demurred. The convinced realist who made such an impact with his state-power theory of trade structures would have rejected the sustained intervening role of regimes. In the traditional state-centric paradigm of realism, the world was best described by the so-called billiard-ball model. The system was comprised of states bouncing off one another like the hard, shiny spheres of a pool table. Outcomes were purely a function of power and interests, not shared understandings. But this was now a more reflective Krasner, willing to reassess his views (and metaphors) in light of recent experience.

Summing up the consensus view of the contributors, Krasner now saw the world more like a cluster of tectonic plates, moving slowly and only under considerable pressure. Modern geology teaches that the earth's mantle is fragmented into plates that are in more or less constant motion, continuously bumping and grinding against one another. Once tensions reach a certain point, the plates shift, sometimes violently. Until an earthquake erupts, though, the tectonic plates determine the configuration of the landmasses above. Regimes, Krasner now suggested, could be visualized in much the same way. If their underlying sources shift enough, regimes will lose their force or even disappear. But until that happens they will continue to exert an independent influence, delivering a measure of governance to interstate relations. In show business lingo, regimes "have legs."

The Supply Puzzle

Rarely has a new concept, once introduced, caught on so swiftly in scholarly circles. "We are witnessing an extraordinary blossoming of academic interest in international regimes," wrote Young (1986, 104), less than half a decade after the first appearance of *International Regimes*. A year later, Keohane and Nye marveled at the alacrity with which the idea had been accepted and applied in the academic literature. Regimes "seem now to be everywhere," they exclaimed (1987, 740).

That wasn't true in Britain, of course, where scholars were more inclined to follow Strange's lead in denouncing regimes as a useless U.S. fad. And even in parts of the world where regimes did get on to the research agenda, the practical objects of study were often quite different from the issues of economic interdependence addressed by Krasner's collective project. In Germany, for example, inquiry tended to focus more on the formation and consequences of regimes in the area of international security—a quite understandable preference given that country's frontline status in the cold war (Rittberger 1993). Regimes were seized on by German specialists in peace and conflict studies, and conceptualized as part of a conflict process model of IR. By contrast, in *International Regimes* only one chapter, by Robert Jervis (1983), was devoted to security matters. U.S. scholars were more concerned with the role that regimes might play in the management of economic affairs.

The concept's appeal for the American school was obvious. In the midst of what appeared to be an irreversible erosion of U.S. power, Americans felt uneasy, even threatened. The world economy was losing its stabilizing hegemon; as a direct result, the depoliticized order that the United States, together with its allies, had sought to put together at the end of World War II seemed to be drowning in a rising tide of tension and conflict. Kindleberger, Gilpin, and the younger Krasner had persuaded many that hegemonic decline could presage a new era of instability and peril. The system "may be fragmenting," Gilpin cautioned (1975b, 259). We were all threatened with "chaos," Krasner warned (1976, 343). So it was comforting to think that there might be something else out there to fill the Control Gap. Regimes held out hope like a lifeboat in a storm. Strange was not wrong in attributing the American school's fascination with regimes to distress over the seeming eclipse of U.S. dominance. But that hardly discredits the concept itself.

The basic rationale for regimes was spelled out by Keohane in his contribution to *International Regimes*, a notable chapter titled "The Demand for International Regimes" (1983). Further elaboration came a year later in *After Hegemony* (Keohane 1984), now rightly regarded as a "truly paradigmatic work" (Murphy 2000, 798). Regimes, Keohane pointed out, can help states overcome problems of market failure that inhibit the realization of collective interests. Market failure, a term familiar to economists, refers to situations in which optimal behavior by individual actors turns out to be suboptimal, both for them and the system as a whole. In a global context, market failure is an ever-present threat because with interdependence, there is always a risk that any one government's policies will generate a variety of "spillover" effects—foreign repercussions and feedbacks—that could significantly impinge on the ability of others to achieve preferred objectives. Economists call these "negative externalities." The prospect of negative externalities means that interests may come into conflict, creating tension and discord. Keohane argued that regimes offer a way to minimize the risk that spillover effects will interfere with the promotion of mutually beneficial interactions.

The value of regimes, for Keohane, lay in their ability to reduce the uncertainty and transactions costs that inhibit effective cooperation. Once up and running, regimes narrow the range of anticipated behavior, thus encouraging compliance with common norms. The more other states can be expected to act in ways that are convergent with the rules of the game, the less will any one government be tempted to diverge on its own. Regimes may also facilitate monitoring by increasing iterations and defining cheating. And they can facilitate new agreements by offering salient solutions, hence shrinking bargaining costs. With a regime already in place, it is unnecessary to renegotiate norms and rules every time a new question arises. As Keohane put it (1984, 90), using economic reasoning, regimes "allow governments to take advantage of potential economies of scale. Once a regime has been established, the marginal cost of dealing with each additional issue will be lower than it would be without a regime." Keohane credits Kindleberger for first alerting him to the salience of transactions costs as a rationale for cooperation. The influence of transactions costs was central to the New Institutional Economics of Douglass North (1981) and others.

In short, regimes make it easier for states to realize their collective interests. As the title of Keohane's chapter in *International Regimes* was meant to acknowledge, however, this insight mainly accounted for the *demand* for regimes—why we would want to have them. It didn't explain the *supply*— why anyone would go to the trouble of providing regimes. The puzzle was this: Why would anyone shoulder the burden of the costs and inconvenience involved?

International Regimes proposed a total of five causal variables to help explain the supply of regimes. Two of these, power and interests, were the old standbys of realist theory and Krasner's obvious favorites. They were, in Krasner's phrase (1983d, 5), "most prominent"—an understandable position coming from one of the progenitors of HST. At least in its security version, HST offered a clear explanation for the development of strong governance arrangements: the self-interest and coercive powers of the hegemon. Even modified to include the possible existence of a leadership core (a privileged group or k-group) that might enjoy a net benefit from cooperating, the incentive was evident. But what if there were no such core? Then any of three other causal variables might come into play: diffuse principles and norms, habit and custom, or accumulated knowledge. Regimes might be adapted from principles and norms prevailing in related or even unrelated issue areas. They might simply ratify regular, long-standing patterns of behavior. Or they might represent a genuine learning process—new consensual knowledge that "can light a clear path in a landscape that otherwise would be murky and undifferentiated" (Krasner 1983d, 20).

None of this, though, added up to a coherent theory of supply. All five variables seemed relevant. But what was their relative importance, how were they related, and what conditions might facilitate their impact? However swiftly the regime concept caught on in the literature, critical questions like these remained unanswered. As an influential survey published a few years later ruefully concluded, "A plethora of contending theories have explained regime creation . . . but the relationship among them is unclear and empirical research has yet to determine which are the more plausible" (Haggard and Simmons 1987, 492). The puzzle seemed daunting. By the end of the 1980s, regime theory appeared to be caught in a cul-de-sac of its own making.

The Compliance Puzzle

Nor was that the only seeming dead end for regime theory. There was also the puzzle of compliance. It is easy to understand the appeal of regimes, assuming everyone plays by the rules. Yet how realistic is the assumption? If regimes may be said to "matter," it is because they truly constrain state behavior. But if the tenet of sovereignty means anything, it is that in extremis, governments can do whatever they wish. They need submit to no higher authority. So what could motivate states to accept the limits imposed by a regime even when they might prefer otherwise?

At issue is the classic problem of collective action. While a group of actors may have a joint interest in cooperating, each actor individually may do better by striking out on its own, taking advantage of the compliant behavior of others. Because of the risk of negative externalities, the incentive to free ride is strong; in the language of game theory, there is a constant temptation to cheat or defect. The challenge for regime theory was to explain why governments might be counted on to resist that temptation, averting market failure.

HST, of course, had an easy answer. Market failure might be averted through the strategic use of power by the hegemon. Compliance may be enforced coercively, through the threat of force or negative sanctions, as suggested by the security version of HST. Or it may be deployed in a more benign fashion, as in the collective goods version of HST, relying on persuasion or the promise of positive sanctions (otherwise known as bribes or side payments). And of course the same possibilities exist even in the absence of a hegemon, if a privileged group is present. A capacity for direct government-to-government influence, whether via coercion or persuasion, is what Scott James and David Lake (1989), inspired by an earlier literature on social power theory, call the first "face" of hegemony. They also distinguish two other faces of hegemony: a second face of market leverage, which favorably alters incentive structures;

and a third face of ideas and ideology, a constitutive influence that structures beliefs about what may be regarded as legitimate or illegitimate behavior. All three faces could be effective in encouraging states to play by the rules.

Another possible answer was offered by game theory, in the form of the so-called shadow of the future. In noniterated strategic interactions, such as the notorious Prisoners' Dilemma game, the temptation to defect is strong. In Prisoner's Dilemma, two prisoners are separately offered the same deal: confess and receive a light sentence while condemning the other prisoner to a heavier punishment; or decline to confess and risk receiving the heavier punishment oneself. Only if both decline to confess will both receive light sentences. When the game is only played once, little incentive exists for either player to risk a "sucker's payoff." But that's not the way the real world works, where most interactions are ongoing—repeated indefinitely, not one-shot affairs. In an iterated game, cheating is much less rewarding, since noncooperative behavior today can be punished by retaliation tomorrow. The future casts a long shadow, putting a premium on considerations of reputation and reciprocity (including promises of reciprocal cooperation as well as threats of retaliation). The greater the value attached to payoffs in the future (technically, the lower the discount rate for the purposes of cost-benefit calculus), the lower is the probability of free riding in the present. The long-term advantage of cooperation will outweigh the short-term disadvantage of compliance.

The shadow of the future is not necessarily specific to regimes, of course. As Stephan Haggard and Beth Simmons rightly insist (1987, 504), "We must distinguish regimes from cooperation, which is clearly possible even in the absence of regimes." Game theorist Robert Axelrod (1984), in a famous computer tournament, vividly demonstrated that the shadow of the future can be effectively self-enforcing, unaided by any kind of institutionalized cooperation. But it is also evident that much is added when convergent expectations are buttressed by the structure of a regime. The point was conceded even by Axelrod himself, writing together with Keohane (1986, 234): "The principles and rules of international regimes make governments concerned about precedents, increasing the likelihood that they will attempt to punish defectors. In this way, international regimes help to link the future with the present." States will be even more encouraged to resist the temptation to free ride.

Finally, a third possible answer came from the logic of Keohane's demand-side theory, which he labeled a "functional" theory of regimes (1984). Functional theory, inspired by the insights of the New Institutional Economics, explains behaviors or institutions by their expected effects. If Keohane was right that regimes reduce the uncertainty and transactions costs that typically inhibit cooperation, the anticipated gains alone might suffice to persuade states to accept the arrangement's limitations. Rational utility maximizers will accept the constraints of a regime simply on the basis of the benefits involved. Compliance, in effect, becomes its own reward.

All three answers seemed plausible. Compliance was not an irrational act, even for nominally sovereign states. Yet therein also lay a fundamental problem: the assumption of rationality itself. Echoing realist theory, the three answers all conceived of state behavior as rational and self-interested, in the sense that governments could be assumed to assess their strategic situations in light of their environment and seek to maximize the expected gains. Even Keohane's functional theory, a foundation stone of neoliberal institutionalism, self-consciously adopted the rationality assumption in order to demonstrate, as Keohane put it (1984, 67), "that the characteristic pessimism of realism does not necessarily follow." But what if governments were not rational in the accepted sense of the term? Worse, what if they were rational but nonetheless forced to defect by the exigencies of domestic or international politics? Toward the end of the 1980s, Robert Putnam and Randall Henning (1989) highlighted a crucial distinction between "voluntary" and "involuntary" defection. In practice, even if policymakers rationally calculate that it is not in the state's interest to abandon cooperation (voluntary defection), they may still be forced to do so because of internal or external pressures (involuntary defection). None of the three answers could offer a reasonable assurance against the risk of involuntary defection. Here, too, regime theory appeared to be caught in a cul-de-sac.

Back to Organizations

By the end of the 1980s, therefore, it seemed that the discourse on regimes might have run its course. As Keohane lamented on the tenth anniversary of Krasner's edited volume (1993, 44–45), "International regimes have been the subject, during the last decade, of substantial research in the United States. . . . Yet there are still huge gaps in our knowledge." The puzzles of supply and compliance remained unresolved. Was there a way out?

Yes, responded Keohane. The way out was to shift focus, folding regime analysis into a more general study of institutions. Starting with his presidential address to the ISA in 1988, Keohane sought to redirect attention from the specific attributes of regimes to the broader question underlying all institutional theory: Why and how do states obey international rules? The new path, promoted in a remarkable series of papers (many collected in Keohane 1989a and 2002), some in collaboration with a former student, Lisa Martin (Keohane and Martin 1995, 2003), quickly led to a renaissance of thinking about the Control Gap, yielding fresh insights into government behavior.

Once more, however, there is an irony in evidence. The longer that scholarship has traveled this path, the more it has led to a renewed emphasis on the kinds of formal arrangements that had dominated research prior to the 1970s. Again, the design and operation of international organizations is taking center stage, just as they had before *Power and Interdependence* and

International Regimes came along. IPE, in a sense, may be said to have returned to its prenatal origins. Effectively, the American school's discourse on system governance has come full circle—from organizations to organizations in three generations.

Redirecting Institutional Theory

The starting point for Keohane was simple. As Keohane summarized it (1989b, 413), the central question was, "Why and under what conditions do governments ever take international agreements seriously?" The issue was not how to create institutions; the system is already shot through with institutionalized forms of cooperation. Nor was it a question of encouraging compliance; states already voluntarily abide by all sorts of rules. The issue, rather, was how to explain observed behavior. It is evident that great variation exists in the degree and kind of institutionalization found in world politics. How do we account for that? In Keohane's words, "We need not only insights into why governments take their commitments seriously, but we also need to understand the sources of variation in this deference to commitments" (413).

Two conditions were apparently key. The first, going back to Keohane's functional theory of regimes, had to do with the issue of uncertainty. The more information an institution can provide that is of relevance to the participants, the less will governments be tempted to disregard prevailing rules. The second, rooted more in the causal explanations of regimes, has to do with the issue of flexibility. The more opportunity an institution affords the participants to adjust commitments in light of changing circumstances, the less will governments be tempted to reject obligations that become inconvenient. Much of the variance of governmental behavior that we observe may be traced to these two issues.

The first condition assumes that information is a variable that may be changed by human agency. According to Keohane and Martin (2003), herein lies the pivotal difference between institutional theory and traditional realism. Institutional theory does accept many of the basic premises of realist theory. States are the primary actors in world politics. They are assumed to be rational and self-interested in their behavior. And they are expected to respond systematically to changes in external incentives. In all such respects, the kinship to realism is close—so close, in fact, that institutional theory might even be regarded as little more than "a half-sibling of realism" (Keohane and Martin 2003, 79).

But on the issue of uncertainty the half siblings diverge sharply. Both institutional theory and realism accept that the information environment facing governments directly affects their incentives for behavior. Both approaches also concede that knowledge of the intentions of other states is apt to be imperfect at best. Realism, however, implicitly assumes that states cannot improve the information conditions in which they operate. Hence governments have no choice but to assume the worst about others, making cooperation difficult. Institutional theory, by contrast, rejects such a view as unduly pessimistic. Information conditions are seen as malleable, particularly where there is a substantial promise of mutual gain on the horizon. The conclusion is obvious. The more that institutions can improve the relevant information environment, the greater will be their ability to facilitate cooperation.

For example, institutions may perform a signaling function. By setting verifiable standards, they make it easier for policymakers to evaluate the intentions of other states. Governments thus gain to the extent that they can more reliably judge what other governments are doing. Governments also gain from making their own activities more transparent, since clarity to others can enhance their credibility and hence the value of their own commitments. It is not just the reputation of other states that is at issue. It is one's own reputation as well. The signaling function works both ways.

Likewise, institutions may perform a mediating function. By constructing "focal points" on which all parties can agree, institutions can resolve distributional disputes that might otherwise inhibit or erode cooperation. The issue was clearly outlined by Krasner in a 1991 article featuring another droll title, "Global Communications and National Power: Life on the Pareto Frontier." When states seek to cooperate with one another, he pointed out, achieving efficiency gains—in technical language, reaching the Pareto frontier where efficiency is maximized—is just one of the challenges they face. Another is to agree on a mutually satisfactory distribution of potential benefits, since many alternative equilibriums may exist along the Pareto frontier. By constructing a focal point that in effect defines the "default" position for all concerned, institutions obviate the need for repeated bargaining over outcomes.

The second condition assumes that rules themselves are a variable that may be changed by human agency. Rules are meant to impart a degree of predictability to state behavior. As Martin and another of Keohane's former students, Simmons, have put it (1999, 105–6), institutions "lock in a particular equilibrium, providing stability." But the lock cannot be too tight if governments are to be persuaded to continue obeying the rules. Institutions must also be flexible enough to accommodate significant changes of circumstance. Keohane concisely framed the dilemma (2002, 7): "In a world without centralized government, why should states comply with obligations that had become inconvenient?" The answer is that their will to comply depends directly on how easy it is to make adjustments when obligations become onerous.

A fundamental premise of institutional theory is that rules and behavior are mutually endogenous (Keohane 1989a, 10; 2002, 1). Back in the 1980s, Cox may have been right in dismissing most mainstream IR scholarship as problem-solving theory, treating structures as immutable. But that is certainly not an accurate characterization of institutional theory as it has developed over the last couple of decades. Institutions, it is recognized, do not come down from the heavens, a holy writ of immutable "Thou shalts" and "Thou shalt nots." On the contrary, they are seen as the product of human action and so can be altered by human action.

If states comply with obligations, it is because governments created those obligations. More important, if the obligations become too inconvenient, they may be changed by governments. Structure and agency interact persistently. As Martin and Simmons summarize it (1999, 103), "Institutions are *simultaneously causes and effects*; that is, institutions are both the objects of state choice and consequential. . . . States choose and design institutions. States do so because they face certain problems that can be resolved through institutional mechanisms. They choose institutions because of their intended effects. Once constructed, institutions will constrain and shape behavior, even as they are constantly challenged and reformed by their member states." Again the conclusion is obvious. The more that institutions can manage pressures for reform, the greater will be their ability to facilitate cooperation.

None of this adds up to a single coherent theory, as Keohane himself was the first to admit (2002, 1): "The resulting conception of how the world works is complex. . . . It lacks parsimony." But his efforts did succeed in releasing discourse from the dead end into which regime theory had seemed to lead it and offered a renewed agenda for the study of system governance. Keohane "was a pivotal figure," writes an informed commentator. "He has provided a theoretical framework and a set of hypotheses that others have used to expand the empirical scope of international relations theory in the sub-field of international political economy" (Griffiths 1999, 189). The path was now set. Many have since followed.

Completing the Circle

In fact, the outpouring of studies since the 1980s has been immense, producing "a vibrant and diverse body of scholarship" in the words of one influential survey (Simmons and Martin 2002, 204). Following Keohane, scholars have sought to refine understanding of the conditions that influence state commitments. At issue is the role that institutions can play in encouraging governments to obey rules. Such a focus has led, quite naturally, to a revival of interest in formal organizations, where questions of information and flexibility may be explicitly addressed. Increasingly, institutional theory has concentrated on the design and operation of international agreements. Is it possible to negotiate cooperative arrangements that will be both mutually acceptable and sustainable?

Like regimes, organizations represent a particular form of international institution. But unlike regimes, which may be informal and based on no more than implicit understandings, organizations are formal and tangible—bureaucratic agencies, often quite large, with their own headquarters, staff, and budget. Organizations are created by negotiation, and have assigned tasks and responsibilities. In practice, organizations function as purposive entities, and may act with varying degrees of authority and autonomy.

The return to organizations completes a circle in the American school's discourse on the Control Gap. The irony is obvious if we recall the dissatisfaction with the earlier postwar literature on organizations that played such a key role in IPE's birth in the United States. The reorientation of IO engineered by Keohane and Nye in the 1970s was a direct response to what they saw as the sterility of standard organizational studies. In retrospect, that early work has stood the test of time better than expected. As Martin and Simmons have suggested (1999, 92), "The early postwar literature . . . was far less naive and legalistic, more politically sensitive and insightful than it is often given credit for being." At the same time, however, it could also be indicted for a lack of any sort of conceptual framework to tie its insights together. In the most fundamental terms, the work was atheoretical. Today's scholarship, by contrast, has the benefit of all the intervening years of theoretical development, which have given more recent research a firmer conceptual foundation.

Critical to the study of international organizations is the concept of legalization—the imposition of legal constraints on governments. Three crucial dimensions are involved in legalization: the degree to which rules are obligatory; the precision of the rules; and the delegation of some or all of the functions of interpretation, monitoring, and implementation to a third party. Legalization may be thought of as a form of institutionalization designed to encourage commitment by raising exit costs. It imposes strong constraints by legitimizing retaliation in the event of cheating, thus strengthening the impact of the shadow of the future. Legalization also provides opportunities for innovative strategies involving legal action. The relevance of all this for institutional theory was recognized early by Keohane, who in yet another manifestation of his pioneering entrepreneurship was instrumental in helping launch a collective research project on legalization in international economic governance. The result of that effort was an important collection of essays edited by Keohane and several colleagues (Goldstein, Kahler et al. 2001). Like the projects that Keohane and Nye conceived in the 1970s, as well as Krasner's *International Regimes* project in the early 1980s, the collection was first published as a special issue of IO.

And what persuades governments to accept legal constraints in the first place? The answer lies in the specific terms negotiated by the participants. The central dilemma has been articulated well by James Fearon (1998), who notes a fundamental trade-off between bargaining and enforcement problems in international agreements. The strengthened shadow of the future may make enforcement of rules easier. But it also gives governments an incentive to bargain harder at the start, in hopes of getting a better deal. The result could be a delay in or even a failure of the negotiations. As Fearon contends, "The more states value future benefits, the greater the incentive to bargain hard for a good deal, possibly fostering costly standoffs that impede cooperation" (296).

The solution clearly lies in the initial design. Another important collection of essays (Koremenos, Lipson, and Snidal2003a), also first published as a special issue of IO, suggests that at least five key dimensions are involved in the rational design of international organizations. These are membership rules, the scope of the issues covered, the centralization of tasks, rules for controlling the organization, and above all, the flexibility of the arrangement. States sign on the dotted line when they are convinced that provisions of an agreement along each of these dimensions are compatible with their own preferences and expectations.

Yet are even these considerations enough? A well-crafted agreement may enhance the prospects for sustained cooperation. In an imperfect world, however, not even the best-designed organization can actually *guarantee* effective governance. Conventional analysis tends to have a normative bias, assuming that once created, organizations will be a force for good in the world—facilitating cooperation, spreading norms, and promoting the rule of law. But that rose-tinted view is sadly unrealistic, ignoring corrupting influences that could beset an organization from either the outside or the inside.

From the outside, an organization could be subject to pressures to accommodate the interests of its most powerful members, even at the expense of broader policy objectives. While "discussed publicly in idealist terms, they are too often manipulated for economic gain by interests capable of influencing their decisions in the same way that other organs of governments or agencies of governance are so utilized," in the words of one critical commentator (Tabb 2004, 4). Indeed, a bias in favor of the strong may be inherent in the very design of organizations, reflecting their origins in human agency. Agreements must be negotiated; one does not have to be a reconstructed realist or Marxist to imagine that as a result, rules might reflect the preferences of those with the most bargaining leverage. Institutional theory accepts the path dependency built into the structure of organizations—"history encoded as rules," as James March and Johan Olsen put it (1984, 741).

From the inside, conversely, an organization could be subject to pressures to promote its own interests, as Michael Barnett and Martha Finnemore (2004) have recently reminded us. As bureaucratic agencies, organizations may take on a perverse life of their own, behaving in ways that could be anything but favorable for the system as a whole. "International bureaucracies are double-edged swords," write Barnett and Finnemore (ix). They may indeed play a positive role. But they may also be prone to all sorts of "pathologies," developing their own ideas and pursuing their own agendas even at the expense of systemic stability. Their self-interested behavior may be undesirable and even dysfunctional.

And so the discourse continues. Coming full circle like a boomerang, back to a focus on organizations, doesn't mean a lack of intellectual progress. As a former senior colleague of mine liked to say at the end of an especially perplexing discussion, we may still feel confused—but at least we are confused at a higher level. For Strange, ever the iconoclast, "international organizations are a big yawn" (1998b, 215). But that severely underestimates the impact that organizations may have in the international system, whether for good or ill. Much has been learned from the evolution of institutional theory, even if many questions remain. Krasner, Keohane, and others have bequeathed to us a rich legacy of insight and understanding.

BEYOND STATES

Yet it is also a flawed legacy. As in the American school's approach to globalization, which was discussed in the last chapter, discourse still accepts what Michael Zürn calls the "shackles of methodological nationalism" (2002, 248). The dominant ontology employed to address the Control Gap is still largely state-centric, reflecting the disciplinary training of the political scientists who from the beginning have held custody of IPE in the United States. As in standard IR theory, national governments are identified as the core actors. The system is still defined in terms of interstate relations. The issue of governance, therefore, is reduced simply to a matter of cooperation among national governments.

But in a world economy still growing increasingly interdependent, such a plain-vanilla approach seems incomplete, perhaps even misguided. Governments still may be core actors, yet they are by no means the *only* actors involved, directly or indirectly, in system governance. It is worth recalling again one of the key messages that Keohane and Nye tried to impart back in the 1970s with their notion of complex interdependence. With the expansion of the global marketplace, they warned, governments were no longer alone in their ability to exercise authority over outcomes. States could no longer monopolize analysis. If we wanted to understand how things work, scholarship would have to catch up with the facts. Regrettably, that message appears to have been largely forgotten as the American school has matured. Scholarship has not caught up with the facts. Indeed, by now, even Keohane has largely cut nonstate actors from the picture. Yet what was true in the 1970s is even truer today. Ever-larger numbers of actors are emerging out of the private sector with a capacity to participate meaningfully in political relationships. Governance increasingly comes in many flavors, some quite exotic.

The message has not been entirely lost on American scholars. For some, the role of private authority is obvious. One example is the venerable James Rosenau (1992), who has long campaigned for a more nuanced understanding of what we mean by governance. "Some of the functions of governance," Rosenau has written, "are now being performed by activities that do not originate with government . . . regulatory mechanisms in a sphere of activity which function effectively even though they are not endowed with formal authority"

(1992, 3, 5). It is inaccurate and misleading to equate de facto governance with de jure government. We must be prepared to think in terms of "governance without government."

Another example is Virginia Haufler (1997), who in an extended case study has examined the role of corporate insurers and reinsurers (companies that provide insurance to insurers) in the governance of international trade and investment. One of the biggest challenges facing insurers is the calculation of political risk, covering possible losses due to actions or inactions by governments. By their judgments about what constitutes acceptable political risk, Haufler notes, insurers may exercise an enormous influence over the formulation and implementation of public policy. And for a third example I might cite myself, in my recent book *The Geography of Money* (1998). Declining barriers between national monetary systems, I argued, have increased competition between currencies. As a result, governments must now share authority over monetary affairs with a select set of private societal actors—namely, those in the marketplace with the capacity and opportunity to choose among alternative monies. Monetary governance is now uneasily shared between the public and private sectors.

But if we really want to find a determined alternative to the American school's state-centric ontology, we must look once again to the British school, where discourse on the Control Gap tends to be far more inclusive. Here too it was Strange who got the ball rolling with her dictum that IR should be viewed as a subset of IPE, and not the other way around. At issue is what we mean by politics in political economy. "Politics is larger than what politicians do," Strange wrote late in life (1996, xiv). In other words, governance is larger than what governments do. Strange's dictum, which harks back to her notion of bargaining maps, meant that governance necessarily encompasses *all* species of actors capable of exercising authority in their respective domains. States should be regarded as just one among many agents with influence over the rules of the game—a heterodox perspective that coincided neatly with the predilections of critical theorists like Cox, who are always happiest thinking in terms of social forces, economic classes, or some other form of private authority. British school scholars have no difficulty at all in disassociating governance from government.

The central question for the British school is this: If governments are no longer in charge, then who is? Answers vary, depending on taste. Perhaps most radical is the extreme pessimism expressed by Strange herself shortly before her death. In her penultimate book, *The Retreat of the State* (1996), she argued that the erosion of state authority had already gone so far that it had, in effect, left *no one* in charge. In Strange's words, "At the heart of the international political economy, there is a vacuum. . . . What some have lost, others have not gained. The diffusion of authority away from national governments has left a yawning hole of non-authority, ungovernance it might be called" (14).

But surely that goes too far. The point emphasized by Keohane and Nye back in the 1970s remains as true as ever. World politics may be anarchic, but it is not chaotic. Something is providing the glue to hold the system together. The state may be in retreat, but there is simply too much order around to suggest that we are now left with nothing more than a "yawning hole of non-authority."

What is that "something"? For some, it is simply "the market." Numerous scholars in the British school speak of market structures reified as a distinct principle in opposition to traditional state authority. Philip Cerny, for instance, writing of the period since World War II, describes a "new hegemony of financial markets" (1994a, 320)—a "transnational financial structure" (1994b, 225) that reduces governments to little more than rivals for market favor. The imagery is reminiscent of the discipline exercised by the institutions of the gold standard in the nineteenth century. Likewise, Randall Germain depicts an increasingly decentralized "international organization of credit [that] has robbed the international monetary system of a single dominant locus of power" (1997, 26). Others, reflecting a Marxian influence, speak of the dominant role of "global" or "transnational" capitalism.

And for yet still others, inspired by Cox's notion of world orders rooted in a state-society complex, the "something" is not markets alone but rather some form of symbiosis with government: market structures acting in concert with, rather than opposition to, traditional state authority. Cox himself, eclectic as ever, likens system governance today to "a *nébuleuse* personified as the global economy . . . a transnational process of consensus formation among the official caretakers of the global economy" (1996a, 298, 301). Along similar lines, Geoffrey Underhill argues that governing authority is now exercised by a "state-market condominium"—an "integrated system [that] operates simultaneously through the competitive pressures of the market and the political processes which shape the boundaries and structures within which that competition (or lack thereof) takes place" (2000, 808).

Cox, as mentioned earlier, owes much of his inspiration to Polanyi's *The Great Transformation* (1944), and so does Underhill. Polanyi's main theme was the inextricable intermingling of markets and states in his celebrated double movement. The two sides are mutually constitutive. Markets are embedded in social networks and institutions, which shape the development of markets over time. In turn, market operations have political consequences, weighing on the evolution of states. Polanyi's concern, of course, was with economic governance at the national level. Both Cox's *nébuleuse* and Underhill's state-market condominium may be understood as updated applications of Polanyi's logic to governance on a broader scale.

Arguments like these are insightful. They help us to move beyond states alone in thinking about the Control Gap. But they may also be criticized for a decided lack of rigor. Most are more than a little obscure in their specification of empirical relationships. Abstract notions of market structures or state-market condominiums may be appealing to the imagination, but they leave us uncertain about precisely who or what actually exercises authority, and how it is done. In other words, they are ambiguous about *agency*. Little guidance is provided for practical analytic purposes. What could be more nebulous than a *nébuleuse*?

More productive would be analysis that is less ambiguous about the actors: studies that focus clearly on specific groups capable of exercising effective authority in their respective spheres of activity. That is what Haufler did in her study of the insurance industry. And that is what Timothy Sinclair has done in his years of research on bond-rating agencies such as Moody's and Standard and Poor. Because they are regarded as authoritative sources of judgment in offshore lending markets, Sinclair contends, rating agencies have come to play "a central role in organizing markets and, consequently, in governing the world" (2005, 5). Murphy elaborates a whole laundry list of "global-level 'private' authorities that regulate both states and much of transnational economic and social life"—a diverse array ranging from industrial cartels to the mafia (2000, 794).

Inquiry along these lines has been promoted in particular by Canadian scholars such as Jennifer Clapp (2001), Claire Cutler (2003), and Tony Porter (2005), aptly illustrating the inclination of many Canadian-based specialists to look for bridges between the American and British schools. Canadians were heavily involved in two recent collections of essays exploring the authoritative role of selected market actors and other nonstate entities (Cutler, Haufler, and Porter 1999; Hall and Biersteker 2002). More work of this kind may be just what is needed to gain an appreciation of the full range of flavors in system governance today.

Chapter 5

THE MYSTERY OF THE STATE

> International political economy remains unintelligible
> without a systematic analysis of domestic structures.
> —Peter Katzenstein

LIKE ANY GOOD RELIGION, the field of IPE has at its core a central mystery—
what might be called the Mystery of the State. The American and British
schools clearly diverge over many issues, including the grand themes of systemic transformation and system governance; as the preceding discussion
makes equally clear, most of their differences, at the most fundamental level,
boil down to the schools' contrasting attitudes concerning a single issue: the
place of the state in formal analysis. Is the sovereign state the basic unit of
interest or just one among many? The question cannot be dismissed merely as
a matter of obscure ontology. It is in fact essential to our understanding of the
real world, which is the ultimate purpose of scholarly inquiry.

Both schools acknowledge that the state is a key actor. In the world in which
we live, they could hardly say otherwise. At the start of the twenty-first century,
it is manifestly impossible to think about the practical connections between
global economics and politics without taking account of the role of national
governments. But is the state the *most important* actor—the only really interesting focal point for analysis? That is the mystery.

Scholars working in the U.S. tradition take for granted that IPE, first and
foremost, is about states and their interactions. In the words of one popular
U.S. textbook, IPE is about "the relationship of the world economy to the
power politics among nations" (Lairson and Skidmore 2003, 6). Public policymaking is the main concern. Analysis is directed largely to understanding
the sources and implications of government behavior. Milner summarizes it
this way (2002b, 214): "The central questions all relate to the interaction of
politics and economics among states in the international system."

As seen from the British perspective, however, the American school approach is far too state-centric—too hostage to Zürn's "shackles of methodological nationalism" (2002, 248)—betraying the school's early capture by political
scientists like Keohane, Gilpin, and Krasner. Scholars in the British tradition
prefer to follow the lead of Strange and Cox, resisting any attempt to subordinate IPE to the study of IR. For them, the field is about much more than
simply the state and its policies; other actors also matter. Summarizes one

representative voice: "In ontological terms, the focus is not simply the state system. . . . Relations across state boundaries in their many forms, rather than affairs of state are the subject of investigation" (O'Brien 1995, 98). The state cannot be allowed to monopolize discourse.

Criticism of the American school's state-centrism is not entirely misplaced. As I have already suggested, methodological nationalism can blind the eye to important elements of change or private authority in the global economy. But the criticism can also be misleading, by confusing the meaning of state-centrism. For the American school, state centrism simply means privileging the state above other units of interest. It does not mean traditional realism—the billiard ball model of rational, unitary actors conceived as closed black boxes driven solely by calculations of national interest and power. States are at the center of the analysis, but they are by no means the sole actors.

In fact, from early on, the black box was gradually opened to admit a much wider range of relevant agents and influences. This is a crucial part of the American school's story, though by no means one that is always fully appreciated. The process of opening began with Keohane and Nye's notion of complex interdependence, which added a growing crowd of transnational actors to the picture. But the truly big breakthrough came with the work of Katzenstein, who emphasized above all the domestic sources of foreign economic policy. From Katzenstein we have learned to appreciate the full range of forces shaping the policy behavior of governments. The youngest of the Magnificent Seven, Katzenstein too is an energetic intellectual entrepreneur whose impact has proved to be long lasting.

OPENING THE BLACK BOX

Given the American school's origins, prioritization of the state as a unit of analysis is scarcely surprising. For all the systemic changes that have occurred since IPE was born, national governments remain the fundamental locus of authority in world affairs. Economies may continue to grow more interdependent, if not globalized; new actors may keep emerging with some degree of influence over outcomes. But no one else enjoys the legitimacy that comes with internationally recognized sovereignty, nor can any other actor legally exercise the ultimate right of coercion. The state is privileged in analysis because it is privileged in reality.

For the American school, therefore, understanding the behavior of states is the central imperative. What motivates government policy in the global economy, and how are policy preferences best explained and evaluated? As in the study of IR more generally, these questions have come to be seen as a matter of "levels of analysis." Most early scholarship tended to view preferences parsimoniously as the product of rational calculus by unitary actors responding to structural constraints and incentives—the black box approach. Katzenstein's signal contribution was to encourage the addition of domestic and, later, even ideational factors to the mix. The black box was opened, taking the newborn field in entirely new directions.

Levels of Analysis

In trying to understand state behavior, IR theory in the United States has long distinguished among three broad levels of analysis, each a general theoretical orientation corresponding to one of Kenneth Waltz's well-known "images" of IR. In his classic *Man, the State, and War* (1959), Waltz sought to categorize the causes of war in as concise a fashion as possible. Any possible casus belli, he suggested, could usefully be ordered under one of three headings: within individuals; within the structure of individual states; or within the structure of the interstate system. The first of his three images stressed defects in human nature; the second, defects in the internal organization of states; and the third, defects in states' external organization (the anarchic interstate system). Today these are referred to as the first, second, and third images of IR, respectively.

Corresponding to Waltz's third image is the familiar *systemic* (or structural) level of analysis, the favorite of realists, which focuses on the sovereign state itself treated as a rational and unitary actor. The methodological value of the approach is that it makes government preferences constants (exogenous) rather than variables (endogenous) for the purposes of analysis. Conceptions of national interest are assumed to be given and unchanging. Thus, inquiry may concentrate exclusively on constraints and incentives for policy deriving from the broader structure of interstate relations. Behavior, as Waltz later put it, may be studied from the "outside-in" (1979, 63).

Conversely, in the tradition of comparative politics, behavior can also be studied from the "inside-out," concentrating on the internal characteristics of states rather than their external environment. That is the object of the so-called *domestic* level of analysis in IR, corresponding to Waltz's second image. Attention is addressed to the strategic interactions among all domestic actors, inside or outside government, with actual or potential influence on a state's foreign actions as well as to the institutional settings through which diverse interests are mediated and converted into policy—in short, the political and institutional basis at home for policy preferences abroad.

Finally, there is the *cognitive* level of analysis, analogous to Waltz's first image, which focuses on the base of ideas and consensual knowledge that legitimate governmental policymaking—an approach that contrasts sharply with the rational-actor models characteristic of the systemic and domestic levels of analysis. As initially conceived, the cognitive level was largely based in psychology and, following Waltz, concerned strictly with the individual. What is in a person's mind? What is the independent influence of personal values and beliefs? Critical in bringing the insights of psychology to IR was Robert Jervis (1976), who emphasized the role that perceptions and misperceptions can play in shaping the mind-sets of key decision makers. Today, the tradition is best represented in the work of Rose McDermott (2004).

In more recent years, the cognitive approach has also spawned a second track under the newly fashionable label of constructivism. The constructivist track is rather more sociological in nature, concerned more with connections between individuals—with learning, intersubjectivity, and social knowledge. How did what is in a person's mind get there, and how do values and beliefs change over time? The spotlight of constructivism is on the independent effect of norms on state behavior.

Variations in the number of levels of analysis have been suggested from time to time, to permit separate considerations of such factors as social organization, bureaucracy, domestic institutions, or economics. Up to as many as ten levels have been suggested in all (Brecher 1999, 229)—not unlike the extra dimensions of the universe added to cosmological studies by the advent of string theory. Until now, however, the consensus view among IR scholars is that three levels are enough. Though some question whether the world can really be divided up so neatly into three distinct images (Gourevitch 2002), few doubt that the trichotomy remains useful as a heuristic device—a handy way to organize discourse.

In earlier years, the most vigorous debates in IR theory were between various systemic and domestic approaches—in particular, between realism and its variants (neorealism, etc.), on the one hand, stressing the primacy of structural variables; and liberalism and its variants (neoliberal institutionalism, etc.), on the other, with their greater emphasis on domestic-level considerations. More recently, discourse has expanded to include a newer debate. On the one side are rationalist theories of all kinds, including both realism and liberalism—labeled "neo-utilitarianism" by Ruggie (1999). On the other side are the two tracks of cognitive analysis, the psychological and the sociological, which go beyond neo-utilitarianism by asking what role ideational factors play in policymaking. On the psychological track, the focus is on individual beliefs: the mapping of mental processes. What ideas motivate state officials and how do they impact on decision making? On the sociological track, otherwise known as constructivism, the focus is on socialization: the construction of shared values and norms. Where do conceptions of identity and interest come from, and how do they become established as matters of common agreement—what constructivists call "social facts"?

In turn, these same debates have spilled over into IPE, enriching the field considerably. And nobody deserves more credit for opening the sluice gates than Katzenstein, who was an early leader in promoting the domestic and, later, cognitive levels of analysis.

The Compleat Academic

Born in Germany at the end of World War II, Katzenstein did not arrive in the United States until the age of nineteen. A summa cum laude graduate of Swarthmore College in 1967 with a triple major in political science, economics, and literature, he went on to earn a master's degree at the LSE before completing his PhD at Harvard in 1973. Ever since, Katzenstein has taught at Cornell University, where he is renowned for his dedication to his students and has won a number of teaching awards.

His first students found him demanding, even intimidating. "He scared the hell out of all us grad students," recalls one of his earliest doctoral candidates. But later generations speak more warmly, suggesting a certain mellowing over time. All remark on the generosity of his intellectual support and guidance. While Katzenstein never hesitates to criticize ideas that he thinks are ill conceived, he doesn't try to force his own ideas on others, preferring instead to bring out the best in each individual. In one former student's words, "He made me the best 'me' I could be." Katzenstein also makes a point of always being available—even during a blinding snowstorm (as another former student tells the story), or while away from Cornell for one reason or another. "Peter is an e-mail machine," says a recent PhD who regularly heard from an absent Katzenstein while working on his dissertation. "Graduate students, including me," confesses another, "used to say that we wanted to be just like Peter when we grew up. He is truly adored."

An intensely private person, Katzenstein can appear reserved, even aloof. But he is also a fierce competitor, driven to excel in everything he does. On the squash court, reports a former student, "nothing pleases him more than beating a strong player who is decades younger." Another student, who played with him often, describes him as "merciless on the court. . . . He loved to win." Katzenstein calls it "my denial about growing old."

Yet when he relaxes he can be remarkably charming, with an Old World, almost courtly air about him. In the words of a younger Cornell colleague, "He has a great warmth about him; he really lights up around children (and gets down on the floor with them), and the Katzenstein home is a mecca for very comfortable dinner parties. . . . He has a sense for what is funny and there is a noticeable twinkle in his eye." He is also devoted to his family, and has been married since 1970 to Mary Fainsod Katzenstein, an accomplished political scientist in her own right. The two "make a dynamic team," says the same colleague.

In many ways, Katzenstein is the compleat academic—someone wholly committed to the life of the mind. The same competitiveness that drives him on the squash court impels him ceaselessly to broaden his intellectual horizons. Alert and inquisitive, he never passes up a chance to feed his curiosity. Strangers, on meeting him, are queried immediately about their interests. "If there is a botanist in the room," a friend comments, "he will take the opportunity to

Figure 5.1. Peter Katzenstein. Courtesy of Cornell University

learn about botany." An avid reader, Katzenstein even enrolls periodically in Cornell courses outside his own department, attending lectures and engaging politely in class discussions. Subjects have included everything from anthropology and sociology to game theory. One could without difficulty imagine him participating regularly in an age of the Enlightenment salon, conversing easily with savants of every stripe.

His wide-ranging, cosmopolitan intellect has not gone unnoticed. In 1987, Katzenstein's accomplishments received formal recognition when he was elected to the membership of the American Academy of Arts and Sciences. A decade later, he was named an International Political Economy Senior Scholar by the IPE section of the ISA. His research productivity has been prodigious, resulting in more than thirty authored or edited books and monographs.

Katzenstein's earliest work was in comparative politics, focusing on central Europe in general and Germany in particular. He himself says that he came to this line of research more or less by accident. But a special interest in Germany hardly seems surprising given his origins. He was born there after all, before becoming a naturalized U.S. citizen in 1979. He also had some Jewish antecedents in his background, which might help to explain why he tried so hard to understand a nation that for all of its extraordinary contributions to Western civilization, could have descended to such barbarities in the 1930s and 1940s. How could it have happened, and was Germany now truly transformed? What role did political institutions play? What governs the relationship between state and society over time? Lessons were sought by comparing and contrasting Germany's experience with other nations in the Central European neighborhood—classic comparative political analysis.

A curiosity about political economy, however, was soon piqued by contact with other key members of IPE's pioneer generation. He never met Keohane during his undergraduate days at Swarthmore, despite two years of overlap after Keohane joined the college's faculty in 1965. But they did soon become acquainted once Katzenstein got to Harvard, especially during Keohane's CFIA fellowship in 1972. And of course he was bound to cross paths as well with Krasner, who was one year ahead of him in his doctoral studies. The three Ks have been friends since the early 1970s and have interacted professionally in many ways—not least, in the editorship of IO. Katzenstein followed Keohane as editor in 1980 before handing the position off to Krasner in 1986. The three were the coeditors of the special issue of IO published in 1999 to celebrate the journal's fiftieth anniversary. In retrospect, it seems only natural that Katzenstein would soon turn his attention to the newborn field of IPE.

Domestic Structures

Katzenstein's contributions to the construction of IPE have been manifold. At Cornell he has mentored literally dozens of now well-established younger scholars, including such familiar names as Joseph Grieco, Lake, and Pauly. As mentioned, he was the editor of IO for six years. And since 1982, he has also edited the Cornell Studies in Political Economy for Cornell University Press, shepherding more than a hundred new books into production.

His earliest impact, though, came through yet another special issue of IO, following much the same path as his friends Keohane (together with Nye) and later Krasner. Keohane and Nye completed their landmark *Transnational Relations and World Politics* in 1972, and were hard at work helping to bring *World Politics and International Economics* to fruition in 1975 when Katzenstein was finishing his PhD. On arriving at Cornell, Katzenstein immediately undertook to organize a collective research project of his own, which appeared under the title *Between Power and Plenty* as a special issue of IO in 1977 (after being vetted by a committee consisting of Nye, Leon Lindberg, and myself), and was published as an edited volume a year later (Katzenstein 1978a). Keohane was instrumental in getting the project initially placed in IO; Krasner (1978b) was one of the collection's best-known contributors. Like *Transnational Relations and World Politics* and Krasner's *International Regimes*, which appeared a few years later when Katzenstein was the editor of IO, *Between Power and Plenty* is today rightly regarded as one of the classics of the American school canon.

The aim of *Between Power and Plenty* seemed simple. In the words of the volume's preface, it was to understand how "domestic structures . . . shape political strategies in the international political economy" (Katzenstein 1978a, vii). The starting point for Katzenstein and his collaborators was the first energy crisis in 1973, which triggered major shock waves throughout the world economy. The blow was common, yet national policy responses diverged sharply. What could account for such striking differences? The answer seemed to lie in the idiosyncracies of domestic political structures, understood to encompass both "the governing coalitions which define policy objectives and the institutional organization which conditions policy instruments" (Katzenstein 1978c, 19). Katzenstein developed the domestic structures theme at length in the volume's introductory and concluding chapters.

In fact, there was nothing simple about this at all. As a matter of intellectual construction, the project's goal was actually quite ambitious, even revolutionary—nothing less than to add a missing level of analysis to the new field of IPE. As Katzenstein explained in his introductory chapter (1978c, 4–5), "The literature on foreign economic policy has, in recent years, unduly discounted the influence of domestic forces. . . . International explanations do not adequately explain why an international challenge, such as the oil crisis, elicits different national responses. Despite the enormous growth of different forms of international interdependencies and transnational relations, the nation-state has reaffirmed its power to shape strategies of foreign economic policy. . . . Today's international political economy remains unintelligible without a systematic analysis of domestic structures." Waltz's second image had to be synthesized with his third image for the picture to be complete.

The perspective of *Between Power and Plenty* clearly reflected Katzenstein's comparativist origins. Comparative politics had always stressed the view from the inside-out, not just from the outside-in, as was most common among IR theorists at the time. In an earlier paper published in 1976, Katzenstein had already criticized standard paradigms in the IR literature for their neglect of domestic factors. "Domestic politics," he wrote, "is very much treated as a residual category in current writings on international relations" (13). If one really wants to understand policy behavior, he went on to argue, one must look to structural characteristics of the policy networks that link state and society in each individual case. In his words, "Domestic structures generate foreign economic policies which express the particular logic inherent in each . . . policy network" (43).

It is a measure of Katzenstein's lasting impact that the necessity to include both levels of analysis, domestic as well as systemic, is now taken for granted in U.S.-style IPE. The centrality of the combination is affirmed in two recent surveys of the field by three of the American school's best-known members: one by Frieden and Martin (2002), and the other by Lake (2006), Katzenstein's former student. Both surveys may be regarded as authoritative. As Frieden and Martin put it (2002, 119–20), "The most challenging questions in IPE have to do with the interaction of domestic and international factors as they affect economic policies and outcomes. . . . [We] need to take into account both the domestic political economy of foreign economic policy and the role of strategic interaction among nation-states." The field's cutting edge, they say, is the "international-domestic research frontier" (119). Lake, adopting the term "Open-Economy Politics" (OEP) from Robert Bates (1997), describes the synthesis of second- and third-image analysis as the "dominant approach [that] now structures and guides research. . . . OEP emerged and came to dominate the study of IPE" (Lake 2006, 757, 762).

Today, even the most hard-core realists concede that genuine value is added by second-image analysis. As no less an authority than Krasner has affirmed (1996, 119), "One of the successes of international political economy as an area of study is that it has integrated international relations and comparative politics." The success is considerable. Credit for it goes, first and foremost, to Katzenstein.

Shrinking Horizons, Again

But the success has also been qualified. Since *Between Power and Plenty*, explorations of the international-domestic research frontier have moved in a number of directions, illustrating the many complexities involved in synthesizing second- and third-image analysis. Yet at the same time, in individual research programs, the scope of inquiry has tended to contract markedly, re-flecting the American school's general drift toward mainly midlevel theory. Hostage to creeping economism, individual studies of OEP tend to focus on more and more narrowly defined relationships and variables. Here too as in approaches to systemic transformation, horizons have shrunk to accommodate aspirations for professional respect. Again, little room is left for holistic think-ing. Analysis has become increasingly partial equilibrium rather than general equilibrium in tone.

This was not true at the start. After *Between Power and Plenty*, Katzenstein himself concentrated on extending and refining his central concept of domestic structures—a research program that reached its zenith with the publication in 1985 of his *Small States in World Markets*, a comparative study of adaptation to economic change in Austria, Switzerland, and five other small European economies. Patterns of adaptation diverged because of differences in domestic structures. But what explained the contrasts in the structures themselves? In *Between Power and Plenty*, Katzenstein had looked to history for an explana-tion. "Contemporary structures," he had suggested (1978b, 323), "are rooted in some of the major historical transformations of the past." In *Small States in World Markets*, he expanded on that theme, detailing the role of the past in shaping dominant social coalitions and the organization of policy institutions. Countries adapt differently, in good part, because their histories are different.

An emphasis on history came naturally to someone whose earliest educa-tional experience had been on the European side of the Atlantic. "Doubtless his German heritage plays a role there," Cox has written to me, expressing great admiration for Katzenstein's historical approach. Cox considers Kat-zenstein, of all the major figures in the American school, closest in spirit to his own historical materialism. By contrast, Katzenstein gives the most credit to his mentor at Harvard, Karl Deutsch—the same scholar whose pioneering work on regional integration (Deutsche, Burrell, and Kann 1957), along with that of Ernst Haas (1958), was so influential in shaping Keohane and Nye's early thinking on interdependence. Katzenstein claims he applied for graduate study at Harvard mainly because of Deutsch, whose publications he had gotten to know during his studies at the LSE. "I was convinced by Deutsch's deeply European perspective," he says. "I certainly work in that tradition."

A broad approach was also taken by others to challenge the use of domestic structures as an independent variable to explain external behavior. Leading the way was another comparativist, Peter Gourevitch (1978), in a memorable essay published in IO just a year after Katzenstein's special issue. Domestic struc-tures could not be treated as though they were exogenous, Gourevitch main-tained. The international system is not just an expression of domestic politics and institutions; it is a cause of them too—described as the "second-image reversed," a colorful term that has now passed into the lexicon. As Gourevitch wrote, "In using domestic structure as a variable in explaining foreign policy, we must explore the extent to which that structure itself derives from the exigencies of the international system" (882). Katzenstein could hardly disagree; his own work clearly acknowledged that some of the historical factors shaping domestic structures were international. But it was Gourevitch who made the endogeneity of domestic structures a central analytic issue.

Studies in the second-image reversed mode have since become commonplace in the American school. Arguably the most comprehensive approach was yet another collective research project organized by Keohane, together with his colleague Milner—a 1996 collection of essays exploring the impacts of growing economic openness (roughly what others mean by globalization) on domestic policy preferences and institutions. "The essential point of this volume," Keohane and Milner wrote (1996c, 7), was that "internationalization is having profound effects on domestic politics, although the forms that these effects take vary cross-nationally due to different institutional as well as political-economic conditions." Three different pathways were identified by which changes in the world economy might alter domestic politics: by creating new policy preferences and coalitions, by triggering domestic economic or political crises, or by undermining government control over macroeconomic policy. In the short run, domestic institutions might have the capacity to block or refract the effects of internationalization. But in the long run, "even institutions change under the pressure of constraints and the lure of opportunities" (Keohane and Milner 1996b, 256).

A third approach, pioneered by Robert Putnam (1988), sought to endogenize both sides of the frontier, focusing on the role of national governments as mediators between internal and external forces. The system, Putnam contended, was like a "two-level game," another colorful term that has passed into the lexicon. One game is played between public authorities and societal actors at the domestic level; a second is played among governments at the international level. State behavior could be understood as the product of policymakers' efforts to intermediate between the two levels. Though the two-level game metaphor has proved popular as a shorthand term for researchers, subsequent attempts to build on it—such as Milner's ambitious *Interests, Institutions, and Information* (1997b)—have tended to disappoint. As Frieden and Martin write (2002, 123), "Treatments of two-level games have not yet made much progress toward full interaction between the two levels." Even proponents of the two-level game approach concede that it fails to produce anything that might be construed as a generalizable theory (Evans, Jacobson, and Putnam 1993).

Still, whatever approach is employed—whether traditional inside-out analysis, second-image reversed, or two-level game—a noticeable trend has set in. Over time, individual explorations at the international-domestic frontier have generally become increasingly small-bore, favoring greater and greater disaggregation of both dependent and independent variables. In lieu of anything as comprehensive as "foreign economic policy," U.S. IPE today tends instead to address more finely defined segments of policy—for example, agricultural subsidies, exchange rates, or the taxation of foreign investment. Likewise, in lieu of anything as broad as "domestic structures," research tends instead to focus more narrowly on specific, identifiable explanatory factors. The reason for the trend should by now be obvious. The more thinly the problem of OEP is sliced, the easier it is to address with a reductionist methodology. Disaggregation helps the American school maintain the rigorous standards of positivism and empiricism.

Interests and Institutions

The disaggregation of domestic structures began with the common distinction between *interests* and *institutions*, two of the hardiest perennials of political theory. In turn, each of these explanatory factors has been further decomposed for greater analytic tractability, accentuating the drift away from general-equilibrium analysis toward mainly midlevel theory building.

On the interests side, the story is the familiar one of pressure group politics. Individuals are assumed to cluster into groups with shared interests, though analysts differ widely on what may be considered the relevant unit of analysis. Are we talking about firms, industries, or sectors? Or are we discussing factors of production? Most analysis makes use of economic theory to deduce what types of individuals can reasonably be assumed to share the same preferences.

Ronald Rogowski set the model for this kind of research in his pathbreaking *Commerce and Coalitions* (1989). Yet another comparativist, Rogowski sought to understand the internal political cleavages that drive external trade policy in different economies. Employing a classic second-image-reversed approach, he began with the well-known Stolper-Samuelson theorem of international trade theory, which posits a direct link between an economy's exposure to foreign trade and the distribution of income between locally scarce and abundant factors of production (land, labor, or capital). The domestic politics of trade, he contended, directly reflect these distributional implications, with trade coalitions forming in the shape of broad factor-owning classes. Rogowski's class-based track quickly became a staple of the literature, usually contrasted with an alternative track focusing on more narrowly defined industry groupings along the lines of the so-called specific-factors model of trade theory, also known as the Ricardo-Viner model. In the specific-factors model, resources are tied to their respective sectors. Hence, trade policy pits all factors in import-competing industries against all those who export their production. More recent research suggests that the relative utility of the two tracks essentially reflects the degree of factor mobility between sectors within each economy (Hiscox 2002).

Paralleling Rogowski's seminal contribution on trade policy, Frieden (1991)—then a colleague of Rogowski's at UCLA—soon pioneered systematic analysis of the role of political cleavages in financial policy. His approach too was classic second-image reversed. Growing international capital mobility, he pointed out, like trade liberalization, has predictable distributional consequences, and these effects, in turn, could be expected to alter systematically the preferences of diverse groups. Coalitions will form to promote or oppose a range of relevant government measures, from the orientation of domestic monetary policy to the choice of an exchange rate regime.

Interest-based analyses have by now become commonplace in the American school. Preferences are inferred by specifying the economic interests at stake in a given issue; policy outcomes are assumed to reflect the relative political leverage of contending constituencies. In turn, political leverage is seen as a function of such elements as preference intensity and organizational ability. And these elements then are further refined to analyze their respective determinants. Preference intensity, for example, may be influenced by the magnitude of the stakes involved or the specificity of actor assets. Organizational ability may be influenced by the size of a constituency or the distribution of potential benefits and costs of mobilizing for collective action. With each step, there has been a further shrinking of horizons.

The story is also much the same on the institutions side. Political scientists have always understood that between pressure groups and policies stand the domestic institutions through which societal preferences are debated and implemented. Institutions aggregate conflicting interests in ways that affect the ability of diverse groups to organize themselves and exercise influence over outcomes. Institutions may also delegate decision-making authority to different actors, changing the weight of various constituencies in the political process. As at the international level, institutions at the domestic level establish the rules of the game, defining and enforcing norms for the allocation of values.

In the emerging field of IPE in the United States, Krasner highlighted early on the importance of domestic institutions in his contribution to *Between Power and Plenty* (1978b). Elaborating on a theme first broached by Katzenstein in his earlier 1976 paper, Krasner stressed the institutionally based capacity of the state in relation to its own society. That capacity, Krasner argued, could be envisioned along a continuum ranging from weak to strong. In weak states, political power is fragmented among many institutional players, including pressure groups of all kinds. Strong states are those where central decision makers can formulate and implement policy with relative autonomy. Subsequently, much effort was put into understanding the "strength" or "weakness" of the policy process—otherwise referred to as state capacity—in a variety of institutional settings. Much of the work was empirical and largely in the comparativist tradition, explaining and debating the merits of alternative organizational structures (Gourevitch 2002).

Here too the problem has been sliced thinner and thinner. Starting with the basic political regime types of autocracy and democracy, finer distinctions are introduced between older and younger regimes, or between transitional and established regimes. Regime institutions, in turn, are subdivided into such categories as electoral, legislative, or bureaucratic, each with its own distinct features and implications for the policy process. Electoral systems (where they exist) may be unitary or federalist, proportional or majoritarian, or based on more or less complex voting rules. Each variation can have a significant impact on the relationship among voters, interest groups, and policymakers. Legislative systems may differ in terms of agenda control, veto points, and other interactions with the executive branch of government, influencing bargaining among politicians. Bureaucratic institutions may vary in the pattern and degree of delegation involved in their mandates, conditioning the way policy is implemented. Again, with each step, there is a further shrinking of horizons.

Thus the black box has indeed been opened, adding the missing domestic level of analysis just as Katzenstein had hoped. His success cannot be denied. As a friend has written to me, Katzenstein brought "the backbone of comparative political economy" to IPE. But even as a new research frontier was created, the scope of inquiry began to contract under the pressure of the American school's allegiance to scientific method. The range of relevant actors and influences has definitely widened. But while the forest has grown, the focus of scholarship has tended to become more and more concentrated on individual trees. In the pursuit of parsimony, relationships and variables are defined ever more narrowly. Methodological rigor is preserved, but at the expense of the bigger picture.

Cognitive Analysis

And what about the cognitive level of analysis—Waltz's first image, now divided between a psychological track and a sociological one? Katzenstein's intellectual entrepreneurship did not end with the synthesis of outside-in and inside-out analysis. Since the mid-1990s, he has joined a determined campaign to promote the study of ideational factors as well, challenging the strict rationalism of traditional neo-utilitarian approaches to international relations theory. To date, the resulting impact on IPE has been limited; the insights of cognitive analysis have yet to make significant inroads into the U.S. version of the field. But signs of a new awareness are emerging. The success that Katzenstein attained with his early work on domestic structures could yet be matched by his more recent work on the role of norms and identity in policymaking.

A Movement Flowers

For Katzenstein, the dominant track in cognitive analysis is the sociological one: constructivism. As an intellectual movement, constructivism is founded on a single critical premise—that reality is socially constructed. As Emanuel Adler summarizes (2002, 95), "The material world does not come classified . . . therefore, the objects of our knowledge are not independent of our interpretations and our language." Ideas matter, not just instrumentally, but also in constitutive terms, as fundamental determinants of identities and interests. Perceptions, values, norms, and beliefs—all rest on a foundation of shared, intersubjective understandings that give content and meaning to the material world. In Ruggie's words (1999, 216), "Constructivism is about human consciousness and its role in international life." What passes for knowledge is socially constructed fact.

Katzenstein was by no means the first prominent figure in IR to take up the cause of constructivism. Indeed, the roots of the constructivist movement are multiple and deep. One source of inspiration came from sociology—in particular, the influential work of Peter Berger and Thomas Luckmann (1966) on the social definition of reality, which in turn built on the classical sociology of Émile Durkheim and Max Weber. Another came from the writings of Antonio Gramsci, with his Marxist take on the origins of hegemonic ideas. And a third came from Haas (1958) and Katzenstein's mentor Deutsch (Deutsch, Burrell, and Kann 1957), whose studies of European integration anticipated constructivism in their emphasis on the critical role of social communications and symbols in the building of transnational collective identities ("we feelings").

From these roots, constructivism has flowered today into one of the main analytic orientations for mainstream IR research. Credit for the movement's early cultivation is usually given to Nicholas Onuf (1989), who first coined the concept of constructivism in IR, and Alexander Wendt (1992), for his now-celebrated article on "anarchy" and what we make of it. Both in turn owed a considerable debt to Ruggie (1975, 1983), who had long urged that more attention be paid to the role of consensual understandings in world politics. It is worth noting that Onuf had studied with Deutsch at Yale University, while Ruggie received instruction from Haas at Berkeley. Later major contributions have included fertile studies by Martha Finnemore (1996) and again Wendt (1999).

Even before Onuf and Wendt, Katzenstein had flirted with some nascent constructivist notions. Katzenstein, in *Small States in World Markets*, laid considerable emphasis on the role of an "ideology of social partnership" in shaping economic policy in the small countries he was studying—"shared interpretations" that helped to define interests (1985, 32). Hence once the constructivist movement formally got under way, he did not wait long to join in. By 1996, he had produced two seminal works addressing the social understandings behind national security policies: an edited collection of essays on norms and identity in world politics, many written by his own former students (Katzenstein 1996b); and a solely authored book on security policy in postwar Japan (Katzenstein 1996a). Today, both are considered pathbreaking accomplishments in the field of security studies.

Central to each volume is the concept of national identity, understood as a society's collective interpretation of itself as a community. Taking issue with the rationalist tradition in IR theory, each book emphasized the political significance of collective identities and norms, which ultimately are culturally determined. "State interests," Katzenstein declared (1996c, 2), "do not exist to be 'discovered' by self-interested, rational actors. Interests are constructed through a process of social interaction. . . . Security interests are defined by actors who respond to cultural factors." Social facts, the two books argued, are as significant in shaping government behavior as are raw power or purely material calculations.

Katzenstein's turn to constructivism was hardly surprising, given his own personal history. Born and raised in a country that was busy redefining its place in the world, then displaced to an entirely different society and culture where he ultimately became a citizen, he could hardly be indifferent to issues of identity formation and transformation. As Katzenstein has written to me, "As a transplant from Europe I never needed convincing about the importance of language in constituting us as individuals. I would have become a very different person in German than I became in English." Constructivism came easy to someone whose own identity had been so profoundly reconstructed.

Constructivism also came easy to someone with Katzenstein's training as a comparativist. Sociological perspectives have always been critical for comparative politics. Undoubtedly, Deutsch planted some seeds when Katzenstein was still a graduate student. But most of all, Katzenstein insists, it was the enthusiasm of his own students that ultimately moved him to take ideational factors seriously. His edited collection *The Culture of National Security* was dedicated to his graduate students at Cornell, without whom, Katzenstein averred (1996d, xv), "I could not have conceived of this project. . . . It was our individual discussions and seminars as well as your research papers and dissertations that made me read in unfamiliar fields and thus lure me in new directions in both research and teaching." Rarely are teachers so generous in acknowledging how much they themselves can learn in the educational process.

And where was IPE in all this? Katzenstein has of course continued to edit the Cornell Studies in Political Economy, encouraging new research in the field by others. But his own emphasis has shifted. The more he has taken up the cause of constructivism, the more issues of political economy have come to be marginalized in his work. Since the mid-1990s his main preoccupations have remained with security policy and increasingly regionalism, seeking a more encompassing characterization of world politics.

Political economy has not been entirely absent, of course. For example, in Katzenstein's *A World of Regions*, a notable study published in 2005, elements of political economy are skillfully interwoven with security and cultural analysis in an effort to understand the role of regions in an increasingly globalized environment. Ours is a world of regions, he contends, each distinct in institutional form, type of identity, and internal structure. In a manner reminiscent of his writings on domestic structures in the 1970s, he stresses the central role of policy networks connecting states and societies both within and between regions. At the same time, in the manner of constructivism, he highlights the role of ideational factors in determining how regions come to be defined. "Regions are politically made," suggests Katzenstein (2005, 9), "collective symbols chosen by groups to dominate specific places in the natural world." Political economy does play a part in the analysis. Salient to the definition of regions, he adds, also are "production processes that separate cores from peripheries" (9). But it is a bit part at best. IPE, clearly, is no longer his main passion.

Yet given Katzenstein's preeminence in scholarly circles, how could there not be an impact on IPE research, too? In effect, his reputation helped legitimize a further opening of the black box to incorporate first-image analysis. If Katzenstein saw merit in adding ideational factors to the mix, why shouldn't others?

First Buds

So far, though, the impact has been limited. As Katzenstein and his friends Keohane and Krasner conceded in their introduction to IO's fiftieth anniversary issue (1999b, 9), "In the field of national security the discussion between rationalism (in its realist and liberal variants) and constructivism has been more fully joined than in the field of IPE." Indeed, in the U.S. version of IPE, the debate has barely even begun. First buds of a constructivist challenge are beginning to emerge but are still far from a full flowering.

The reason is not difficult to fathom. Ideational factors sit uneasily in a hard science model. Like economists back when IPE was first born, U.S. specialists in the field today instinctively resist a theoretical approach that runs against the grain of accepted methodological standards. How can formal analysis account for the inherent uncertainties of the human mind? How can existing empirical methods cope with the vagueness of notions like socialization and social facts? Here, too, mainstream scholars have preferred to ignore what cannot be objectively observed or systematically tested. For confirmation, one need look no further than the two recent surveys by Frieden and Martin (2002) and Lake (2006). Remarkably, neither even mentions the cognitive level of analysis. Both, demonstrating the powerful grip of creeping economism, define IPE strictly in terms of neo-utilitarian rationalism.

Not that ideational factors were ever entirely excluded by the American school. As early as 1979, Odell was stressing the role of policy beliefs and subjective perceptions in the shaping of U.S. monetary behavior in the period after World War II. "In analyses of policy change," argued Odell (1979, 80), "beliefs should be elevated to an equal theoretical level." Odell's focus was on the individual policymaker, representative of the psychological track of cognitive analysis. His aim was to demonstrate the degree to which state behavior could be traced to the mind-set of senior officials. As Odell expanded in a subsequent book (1982, 58), "Behavior depends not on reality but on how reality is perceived and interpreted. . . . Substantive ideas held by top policy makers and advisers [are] decisive or necessary elements of explanation."

Likewise, a few years later Judith Goldstein (1993) was stressing the role that ideas have played historically in U.S. trade policy and the creation of trade institutions in the United States. Ideas, Goldstein contended, play a dual role: first, as focal points or road maps, providing strategic guidance to policymakers; and second, once adopted, as rules that survive to bind future political choices. Sometimes free trade thinking has prevailed in Washington, DC; at other times, more emphasis has been placed on fair trade or the legitimacy of domestic distributional considerations. Proceeding from the assumption that the organizational structure of the state has a significant influence on the orientation of policy, Goldstein examined the sources of each of these key ideas and how they have been inculcated over time into law, thus helping to explain the often-contradictory stance of U.S. policymakers.

Contributions like these, however, were few and far between, failing to inspire much emulation. Even scarcer were efforts to take the sociological track, highlighting processes of social construction and the constitutive role of norms. The major exception was Ruggie, who long wandered in the desert preaching the cause of constructivism even before the movement had a name. Most memorable was Ruggie's chapter in Krasner's *International Regimes* volume. Central to the "compromise of embedded liberalism" was his notion of a normative framework, understood as an "intersubjective framework of meaning" (Ruggie 1983, 196). Regimes, Ruggie argued, are social institutions. "We know international regimes not simply by some descriptive inventory of their concrete elements, but by their generative grammar, the underlying principles of order and meaning that shape the manner of their formation and transformation" (196). The impact of Ruggie's reasoning could be seen in the inclusion of three constructivist-type elements—diffuse principles and norms, habits and customs, and accumulated knowledge—among the causal variables proposed by Krasner to explain the origins of regimes. But subsequent work on regime theory or its successor, institutional theory, made little use of Ruggie's perspective.

Only in the most recent years have studies of ideational factors begun to blossom in the American school. Leading the way on the psychological track, once again, is Odell, following his stint as editor of IO. In a thoughtful exploration of international economic negotiations, Odell (2000) built on the insights of his earlier work to underscore the role of negotiators' beliefs as an independent influence on bargaining strategies and outcomes. The critical issue, he suggested, is what Nobel Prize–winning economist Herbert Simon called "bounded rationality"—a variant of "rational choice that takes into account the cognitive limitations of the decision maker, limitations of both knowledge and computational capacity" (1997, 291). Given the constraints of bounded rationality, negotiators typically make use of cognitive shortcuts, convenient heuristics that rely heavily on subjective beliefs to guide their behavior. To understand economic diplomacy, therefore, it is vital to understand the ideas of the diplomats. In Odell's words (2000, 3), "If the real world is one of bounded rationality, identifying such key beliefs and their effects become a productive way to advance knowledge about, and the practice of, economic bargaining." A later paper by Odell expands on the theme, arguing for more use of the bounded-rationality premise in IPE generally. "Political economy knowledge would be better," Odell writes (2002, 168), "if we paid more attention to how economic policy decisions are actually made. Theoretically, a new [approach] rebuilt upon a bounded-rationality microfoundation would be more complete and better able to account for change."

Systematic studies have also begun to appear on the sociological track, albeit still at a modest pace—mostly, as it happens, on monetary or financial matters. Kathleen McNamara (1998), for example, has carefully explored the "currency of ideas" as a driving force in the process of monetary integration in Europe. The key to understanding the evolution of European monetary politics in the 1970s and 1980s, McNamara suggests, lay in a new "neoliberal" policy consensus that took hold among policy elites, redefining state interests. Jeffrey Chwieroth (2007) identified a similar dynamic in a constructivist study of financial liberalization in emerging market economies in the 1980s and 1990s. Capital markets were opened, Chwieroth argues, because of a new set of neoliberal norms that were diffused through a network of knowledge-based experts once they came to positions of authority in governments and international organizations. Other constructivist research has underscored the social sources of financial power and monetary leadership in the global community (Barkin 2003; Seabrooke 2006). Most of this work has been fairly specific in terms of issue area, highlighting the influence of particular policy programs or economic ideologies.

Perhaps most ambitious have been broad efforts to relate strategies of foreign economic policy back to the general notion of national identity, much as Katzenstein did in his pathbreaking work on security policy (1996a, 1996b). Renewed interest in the economic role of national identity was sparked initially by the strikingly divergent policy paths followed by various successor states after the breakup of the Soviet Union in 1991. While some of the former Soviet republics quickly embraced a Western orientation in trade and finance, others struggled to reintegrate as much as possible under the banner of the newborn Commonwealth of Independent States (CIS). What could account for such marked differences? Studies by Rawi Abdelal (2001) and Andrei Tsygankov (2001) located the explanation in variations in each new state's sense of self. The stronger the sense of a genuine national identity, the more likely a government was to distance itself from the CIS. It is hardly a coincidence that Abdelal happened to be a student of Katzenstein's, while Tsygankov was mentored by Odell.

Subsequently, the national identity theme was extended to cases in other parts of the world as well in a collection of essays coedited by Helleiner and Andreas Pickel (2005). National identities, Helleiner wrote in the concluding chapter (2005, 220), "influence economic policies and processes in very significant ways." Helleiner specifically credits Katzenstein's work on security issues for inspiring his group's focus on national identity (230). Along similar lines, another recent collection (Roy, Denzau, and Willett 2007) has emphasized the importance of distinct sociopolitical contexts in accounting for the timing and diversity of neoliberal policy experiments around the world, highlighting the role played by "intersubjectively accepted mental constructions" in determining perceptions of interest. This analysis is based on the Shared Mental Models framework first proposed by economists Arthur Denzau and Douglass North (1994).

How successful all these efforts at cognitive analysis will turn out to be is still an open question, of course. But it is clear that the black box is now increasingly open to ideational factors in addition to the more traditional systemic and domestic variables. U.S. IPE may still privilege the state as the basic unit of analysis. Yet the field has definitely come a long way from the simple billiard ball model of old.

DEMOTING THE BOX

Once again, the contrast with the British school is stark. From the British point of view, it doesn't matter how open the black box is. The problem is the box itself, which must be demoted. Other units are of interest too.

The logic is simple. The question, we are told, is not how many levels to employ in analyzing state behavior. Rather, it is the privileging of the state itself that is at issue. Treating the state as the most important unit of interest unduly cramps analysis, leaving out much of what makes the study of IPE worthwhile. As one British scholar declares, "Political economy cannot be reduced merely to policy studies" (Watson 2005, 28). In the spirit of Strange's open range, the British version of IPE aims to be far more inclusive, adding many more characters to the story—players that are of interest in their own right, not just as some kind of influence on government behavior. For the British school, that is the only way to solve the Mystery of the State. The state must be treated as just one agent among many, if it is to be included at all.

Sub-field or Inter-discipline?

From the start, British scholars have resisted the American school's tendency to define IPE more or less as a subset of IR. Geoffrey Underhill best posed the question (2000, 805): "Sub-field or inter-discipline? Should [IPE] focus on the special nature of the system of states, along the lines of more traditional International Relations, or should it develop . . . branches across a broad range of social science traditions?" The British school's response is unmistakable. IPE is an "inter-discipline," not just a minor specialty within political science. The British version of the field, Underhill concludes, "has long since burst the boundaries of traditional IR and has taken a place on its own among the social sciences" (815).

The contrast was drawn early. At first, the ambition in Britain was not much different from that of the American school. It was simply to build a bridge between international economics and international politics—to find the "middle ground" that Strange called for in her "Mutual Neglect" manifesto (1970, 307) and that so excited the fabled Cumberland Lodge Conference (Brown 1973). Though governments would still figure prominently, they would now share the stage with markets—a relationship that Strange sought to codify in books like *States and Markets* (Strange 1988b) and *Rival States, Rival Firms* (Stopford and Strange 1991). For the American school, that is still as far as the inquiry need go. When Lake (2006) defines IPE as a "true interdiscipline," it is the middle ground between economics and IR that he has in mind—something quite different from what Underhill means when he uses the word inter-discipline (with its alternative British spelling).

But then, during the 1980s, perspectives in Britain began to broaden dramatically, distancing scholarship on the other side of the pond even more from a narrow attachment to the state. The trend was evident in the essays that Strange commissioned for *Paths to International Political Economy* (1984a), which called for new bridges to be built to an ever-widening range of disciplines. Specialists now talked freely of a "clash of paradigms" (Tooze 1985, 112).

By the 1990s, the differences between the two sides of the Atlantic had become entrenched. Surveys of British and American universities at mid-decade (O'Brien 1995; Denemark and O'Brien 1997) found a competition between two quite distinct conceptions of IPE: a "traditional" approach, which "views IPE as a subdiscipline of political science"; and an "inclusive" approach, which "opens up and includes new areas of investigation [and] threatens to outgrow the traditional boundaries of state-centric international relations" (Denemark and O'Brien 1997, 215). Not surprisingly, the "traditional" approach appeared to predominate in the United States—an observation confirmed by a more recent survey of IPE syllabi in U.S. universities (Paul 2006). The survey found "little evidence to suggest that political economy as it is studied and taught in sociology, geography, anthropology, law . . . has found its way into American classrooms" (729). The "inclusive" approach, meanwhile, had by the 1990s become the overwhelming favorite of British academics. In Britain the theme of eclecticism now predominated, much as Strange had hoped.

Behind the preference for a more ecumenical approach lie all the factors noted in chapter 2, including of course Strange's memorable powers of persuasion. Underlying everything, from the start, was the basic divergence of broad intellectual cultures. Not only have international studies traditionally been addressed differently—with the U.S. side emphasizing the norms of conventional social science, and the British side drawing more from a "historical-relativist paradigm" (Tooze 1985, 121). In addition, British academics were much more amenable to the siren call of critical theory, questioning orthodoxy of all kind—not least, U.S. orthodoxy. And this predilection, in turn, was undoubtedly reinforced by the considerable, albeit latent, anti-Americanism that was to be found in many British universities at the time.

In a Gramscian fashion, some in the British school today even speak of their more heterodox approach as a "counter-hegemonic movement" in order to underscore their determined resistance to the orthodoxy of the American school (Gills 2001, 237). Indeed, as also noted in chapter 2, many go so far as to call for an entirely different name for the field—GPE rather than IPE—in order to avoid any taint of the "traditional" approach. In the words of Ronen Palan (2000b, 1), "IPE is generally adopted by those who view it as a subfield of International Relations, whereas GPE is normally the preferred label for those who view it as a transdisciplinary effort." The rejection of the "traditional" approach has by now become almost universal in British academia. Few scholars in Britain these days would even think of trying to defend the state-centrism of U.S. IPE.

Alternatives

Rejecting state-centrism did not mean abandoning the state altogether. For some in the British school, the state remains a key focus of analysis, converging around the notion of the "competition state"—a term first coined by Philip Cerny (1990). An increasingly open world economy, it is argued, is transforming the architecture of global politics, forcing governments to use new forms of intervention to promote the competitive advantages of their own national industrial and financial activities (Palan and Abbott 1996; Weiss 1998). The competition state is not just the rival of transnational markets, struggling to sustain its authority against a widening Control Gap. By redefining the national interest to embrace interdependence, governments in effect transform themselves, becoming active participants in the promotion of globalization. Hence even if the state should be demoted as an object of research, no longer allowed to hog center stage, it must be studied seriously. As Angus Cameron and Ronen

Palan put it (2004, 8), "The state continues to play an important role: but it is a very different state."

But if the state is no longer central, where should we look for an alternative? That is where matters get murkier. Though British school scholars are united in their rejection of state-centrism, they divide sharply over where the spotlight should instead be directed. Here too, as in their discussions of the Control Gap, the answers vary depending on taste, all competing for primacy. To say that the British school's ontology lacks a certain consonance would be an understatement. In their determined insistence on an all-inclusive eclecticism, theorists have highlighted and promoted a gaggle of candidates to replace the state as the leading player. Even the British school's most ardent champions acknowledge the "pitfalls of over-fragmentation" (Gills 2001, 238).

At one extreme are those who, following Strange, insist on the centrality of the individual. Strange's intense engagement with social issues was no accident. As one former student has testified, "She cared deeply about people" (Lorentzen 2002, ix). Methodological individualism came naturally to someone whose only formal university training was in economics. Many others, such as Barry Gills (2001) and Matthew Watson (2005), continue to conceive of IPE in the same way. For Gills (2001, 235), the field is all about a "discourse of freedom . . . a sustained and serious concern for human emancipation, liberation, and empowerment." Whatever else we look at in IPE, Gills says, "we must elevate this question to the first order" (235). Echoes Watson (2005, 5), IPE "should be the study of individual action within the context of institutionalized economic norms."

At the opposite extreme are those who, following Cox, identify IPE with the study of historical structures. Many are happy to adopt Cox's preferred term of world orders. Others, as we saw in the last chapter, fashion distinctive labels of their own, such as Underhill's catchy state-market condominium (2000); while yet others, in the Marxist tradition, simply equate the international system with global or transnational capitalism. Whatever the terminology, the message is the same. Analysis should concentrate on the systemic level, where the rules and norms for human behavior are determined. As Cox himself expressed it (1995, 32), "Political economy . . . is concerned with the historically constituted frameworks or structures within which political and economic activity take place."

Finally, in between are those who prefer to focus on specific, tangible actors—the kinds of institutionalized "private authorities" that we encountered in discussing the Control Gap. The approach builds on Strange's theme that politics is larger than what politicians do. All agents with structural power should be included, from multinational corporations to the mafia. Strange herself, in her last books (1986, 1996, 1998a), laid stress on banks, insurance companies, and other critical players in casino capitalism. Younger scholars, following in her footsteps, add still more actors—labor unions, social movements, and nongovernmental organizations of all types. The cast of characters is potentially endless, all crowding alongside the state and clamoring for attention.

That this dissonant chorus leaves the British version of IPE a bit unfocused is undeniable. More than two decades ago, Roger Tooze suggested that "the British 'historical' approach could benefit from a more coherent, comprehensive and articulated conceptual basis" (1985, 124). If anything, the lack of intellectual coherence has actually grown worse with time. The British school's harmony of opposition to state-centrism breaks down when it comes to providing a compelling counterpoint.

COMPLEMENTARITY, AGAIN

So the mystery remains. The American school persists in privileging the state above all other units of interest. The black box has been opened, adding domestic and even ideational factors to the picture. But ultimately public policy remains the main concern—understanding government behavior. The British school, meanwhile, resists the subordination of IPE to the study of IR, insisting on a much more heterodox ontology. Yet ultimately the welter of alternatives blurs the vision and threatens MEGO—"My eyes glaze over." If the American school can be criticized for leaving too much out, the British school is vulnerable to the charge that it tries to bring too much in—everything but the kitchen sink, one might say.

Once again, we are reminded of how complementary the two schools are. Where the "traditional" approach of the American school, with its single-minded preoccupation with the state, narrows the focus enough to preserve the principles of positivism and empiricism, the "inclusive" approach of the British school, in its ecumenism, broadens perspectives sufficiently to keep us sensitive to a fuller range of analytic concerns. Conversely, where the British school, with its emphasis on grand historical narratives, threatens to lose us in the forest, the American school, in its preference for reductionism, risks limiting our vision to individual trees. The American school prefers parsimonious specialization. The British school encourages ambitious generalization.

One is reminded of the old adage explaining the difference between specialists and generalists. Specialists, it is said, are those who learn more and more about less and less until they know everything about nothing. Generalists, on the other hand, learn less and less about more and more until they know nothing about everything. Both schools could benefit from keeping that bit of wisdom in mind.

Chapter 6

WHAT HAVE WE LEARNED?

What is the answer? [I was silent.] In that case,
what is the question?
—Gertrude Stein's last words, as reported
by Alice B. Toklas

SO WHAT HAVE WE LEARNED? Enormous effort has gone into the construction of IPE. Whole forests have been sacrificed to produce innumerable books and articles on every conceivable aspect of the subject. Inquiry has been promoted; ideas have proliferated; debates have raged. As in any academic field, the aim of the collective enterprise, ultimately, has been to create a coherent body of knowledge. So how successful has the attempt been? What do we know now that we didn't know before?

In the manner of Bill Clinton—who famously answered a question about his private life by suggesting that much depended on "what the definition of 'is' is"—much depends on what we know the definition of "know" to be. If knowledge is measured by our ability to make definitive statements—to generalize without fear of dispute—the field's success may be rated as negligible at best. Many theories have been developed, from HST onward. But none are universally accepted, and disagreement persists over even the most basic issues of process and structure. An old jibe about the economics profession has it that if you laid all the economists in the world end to end, you still wouldn't reach agreement. The same regrettably may be said of IPE. As Krasner ruefully acknowledged in a reflection on the field (1996, 110), explanations "have, in some specific cases, been deeply illuminating, but no one has presented a coherent general theory."

Yet is that the best way to measure knowledge? Perhaps Gertrude Stein, on her deathbed, got it right. We may not know the answers but at least we can learn to ask the right questions—to define an appropriate research agenda. For many, that is the true test of an academic field like IPE. "I use the term 'political economy,' " Gilpin once wrote (1987, 9), "simply to indicate a set of questions to be examined." Concurs a more recent British source, IPE is best understood as a "question-asking field" (Watson 2005, 15). Specialists may never agree on how the world works. But at least it should be possible to agree on what it is about the world that we want to study—what is often referred to, especially in the British literature, as the field's "problematique."

Unfortunately, even by that test IPE's success must be rated as less than stellar. At the broadest level, we all accept that the field is about the nexus of global economics and politics, an amalgam of market studies and political analysis. But try to get any more specific and differences quickly emerge. Two decades after Strange issued her "Mutual Neglect" manifesto, two of her followers were lamenting that "scholars still debate what exactly should be included in the set of questions that defines IPE" (Murphy and Tooze 1991, 2). Matters have not improved much since. Specialists today still differ sharply over what is the field's core problematique. Is it any wonder that IPE has been characterized as "schizoid"?

Here again, the diversity of the field is well illustrated by the contrasts to be found between IPE's American and British versions. Both schools have accomplished much; our understanding of the world now is certainly much better than it was when the field first began. But since the agendas of the two schools are so divergent, so too is what we have learned from each. Students in the two traditions are taught to ask distinctly different sets of questions. Whereas the state-centric U.S. style is most concerned with the causes and consequences of public policy, the more inclusive British approach is inclined to encompass a rather broader range of social issues and concerns. The body of knowledge that has been created is large, but hardly tidy.

THE AMERICAN SCHOOL

For the American school, the agenda remains much as I described it nearly two decades ago in the article that so provoked Craig Murphy and Roger Tooze (Cohen 1990). Despite their objections (Murphy and Tooze 1991), noted back in chapter 2, mainstream scholarship in the United States continues to concentrate on the two broad questions of *actor behavior* and *system governance*, in traditional state-centric fashion. What motivates government behavior, and how do sovereign nations manage their economic interdependence? Between them these two questions, both focused on public policy, form the core problematique for the U.S. version of IPE.

In substantive terms, the problematique in turn is broken up into more discrete issue areas, again reflecting the American school's general drift toward mainly midlevel theory. The school's early pioneers, as I have already noted, had dared to Think Big. When Keohane and Nye wrote about complex interdependence, Gilpin about his three models of the future, Kindleberger about hegemony, Krasner about regimes, or Katzenstein about domestic structures, they all had in mind the entire range of economic relations between states, not finely defined subcategories. Their questions were general, not specialized. But as part of the more recent trend toward a greater disaggregation of analysis, promoted in the name of professionalism, successor generations have narrowed their inquiries to less comprehensive notions of political economy. Today, scholarship typically focuses on individual segments of policy, not foreign economic policy in general.

Manifestly, something is lost when horizons are shrunk in this way. The Big Picture tends to get obscured, if not forgotten. It is significant that of the American school's original Big Thinkers, only Gilpin (2001) continued to work at the same level before joining Kindleberger in retirement. By contrast, the three youngest of the Magnificent Seven all eventually chose instead to abandon IPE in favor of other pursuits. Keohane (2002), as noted, moved on to institutional theory and other approaches to issues of governance in world politics. Krasner (1999) took up the subject of sovereignty in historical context, while Katzenstein (1996a, 1996b, 2005), as we have seen, turned to constructivism as well as questions of security policy and regionalism. As Keohane has written to me, "I think our departures from IPE reflected the narrowing and increasing methodological rigor: either we had to bone up on economics and focus at the micro-level, or go into another, more fertile territory. All three of us did the latter."

Yet the utility of disaggregation should not be underestimated, despite its limitations. The value added is unmistakable. Years of research have taught us much about what causal variables to look for to explain government behavior; we also know more now about the potential contributions as well as limitations of alternative modes of system governance. In the end, we have acquired a firmer basis for the cumulation of knowledge. We may still not have definitive answers, but we have certainly gotten a better handle on how to frame our questions.

A Conspicuous Asymmetry

Following the lead of the economics profession, which for the most part divides its subject material neatly into the two spheres of microeconomics and macroeconomics, most substantive work in the U.S. style is segregated under the rubric of either trade or finance. International trade, with its focus on markets and the terms of exchange, may be regarded as the external extension of domestic microeconomic activity. Likewise, international finance, with its concentration on money and credit, may be regarded as the external extension of domestic macroeconomic activity. The policy studies that define the main themes for theorizing in the American school are largely variations on either trade or financial policy.

Other topics attract attention from time to time—for instance, foreign direct investment, migration, or economic sanctions—but remain at the periphery of the field's scope. So too does the broad issue of development for the poorer economies of the world. Among economists, the earlier treatment of development as a specialized area of inquiry has long since gone out of fashion. As

Paul Krugman has written (1996, 7), "There was a field called development economics. . . . That field no longer exists." The same is now true of U.S.-style IPE. Developing countries receive their share of attention, but mainly as a group with distinctive characteristics that may be contrasted with the more advanced economies of Europe, North America, and East Asia. The development process as such receives little emphasis. Instead, U.S. scholars are inclined to focus their research most on the advanced economies—perhaps, as Sylvia Maxfield has suggested (2002, 471), because of the greater availability and reliability of data with which to test theoretical propositions.

In each variant of policy studies, much effort has gone into the analysis of both state behavior and system governance. Relative emphases, however, have differed considerably, creating a conspicuous asymmetry between the trade and financial sides of the literature. On the trade side, research has focused more on the underlying sources of policy. On the finance side, by contrast, the reverse is true. Question asking in matters of money and finance tends to concentrate more on issues of interstate cooperation and the management of interdependent relations. As one source has observed, "Interest in the domestic and transnational (rather than strictly state-to-state or international) politics of trade is longstanding in international political economy. . . . Unfortunately, immersion in a similar politics for money and finance is often lacking. . . . The class or sectoral politics of money are sidelined" (Paul 2006, 731). Trade specialists, it seems, prefer to theorize most about what motivates governments. Specialists in international finance, conversely, are inclined to think more about how to govern what governments do.

What explains the asymmetry? Most likely, it reflects the greater transparency of distributional issues in the trade area than in finance. Trade encompasses the full range of goods and services that are bought and sold across national frontiers, including the increasing volume of intracorporate flows that course through the complex supply chains created by multinational enterprises. When trade barriers are increased or decreased, incomes and market shares are directly affected. There are obvious winners and losers, both domestically and internationally. The political cleavages that result were bound to attract the attention of the political scientists who, from the start, have dominated the American school. Distributional conflict lies at the heart of political theory; analyzing how such tensions are resolved through the institutions of government has been the hallmark of the political science discipline ever since its divorce from economics in the nineteenth century. It is therefore hardly surprising that scholars attracted to the study of trade issues might naturally gravitate more toward research at the domestic level, addressing the roots of state behavior.

On the finance side, by contrast, distributional issues tend to be more opaque, owing to the higher level of aggregation involved in the study of economic activity at the macroeconomic level. Finance encompasses all the main features of monetary relations between states: the processes and institutions of financial intermediation (the mobilization of savings and allocation of credit) as well as the creation and management of money itself. In contrast to the trade side, it is not so easy to identify clear winners and losers when, say, interest rates are raised or credit markets are liberalized. Hence policy on the finance side tends to appear less overtly politicized, seemingly driven more by technical analysis than by the exigencies of politics per se. As Odell long ago observed (1979, 80), "The formation of international monetary policy bears more resemblance to the making of traditional diplomatic-military strategy than to trade policy."

Appearances may be misleading, of course. Beneath the surface, politics could be boiling along merrily. And sometimes the steam even breaks out into the open, with roaring political debates over exchange rates or the opening of capital markets. Nevertheless, for many—especially those mystified by the complexities of money and credit—a less domestically oriented perspective is a convenient starting point for analysis. Given that starting point, the more salient challenge in finance seems to lie not at home but at the international level, where divergences among national policies must somehow be reconciled or accommodated. Research naturally follows, gravitating more to questions of system governance.

As a result of these differences, the contributions of the two variations have been asymmetrical as well. While specialists on the trade side have made significant advances in spotlighting the determinants of government policy, progress has been slower in formalizing analysis of arrangements governing the trading system. Conversely, while specialists on the finance side have developed an extensive literature on the management of international money and credit, relatively less effort has gone into conceptualizing the forces motivating state behavior. In none of these areas have the answers been to everyone's satisfaction. But it is evident that on some questions we have managed to learn a lot more than on others.

A few words on each variation will illustrate how much has been learned in each area—and alas, also how much remains to be learned.

TRADE

Historically, at the time of IPE's birth, interest in trade issues was first stimulated by conflicting trends in government policy in the 1960s and 1970s. Cutting across the grain of postwar liberalization, which had generated such a remarkable spread of interdependence, was a rising tide of protectionist sentiment as well as a new interest in trade regionalism stimulated by the successful launching of Europe's Common Market (now the European Union). What might account for these conflicting trends, and how could they be managed?

By the 1980s, questions like these were being addressed by a growing number of scholars in the American school.

Preferences

Consider, first, actor behavior. What explains the trade preferences of states? In principle, three broad policy options are available: openness, protectionism, or regionalism. Openness means commitment to a liberal and multilatal global trading system, reducing tariffs or nontariff barriers to a minimum. Protectionism means the reverse: unilateral closure and insulation from foreign competition. And regionalism means joining together with one or more partners in some form of preferential trade agreement (PTA). In practice, of course, among these three polar alternatives, many variations and combinations are possible.

For economists trained in the conventional neoclassical tradition, the question of trade preferences is inherently puzzling. Their profession's prevailing theories, descended from Adam Smith and David Ricardo, stress the many benefits of unrestricted exchange between economies based on underlying differences of comparative advantage. Openness should be the obvious choice. Yet in the real world, forces of protectionism and regionalism seem forever rampant, if not overwhelming. Governments appear to oscillate unpredictably among the three polar alternatives. The dissonance between theory and practice is deafening and seemingly inexplicable. In chapter 1, I noted the reluctance of most economists to look into the details of policymaking, so much like sausage making. Frustrated, they are tempted simply to throw up their hands and proclaim, "It's all politics!"

That of course is where IPE came in. For political scientists, with their distinctly different disciplinary training, it was far less unnatural to think of logical reasons for behavior that traditional economics would reject as irrational. No doubt that is why political scientists were more attracted to the newborn field in the first place. Any student of standard IR theory could see that the mercantilist elements of trade policy are not aberrant exogenous variables to be deplored but rather central endogenous factors to be explained. Policy is the outcome of a complex process of bargaining and compromise. Yes, it may all be politics—or nearly so. But no, it is not inexplicable, at least not in principle.

In fact, after decades of discussion, a fair amount of consensus has developed in the American school over what explanatory factors are likely to matter most, even if the invisible college continues to disagree over their relative importance or even about the sign of some relationships. Since the list of possible causal variables is long, it would be difficult, if not impossible, to catalog them all here. But a brief survey of a representative sample may suffice to illuminate the progress that has been made as well as what remains unresolved.

The basic approach is what Lake (2006) calls OEP. Analysis focuses mainly on the international-domestic research frontier, which Frieden and Martin (2002) described as the cutting edge of U.S.-style IPE. Explanations are sought at either the systemic or domestic level of analysis, and tend to be neo-utilitarian in spirit, stressing rational calculation in response to material incentives and constraints. As noted in chapter 5, only rarely—as in the early work of Odell (1979, 1982) or Goldstein (1993)—have ideational factors been added to the equation.

The Systemic Level

At the systemic level, where realists are most comfortable, states are assumed to act on behalf of some more or less well-articulated conception of national interest. Both economic and political incentives are cited, corresponding roughly to Gilpin's pursuit of wealth and pursuit of power (1975b, 43), or to what Viner (1948) meant by power and plenty. The decisive variable is the global strategic setting. Policy preferences, it is assumed, may be derived from the structure of the international economy or polity.

Critical to the pursuit of wealth are possible market "imperfections"—departures from the economist's textbook model of "perfect" competition—that could justify state intervention to restrict exchange. The traditional case for free trade assumes all the conditions of perfect competition, such as large numbers of rival buyers and sellers, no barriers to entry, and undifferentiated products. More important, it assumes constant returns to scale and costs that are fully internalized by individual enterprises. In the presence of monopoly elements, however, including especially the possibility of economies of scale or significant externalities, openness might not in fact maximize a country's economic gains; quite the opposite, in fact. In the early 1980s, a new generation of contrarian trade economists began to argue that in situations such as these, some degree of protectionism in the pursuit of wealth might not be so illogical after all. Their approach went under the label of the "new international economics" or "strategic trade policy." By the end of the 1980s, specialists in IPE were already adopting strategic trade policy as their own (Stegemann 1989).

Critical to the pursuit of power is the distribution of capabilities among states, which can have grave implications for national security. Central is Joanne Gowa's notion of "security externalities": the positive impact that trade may have on a country's military potential. In Gowa's words (1994, 6), "These externalities arise because the source of gains from trade is the increased efficiency with which domestic resources can be employed. As a consequence, trade frees economic resources for military uses." Different configurations of power pose different risks of armed conflict. The greater the risk of conflict, the less will be a government's incentive to promote trade relations that might, in the end, be of greater benefit to potential adversaries.

An emphasis on the distribution of state capabilities was evident in the American school's long-running debate over HST. The main message of HST was that trade preferences could be assumed to derive from the broader structure of international politics. In contemporary discourse, the argument lives on in what Lake (1993) called the hegemony-theory strand of HST, which links trade policy directly to each country's position within the global system. Particular stress is laid on the degree of polarity or concentration of power in the system. Gowa's notion of security externalities suggests that multilateral liberalization will be favored only at times of low security threat. In a more hostile environment, governments are most likely to favor either unilateral protection or else PTAs with allies, in order to help friends and shut out foes. Striking evidence is provided by Edward Mansfield (1994), who found a U-shaped relationship between concentration and trade in the historical data. Policies tend to be most open in both highly concentrated systems—in effect, hegemonies—or systems of low power inequalities, because of their relative political stability. By contrast, protectionism or regionalism tends to prevail more at intermediate levels of concentration where security relationships are apt to be least tranquil.

The Domestic Level

At the domestic level, where comparativists are more comfortable, we return to the mix of interests and institutions that is already familiar from the last chapter. States are assumed to act in response to the more or less well-articulated preferences of diverse societal agents as mediated through the nation's political institutions and processes. The decisive variable is the *internal* strategic setting—what Katzenstein meant by the domestic structure. Preferences are assumed to be driven from the inside-out, rather than from the outside-in.

Interests, as we saw in chapter 5, are typically inferred using a classic second-image-reversed approach, following the lead of Rogowski's *Commerce and Coalitions*. Where any group stands on trade policy depends on what its stake is in the outcome. Most studies employ some variant of either Rogowski's class-based track, derived from the Stolper-Samuelson theorem, or else the alternative track of more narrowly defined industry groups echoing the Ricardo-Viner model. Which constituencies should receive the most attention depends very much on the taste of the individual researcher.

Among societal agents with an interest in trade policy, perhaps none is more influential than the multinational corporation, that giant of the contemporary market system. By definition, multinational corporations have a vital stake in government measures that may affect their ability to operate in the global environment. In principle, therefore, we might expect corporate trade preferences to be very much opposed to protectionism, whether unilateral or regional—a force for multilateral free trade—even if some of the benefits of liberalization accrue to foreign rivals. In practice, however, generalization is difficult, owing to the considerable diversity to be found in the characteristics of individual industries. Corporations that depend broadly on foreign markets might well, as expected, lobby their home governments for liberalization. But as Milner and David Yoffie (1989) once pointed out, they are likely to do so strategically, making their support contingent on reciprocal liberalization by governments elsewhere. Alternatively, they might lobby for selective PTAs, freezing out their most threatening foreign competitors, as the best route to greater market share. Such a strategy is especially likely in industries subject to sizable economies of scale, as Milner suggested in a later paper (1997a). Multinationals might even turn protectionist if they have costly foreign investments intended to serve a local market that they want to shelter from untoward competition.

Institutions, in turn, are assumed to mediate the influence of interests by the way they aggregate societal preferences and delegate decision-making authority. Again, which specific institutions should receive the most attention depends greatly on the taste of the individual researcher. A useful starting point, as noted in chapter 5, is the distinction between autocracy and democracy. Is democracy more or less conducive to open trade than autocracy? Some sources, such as Daniel Verdier (1998), say less. Verdier argues that because of the political tensions engendered by trade, democracies are less likely to liberalize and more likely to adopt protection against each other. But many other sources disagree, citing abundant evidence that democracy actually appears to be more conducive to open trade.

If so, what is it about democracy that favors liberalization? For Mansfield, Milner, and Peter Rosendorff (2000), the reason is that in democracies, there is a popularly elected legislature with the capacity to constrain a country's chief executive through its ratification responsibilities. Since legislatures are apt to be more protectionist than the executives, the executives in democracies will be inclined to search for lower mutually acceptable levels of trade barriers, making liberalization agreements more likely. But for Milner and Keiko Kubata (2005), the reason lies instead in the ability of democracies to give voice to proliberalization constituencies that in autocracies are normally excluded from the corridors of power.

Clearly, the analysis of trade preferences has come a long way. Equally clearly, it also still has a long way to go.

Governance

What about the governance of trade relations? The basic question, as we saw in chapter 4, is the classic problem of collective action. Somehow, in the absence of a world government, means must be found to promote and sustain cooperation in the common interest. In the trading system, the challenge above all comprises two major issues: import liberalization and dispute resolution. Rules, formal or informal, are needed to promote open markets and defend them against the ever-lurking forces of protectionism. Starting soon after World War II these responsibilities were delegated to GATT, succeeded a half century later by a greatly expanded World Trade Organization (WTO). What insights are offered by the experience of GATT and the WTO?

The accomplishments of GATT and its successor are like the proverbial glass of water: half empty or half full? Admittedly, the two organizations have not been entirely successful in their objectives. Protectionism has by no means been eliminated, nor have the established mechanisms for the settlement of trade disputes worked to everyone's satisfaction. Yet as compared with what came before, when there were no international trade organizations, it is clear that much has been accomplished. On the one hand, an unprecedented amount of import liberalization has been achieved as a result of successive rounds of multilateral negotiations; on the other, considerable improvements have been introduced into dispute-resolution procedures, especially under the enhanced powers of the WTO. The governance functions performed by the two organizations may have fallen short of aspirations, but they have hardly been negligible. The glass is by no means dry.

Unfortunately, research on GATT and the WTO has long tended to be more applied than theoretical—more concerned with assessment of their empirical record than with formal analysis of their role in political behavior. It was only in the 1990s, with the renaissance of institutional theory led by Keohane, that significant progress began to be made in understanding conceptually what the two organizations can or cannot do to manage trade relations among sovereign states. Insights have accumulated, though by means matching the advances that have been made in the area of trade preferences.

As institutional theory teaches, the role of organizations like GATT and the WTO is essentially to aggregate preferences and enforce compliance. Mutual concessions must be encouraged to open markets to competition; defection or cheating must be discouraged to keep disputes from escalating out of control. Recent scholarship highlights four main channels through which the two organizations have sought to carry out those objectives.

First is through their ability to provide information to member governments, thus reducing strategic uncertainties. This is an old theme in institutional theory, going as far back as the 1980s literature on regimes. Keohane's functional theory of regimes always stressed the salience of the information environment. The more international institutions could aid nation-states in evaluating each other's intentions, the easier it would be to facilitate cooperative behavior.

GATT and later the WTO have aimed to ease reciprocal misgivings in a variety of ways. In the context of multilateral negotiations, they have helped to reduce bargaining costs by facilitating communication among negotiators; they have also been in a position to mediate distributional conflicts by offering solutions that could serve as focal points for mutually acceptable agreements. Likewise, in the context of dispute resolution, the two organizations have tried to reinforce compliance by monitoring state behavior and clarifying existing standards. And since the expanded WTO replaced the earlier GATT, enlarging the available staff, a mechanism has been put in place to conduct country-by-country reviews of trade policy. A variety of studies confirm the importance of these kinds of activities in making governments think twice (or more) before reneging on their commitments. Summarize Frieden and Martin (2002, 144), "These functions [of GATT and the WTO] enhance the value of having a reputation of living up to international agreements and allowing decentralized enforcement of cooperative agreements to take place."

A second channel is through the legalization of obligations—a relatively newer theme in the literature, as noted in chapter 4. In joining an organization like GATT or the WTO, governments formalize their commitments to one another. For Goldstein and Martin, the effect might actually prove to be counterproductive, owing to perverse incentives that international legalization could create at the domestic level. "A more legalized trade regime will provide more and better information about the distributional implications of commercial agreements," observe Goldstein and Martin (2001, 220), adding, "We believe that better information will empower protectionists relative to free traders on issues relating to the conclusion of new agreements." But even Goldstein and Martin concede that once states have signed on the dotted line, the effect is likely to be more positive, empowering free traders relative to protectionists. The legalization of commitments, to repeat, encourages compliance by raising exit costs.

Third is the flexibility that was built into the rules of the two organizations, another relatively new theme in formal studies. Commitments are easier to accept if states are assured that new circumstances can be satisfactorily accommodated in a timely fashion. Barbara Koremenos, Charles Lipson, and Duncan Snidal (2003b) speak of two forms of institutional flexibility: adaptive flexibility, which permits specific obligations to be relaxed should they become overly onerous; and transformative flexibility, which allows for more general changes in the rules of the game. Rosendorff and Milner (2003) provide a particularly apt example of the former, stressing the importance of well-crafted escape clauses in inducing governments to commit to liberalization agreements. Escape clauses allow states more leeway in implementing their commitments by authorizing a reversal of policy, within limits, in the event of a rush of imports that causes "serious injury" to a domestic industry. Without escape clauses, Rosendorff and Milner contend, "many trade agreements would never be politically viable. . . . Increased flexibility lessens the problems of bargaining and distribution" (72). An obvious instance of transformative flexibility was the capacity of GATT to sponsor its own metamorphosis into the WTO.

Finally, there is the constitutive role that the trade organizations have played in shaping identities and interests—a constructivist theme that is just beginning to enter the literature. As Milner has suggested (2002a, 456), the two organizations have facilitated learning by "encapsulating the norms by which countries agree to play the trading game." From the beginning, GATT and the WTO have sought to heighten appreciation of the benefits of open markets and mutual restraint. After more than a half century of experience, social values have clearly shifted toward greater acceptance of the premises of neoclassical economic theory. No longer is protectionist free riding accorded the same legitimacy as it was in previous eras. As Kahler has observed (1990, 104), "Few governments are willing to argue any longer for the benefits of economic closure." Today the burden of proof is on those who would disrupt the liberal trading system, not those who would preserve it.

None of these channels is foolproof, of course. As crucial as they may be in principle, their practical ability to rule the behavior of sovereign states is imperfect at best. That the glass of water is no more than half full is by no means an accident. But at least we have begun to acquire a better understanding of where the water comes from and what might be done to raise its level toward the glass's rim. Here too we now have a better grasp of what questions to ask.

FINANCE

As in trade, interest in issues on the finance side was first stimulated by developments in the real world—including, not least, America's accumulating payments crisis throughout the 1960s, which by the early 1970s led to termination of the dollar's gold convertibility and, finally, the collapse of the Bretton Woods exchange rate system. Monetary chaos seemed to threaten, especially after the first oil shock in late 1973, which generated unprecedented payments imbalances and financing problems around the world. How could scholars not take an interest?

Preferences

Again, I will start with actor behavior. On the finance side, policy in the broadest sense is concerned with the challenge of macroeconomic management. Among the tools available to officials to meet that challenge are monetary policy (the money supply and interest rates), fiscal policy (the government budget), the exchange rate, and capital-market regulation. At issue are what economic theory has historically labeled the twin goals of "internal balance" (full employment with low inflation) and "external balance" (equilibrium in the balance of payments)—two objectives that are often in conflict with one another. What explains the choices that governments make in their pursuit of these two goals?

Economic theory, regrettably, is no more useful in answering this question than it is in explaining trade preferences. As suggested earlier, it is tempting simply to assume that financial policy is driven by technical analysis rather than by politics. The problem with that premise, however, is that technical analysis does not always provide clear-cut guidance to policymakers. In fact, different macroeconomic models yield sharply divergent views of what might be regarded as an optimal policy mix for an open economy. Choices must still be made. As Jonathan Kirshner has maintained (2003, 7), "Economic theory rarely tells us anything definitive. . . . In any given setting economic logic will effectively rule out certain options. But there will also almost always remain a range of policies that are plausible—that is, economically coherent. And here economic theory will have little to tell us about the path chosen from this plausible set." Once again, that is where IPE comes in, to help explain what options are selected from within those plausible sets.

As indicated, study of the sources of state behavior has actually been more advanced on the trade side than on matters of money and credit. But this does not mean that the issue of preferences here has been wholly ignored. Not all specialists automatically assume that financial policy is mostly depoliticized. In fact, much serious work has been done, and as a result a fair amount of consensus has developed on the finance side, too, over what explanatory factors are apt to matter most. Moreover, here also analysis focuses mainly on the international-domestic research frontier of OEP and tends to be typically neo-utilitarian in spirit, although as noted in chapter 5 more recent years have seen a budding interest in ideational factors as well. Again, a brief selective survey can illuminate how much has or has not been accomplished.

The Systemic Level

At the systemic level, security considerations typically receive less attention than they do in trade studies. No one doubts that global politics matters in financial relations. Furthermore, applied analyses abound, such as my own research of a couple of decades ago on the impact of international banking on U.S. foreign policy (Cohen 1986). But among specialists on the finance side, efforts to conceptualize the pursuit of power in more formal terms were, until lately, most conspicuous in their absence.

Monetary issues did figure in the early debates over HST, which Gilpin and Krasner taught us clearly had a political dimension, but failed to lead to any generalizations comparable to what scholars like Gowa (1994) and Mansfield (1994) were able to develop on the trade side. Subsequently, the global strategic setting was pushed to the periphery or not even discussed at all. As Kirshner has remarked (1995, 3), the political dimension of international finance became "a neglected area of study." One notable exception was Kirshner's own *Currency and Coercion* (1995), which sought to understand how states might use their currency relations as an instrument of coercive force. Another is a recent collection of essays edited by David Andrews (2006) that focuses systematically on the sources and uses of international monetary power. Overall, though, the impact of security concerns on financial behavior remains relatively underexplored.

By contrast, greater attention has been paid to the purely economic dimension of the international environment—the pursuit of plenty. Here, most critical is the impact of capital mobility: the massive expansion since the late 1950s of cross-border financial flows, often referred to as financial globalization. First came the growth of offshore currency markets, and then a gradual liberalization of controls at the national level that for many countries has led to a degree of financial integration not seen since the end of the nineteenth century—a veritable phoenix risen after the demise of international finance in the interwar period (Cohen 1996). The influence of financial globalization today is pervasive. If specialists agree on anything, it is on the importance of capital mobility for every aspect of international financial policy, from the choice of exchange rate regime to the design of domestic monetary institutions.

The question is, How important? Greatest attention has been paid to the broad impact of financial globalization on policy autonomy. Does capital mobility irreversibly compromise the authority of the state in macroeconomic management? The core issue is what in an early paper (Cohen 1993) I labeled the "Unholy Trinity": the fundamental incompatibility of the three desiderata of autonomy of national monetary policy, exchange rate stability, and the free movement of capital. The logic of the Unholy Trinity is based on the so-called Mundell-Fleming model long familiar to economists, which suggests that in an environment of fixed exchange rates and fully integrated financial markets, a government loses all control over its domestic money supply and interest rates. Is the logic inescapable?

Initially, for many there was no doubt. Global finance, it was said, had become something akin to a structural feature of world politics—an exogenous attribute systematically constraining state behavior, rewarding some actions and punishing others. The ever-present threat of capital flight created irresistible pressures for a convergence of national policies. Andrews, in a salient contribution, called this the capital mobility hypothesis (CMH) (1994, 203): "The central claim associated with the capital mobility hypothesis is that financial integration has increased the costs of pursuing divergent monetary objectives, resulting in structural incentives for monetary adjustment."

Yet not all analysts agreed with the CMH. Andrews himself urged caution, directing attention to qualifications and limits of the proposition; others were even more adamant. There can be no doubt that capital mobility increases the costs of going it alone. But it also seems reasonable to assume that some room for independent policy choice may yet remain, depending on the priorities of policymakers. The logic of the Unholy Trinity can be escaped—or at least evaded to a degree—if governments are willing to make trade-offs. Officials might sacrifice fixity of the exchange rate or financial openness. Alternatively, they might substitute fiscal policy for monetary policy in their management of the domestic economy. They can steer markets in new directions or win breathing space for necessary political adjustments. As Pauly has insisted (1995, 373), "Capital mobility constrains states, but not in an absolute sense. . . . States can still defy markets," if they are willing to pay the price. A survey of recent research suggests that the discipline imposed on governments by mobile capital, while real, is quite a bit less than earlier imagined (Cohen 2002). How much less is still hotly debated.

The Domestic Level

At the domestic level, we again return to the familiar mix of interests and institutions. The pioneer of interest-based analysis of financial policy, as noted in chapter 5, was Frieden (1991), emphasizing the distributional implications of growing capital mobility. Pinpointing the preferences of particular groups, however, has not proved easy. As already mentioned, the higher level of aggregation involved in macroeconomic issues, as compared with the trade side, makes it more difficult to distinguish clear winners or losers.

Following Frieden, most sources today concur that in general, the key cleavages are likely to run along lines determined by the degree of involvement in the world economy. Producers of traded goods and international investors, for example—those who Frieden (1991) refers to as "integrationist" interests—might be expected to prefer stable exchange rates. By contrast, producers of nontradables and labor unions—"anti-integrationist" forces—are more apt to favor flexible rates because of the greater leeway provided for an autonomous monetary policy to cope with local circumstances. But beyond such broad generalizations, theorists continue to disagree over the specific configurations of interests involved. Some stress partisan preferences (Oatley 1997), while others highlight the role of specific sectors such as banking (Hall 2005) or heavy industry (Hefeker 1997). Simmons (1994), in a widely cited study of adjustment policies in the interwar period, puts most emphasis on the contrasting interests of conservative investors and creditors, on the one hand, and organized labor, on the other.

Institutions, by contrast, appear to have offered a somewhat more fruitful avenue for research. When dealing with macroeconomic issues, governments face a persistent tension between promoting the credibility of policy and preserving flexibility for policymakers—what economists call the rules versus discretion issue. Domestic political institutions in this context, particularly electoral and legislative arrangements, can be expected to play a critical role.

William Bernhard and David Leblang (1999), in a representative study focusing on industrial democracies, have provided evidence that in systems where the cost of electoral defeat is high and electoral timing is exogenous, officials tend to be less willing to forego discretion over monetary policy by choosing a fixed exchange rate. In proportional systems, by contrast, where the costs of electoral defeat are lower and electoral timing is endogenous, policymakers are more likely to adopt a fixed rate regime. Separately, Leblang (1999) has demonstrated an equally close relationship between exchange rate choices and political institutions in a large sample of developing economies. Floating rates are more likely to be found in democracies than in autocracies, Leblang discovered, and in democratic polities, floating is adopted more often in systems of proportional representation than in majoritarian electoral regimes.

One domestic institution of particular salience in this context is the central bank. For governments determined to promote their policy credibility, an obvious alternative to fixing the exchange rate is central-bank independence (CBI): granting full autonomy to the country's monetary authorities to operate free of political interference, as long advocated by many economists. Recognizing that the two institutions, an exchange rate peg and CBI, are to some extent interchangeable forms of monetary commitment, a recent collection of essays insists that they must in fact be analyzed together as a joint policy choice (Bernhard, Broz, and Clark 2003). Like so many other noteworthy contributions to the American school, this collection too was first published as a special issue of IO.

In one essay, William Clark (2003) models the choice of monetary institutions from the point of view of a survival-maximizing government, highlighting the conditions under which policymakers will view fixed exchange rates and CBI as direct substitutes for one another. In his model, the government's choice depends both on the availability of fiscal policy as a substitute for monetary policy and on such contextual factors as the magnitude of political pressures or inflationary expectations. Another key paper comes from Lawrence Broz (2003), who emphasizes the issue of transparency in choosing monetary regimes. While CBI is opaque and difficult to monitor, he notes, a commitment to a fixed exchange rate is easily observed. Hence, the transparency of monetary commitments and of political systems might be considered substitutes for one another: the greater the obscurity of political decision making (autocracies), the greater will be the need for transparency in monetary institutions to ensure anti-inflation credibility. Like Leblang (1999), Broz finds that floating rates (with an independent central bank) are more likely in democracies and fixed rates more likely in autocracies.

Finally, there are the constructivist elements that have begun to show up in recent research on financial policy (e.g., McNamara 1998; Chwieroth 2007). It is hardly surprising that an interest in the role of values and norms would arise more quickly on the finance side than on the trade side. In matters of money and credit, reputation and perception are basic. As Kirshner has observed (2003, 12), "With regard to money, the power of ideas does more than just shape the possible. It defines the feasible." If a currency gains acceptance, it is because of confidence in its value; if loans are made, it is because creditors trust the debtor to make good on obligations. Macroeconomic policies, therefore, must necessarily take account of "market sentiment" if they are to be effective. In the words of Jacqueline Best (2004, 404), "Financial stability depends on confidence, and confidence is a matter of faith—not simply in the efficiency of institutions, but also in the robustness and legitimacy of the norms that inform them."

Understandably, given the constructivist movement's late entry, there is to date still little accord on which ideational factors are likely to be most influential in this context—let alone where they come from or how they gain legitimacy. It is clear, however, that as the study of behavior on the finance side continues to develop, traditional neo-utilitarian analysis will have to be expanded to include the influence of ideas and social facts.

Governance

Concerning matters of governance, the basic question is of course the same as on the trade side: how to promote and sustain cooperation in the common interest. In international finance, the challenge comprises all aspects of macroeconomic management as they bear on payments relations between states. The balance of payments, encompassing all transactions between a country's residents and the rest of the world, is by definition a mutual experience. One economy's surplus is someone else's deficit. Spillover effects are thus inevitable: one country's choice of policies in pursuit of internal and external balance may easily come into conflict with another's. Formal or informal rules are needed to ensure that the preferences of many diverse governments may be effectively reconciled. In my earliest full-length effort to explore the political economy of monetary relations, *Organizing the World's Money* (Cohen 1977), I called this the consistency objective: the goal of attaining and preserving some minimum degree of compatibility among national policies.

Organizing the World's Money outlined four alternative principles by which the global financial system might be constituted to realize the consistency objective. These were: automaticity—a self-disciplining regime of norms and rules binding for all governments; supranationality—a regime founded on collective adherence to the decisions of some autonomous international organization; hegemony—a regime organized around a single state with acknowledged responsibilities and privileges as leader; or negotiation—a regime of shared responsibility and decision- making. Effective governance, I argued, had to be based on one or some combination of these four organizing principles.

Following the Great Depression of the 1930s—and even before the end of World War II—a collective effort sought to take command of the international monetary system. That was of course the 1944 Bretton Woods conference, which resulted in the creation of the IMF. The Bretton Woods system, as it came to be known, had two major features. One was a new centralized pool of gold and national currencies, intended to provide liquidity to governments when needed to finance external deficits. The pool, based at the IMF, was meant to supplement an already well-established gold-exchange standard—an international reserve system based on the U.S. dollar, the only currency still convertible into gold. The other feature was a brand-new system of pegged exchange rates, intended to minimize the kinds of currency instabilities and competitive manipulations that had been so prevalent in the interwar period. Each government pledged to fix a par value for its money, to be maintained within narrow limits, while also introducing convertibility for trade transactions. The IMF itself was expected to perform three important functions: regulatory (administering the rules governing exchange rates and currency convertibility), financial (supplying liquidity to deficit countries), and consultative (providing a forum for the cooperative management of monetary relations). In effect, the blueprint for the Bretton Woods system embodied three of the four organizing principles outlined in *Organizing the World's Money*—all but the politically sensitive notion of hegemony.

In practice, as we know, events didn't work out quite as intended. Owing to the unexpected severity of postwar dislocations as well as the paucity of the IMF's own initial resources, much of the burden for stabilizing the system fell on the United States—first with the Marshall Plan and related aid programs, and then via America's payments deficits, which effectively supplied needed liquidity to many other countries. Hegemony prevailed after all, triggering the ruminations of Kindleberger and Gilpin, and setting the stage for two decades of debate over HST.

Ultimately, starting in the 1960s, the IMF did begin to play a greater role in system governance, continuing even after the collapse of the par value system in the 1970s. I remember telephoning a friend at the IMF after currency floating began to ask him how he felt about working for an organization that no longer had a function. But I was wrong, of course. There was much more to the Bretton Woods system than just a set of exchange rate rules; on all other payments-related issues, the IMF retained as much authority as ever. Moreover, without the practical coordination enforced by the par value system, there was now even more reason to worry about the consistency objective. Since the IMF seemed a natural place to look for solutions, the principle of supranationality received renewed emphasis. The organization's mandate has been repeatedly expanded in scope.

Admittedly, as with GATT and the WTO, the glass has been at most half full. Despite its best efforts, the IMF has failed to prevent major dislocations such as the Latin American debt crisis of the 1980s or the Asian financial crisis of the late 1990s. Nor has the organization been free of the sorts of "pathologies" identified by Barnett and Finnemore (2004). But neither has it been wholly ineffectual. For all the trials and tribulations of recent decades, the broader system has remained intact. Here too, as with the trade organizations, the IMF's governance function has been something more than negligible, even if falling short of its aspirations.

What insights are offered by the IMF's experience? Research affirms the importance of the same four channels as are highlighted by the experience of the trade organizations. In the first place, the IMF has had a salutary effect on the information environment. Valuable intelligence is provided through the organization's many publications as well as its regular schedule of meetings, thus making it easier for governments to keep track of one another's intentions. Useful focal points are constructed through the IMF's policy recommendations, whether addressed to global issues or in relation to the problems of individual members. And as Pauly (1997) has rightly emphasized, a critical role is performed in monitoring behavior through the organization's multilateral surveillance function, which includes regular country consultations. Compatibility among national policies may not be assured as a result, but the probability of some measure of consistency is certainly enhanced.

Second, the IMF has an effect through its legalization of obligations. As with GATT and the WTO, membership brings with it formal commitments that raise exit costs. In the words of Simmons (2001, 190), the Bretton Woods system ushered in a new "public international law of money." The legal constraint is by no means absolute, of course. Despite the pledge to maintain stable par values, pegged rates were quickly abandoned after the United States closed the gold window in 1971. But the bite does seem to have some teeth to it, at least with respect to such issues as multiple exchange rates or currency convertibility. Simmons demonstrates that governments have generally stuck to the rules on these issues despite the lack of direct IMF enforcement. The reason, she argues, is a desire to avoid reputational costs. In her words: "Costs are higher if comparable countries are complying, and if a state is heavily invested in maintaining a strong reputation for respecting the rule of law. In short, legalization strengthens commitment" (190).

Third are the elements of flexibility, both adaptive and transformative, which are as prominent in the IMF's structure as they have been in GATT and the WTO. The articles of agreement on which the IMF was founded were deliberately crafted to leave ample room for maneuver over time. Adaptive flexibility was manifest in the loopholes built into many of the individual rules. The pledge to maintain par values, for example, was qualified by an acknowledged right to shift currency pegs under selected circumstances. Likewise, the obligation to assure convertibility of currencies for trade transactions was qualified by the right to sustain controls over capital movements. Transformative flexibility was evident in the leeway provided to amend or liberally reinterpret any of the articles themselves, should the circumstances seem to warrant it. One case in point was the Second Amendment, adopted in 1976, which formally ratified the end of the par value system. Another can be found in the plethora of financing "facilities" that have been added since the IMF's founding, allowing the organization to lend vastly larger sums to member governments than had been originally envisioned. The principle of automaticity has been enforced by the IMF, but not rigidly.

Last is the constitutive channel—the role that the IMF, like GATT and the WTO, has been able to play as a purveyor of policy standards. As Pauly writes (1999, 402), the IMF has "emerged as the chief promoter of certain behavioral norms in the management of markets." In its early years, the IMF's message was essentially Keynesian in spirit—not at all surprising in view of the fact that John Maynard Keynes was one of the principal negotiators at Bretton Woods. Ruggie (1983) captured the idea in his notion of embedded liberalism. Governments were encouraged to take an active part in promoting internal balance even while dealing with problems of external imbalance. Over time, however, the organization's tone has changed, moving closer to the neoclassical philosophy of GATT and the WTO. The IMF's values have veered more toward what the economist Joseph Stiglitz (2002), a Nobel laureate, labels "market fundamentalism"—a "free market mantra" emphasizing less government intervention and more reliance on deregulated private enterprise to sustain domestic prosperity. The original Keynesian norms, in Best's words (2004), have been "hollowed out."

And why did the change occur? Opinions, not surprisingly, differ. Best sees the development as driven mainly by events—the avalanche of crises that struck the international monetary system. Fund officials, she avers (2004, 403), were forced to "focus on providing functional solutions to technical problems." By contrast, Stiglitz blames it all on "commercial and financial interests"— the few "who benefit . . . at the expense of the many" (2002, 20). And in between is Pauly (1999), who sees a more subtle process of socialization at work reflecting the dominant position of the IMF's strongest members. First a new consensus of views emerged among key governments. Then that consensus was conveyed to weaker states through whatever channels were available, including the IMF. In Pauly's words, the organization provides "a handy mechanism for propagating new norms" (404). Whatever the explanation, though, on one point most sources agree. As the central institution in international finance, the IMF clearly does have the capacity to influence intersubjective understandings and perceptions of interest.

Monetary Cooperation

In the end, however, the IMF has been only part of the story. For all the renewed emphasis that the principle of supranationality received from the 1960s onward, the IMF's writ has come to run mainly to smaller and poorer member countries, where authority can be exercised through the organization's control of access to credit as well as through the policy conditions attached to its loans. For larger and wealthier states, by contrast—arguably the most critical actors from a systemic point of view—the direct role of the IMF has dwindled over time, in good part because of the privileged access that these countries have come to enjoy as borrowers in the resurrected global capital market. As I noted more than two decades ago (Cohen 1981, 1983a), financial globalization effectively "privatized" payments financing for the most creditworthy states, thus minimizing their dependence on IMF resources. The last advanced economy to borrow from the IMF was the United States, during a run on the dollar in late 1978.

So how is the consistency objective promoted among the advanced economies? In practice solutions have been sought directly, through the development of collective approaches that largely bypass the IMF—effectively substituting negotiation for the principle of supranationality. Most prominent in this regard is the regularized process of consultation that has grown up under the aegis of the so-called Group of Seven (G-7), comprising the United States, Britain, Canada, France, Germany, Italy, and Japan. The G-7's origins go back to a historic gathering of finance ministers in Rambouillet, France, in November 1975, called by the French government in hopes of breaking a deadlock in negotiations on world monetary reform. (Only six governments were included at the time; Canada was added later.) Its role was intensified after the celebrated Plaza Agreement of September 1985, which formally pledged participants to a coordinated realignment of exchange rates. G-7 finance ministers now meet regularly to discuss the current and prospective performance of their economies, and evaluate policy objectives and instruments for possible linkages and repercussions.

More than anything else, it is the existence of these less institutionalized mechanisms that accounts for the greater advances that have been made on the finance side, as compared with the trade side, in theorizing about governance issues. Not that the record of the G-7 or other negotiating forums is all that much to boast about; here too the glass is half full at most. But much research has been stimulated, adding considerably to our understanding of the possibilities as well as the limitations of monetary cooperation.

The case for monetary cooperation is clear. In fact, it is the standard case for avoiding or correcting market failure, as first outlined by Keohane more than two decades ago (1983, 1984). Dangerous spillovers through the balance of payments can, in principle, be controlled by a mutual adjustment of policies. But over time the practical impediments to effective cooperation have become equally clear. Four barriers stand out in particular.

One possibility is that agreement will be impeded by distributional disputes. The challenge of cooperation is not just to achieve an efficient outcome but also to agree on the sharing of gains. Much depends on whether governments are more interested in absolute or relative gains—the familiar, now-shopworn question highlighted by Joseph Grieco's notorious neorealist attack on neoliberal institutionalism (1988). Are states primarily concerned with market failure or distributional conflicts? In reality, it is most likely that they worry about both. As Krasner put it in his characteristically colorful manner (1991), negotiators must do more than aim for a happy life on the Pareto frontier. They must also arrive at some mutually satisfactory location somewhere on that frontier—an issue that cannot be easily resolved in a world of many jealous "defensive positionalists" (as Grieco referred to security-conscious governments). Differences over the costs and benefits of alternative policy packages give states incentives to act strategically, complicating bargaining.

A second possibility is that governments are able to reach agreement—but only by choosing policies that are more politically expedient than economically sound, thus leading to suboptimal outcomes. In an early paper, economist Kenneth Rogoff (1985) pointed out that formal coordination of monetary policies could, perversely, lead to higher inflation. Authorities might agree to expand their money supplies together in order to evade the external deficits that would otherwise discipline any one country trying to inflate on its own. Policy may well be successfully coordinated, but in the service of an inferior result. It is also possible that dominant interest groups at the domestic level might exploit the process of negotiation to promote particularist or even personal ambitions at the expense of broader collective goals.

A third barrier is posed by the so-called time-inconsistency problem—the chance that agreements, once negotiated, will later be violated. As I once wrote (much to my wife's chagrin), "International monetary cooperation, like passionate love, is a good thing but difficult to sustain" (Cohen 1993, 134). In fact, it is always difficult to secure durable compliance in relations among sovereign states. Defection may be voluntary, as interest-maximizing governments are tempted by changing circumstances to renege on their commitments. In my own work, I have emphasized the episodic nature of monetary cooperation initiatives, which I attribute to changing perceptions of the costs and benefits of agreed policy compromises. Concessions that seem acceptable at moments of crisis may come to be seen as increasingly onerous once stability is restored (Cohen 1993). Alternatively, as noted in chapter 4, defection may be involuntary, forced on officials by discontented constituents. Promises abroad may be sacrificed on the altar of politics at home.

Finally, there are the complications introduced by the growth of capital mobility. Michael Webb (1995) was among the first to note the increasingly demanding nature of cooperation as financial markets become more deeply integrated. Earlier in the post–World War II period, when domestic insularity was still the rule, coordination efforts could concentrate mainly on the "external" issue of payments disequilibrium—the management of destabilizing imbalances. Under the "compromise of embedded liberalism," little adjustment of policies was expected internally, within individual countries. Instead, the spotlight was on finding needed deficit financing and perhaps an occasional adjustment of par values. Macroeconomic divergence might have been the root cause, but for the most part remedies could be directed merely to the symptoms.

Today, however, with floods of capital free to move from market to market, domestic policy cannot be so easily protected, just as the capital mobility hypothesis suggests. Payments disequilibriums may well be far too big to deal with symptomatically. Now there is pressure to go to the root cause itself—to address the effects of macroeconomic divergence directly via changes of monetary and fiscal policy, intruding on sensitive domestic priorities. Plainly this makes cooperation a much tougher challenge. As Webb observes (1995, ix), "Monetary and fiscal policies are difficult to coordinate . . . because they are economically and politically the most important domestic economic policy levers available to governments." Policymakers are naturally loath to give up the best tools they have.

THE BRITISH SCHOOL

To all this extensive scholarship, the British school responds with something approaching disdain. Yes, the American school's efforts have taught us much. Yes, we now have a much better handle on how to frame questions about public policy. But for scholars in the British tradition, much of that is simply beside the point. U.S.-style IPE defines the agenda far too narrowly. We need, it is said, a much more inclusive interpretation of the field's problematique.

The Narrow Agenda

To a large extent, the criticism goes back to the origins of the American school. With political scientists taking custody of the infant field and raising it as a branch of their own discipline, it was natural to define the problematique in the same manner as IR. That meant the two questions of actor behavior and system governance—the same two questions that the subfield of IR had always asked. Scholars like Keohane, Gilpin, and Krasner were trained to think about world politics in terms of public policy: to explain what states do and explore how relations among them might be managed. So why not think about the world economy in the same way? In effect, the agenda was preordained.

For the British school, however, that is all too narrow. Why, for example, in thinking about what actors do, should we limit ourselves just to *explaining* behavior? The American school's fascination with causal variables, in British eyes, pays undue deference to the principles of positivism and empiricism. IPE ought to be about more than formal modeling or hypothesis testing. It should also be about *evaluating* behavior and its consequences—about *normative* analysis. In line with Strange's dictum, research should always be prepared to ask the question, *Cui bono?* For whose good? Scholarship, Strange insisted, is inseparable from values. Scholars must do more than merely observe. They must also *judge*—to denounce inequity and seek justice. The spirit was captured well by a British school friend of mine who said one day, "I don't do findings. I do interpretation."

Likewise, in thinking about governance, why should analysis be limited just to economic relations? Why should theory be restricted just to what Cox called problem solving within the existing system? IPE, for the British school, is about more than the care and protection of economic interdependence. Much more fundamentally, it is about underlying social patterns and structures—about the way that society itself is ordered and governed. Inspiration comes from classical political economy, to which the British school traces its roots. The world economy, it is said, cannot be studied on its own, apart from other social processes. Rather, it must be seen as embedded in a wider "social whole" (Krätke and Underhill 2006, 32), part of a broader conception of the totality of human experience. The goal of inquiry, concludes one source, is "to devise a programme giving a holistic account of the world we inhabit" (O'Brien 1995, 101).

In terms of both questions—behavior and governance—the difference is not just about defining the basic units of interest, as discussed in chapter 5. The issue goes beyond ontology and has everything to do with the fundamental purpose of intellectual inquiry. All scholarship is presumably truth seeking. But whereas the American school aims to maintain a certain distance between the researcher and the subject of research, in hopes of preserving objectivity, the British school prefers to become fully engaged, in order to make the world a better place. In the words of Murphy and Tooze (1991, 27), inquiry is (or should be) about "the pursuit of the ethical life." The aim is not just to understand but where possible to improve. And that higher calling demands a problematique that is both normative in tone and universal in aspiration. Anything less may be dismissed as idle chatter—merely "academic," in the worst sense of the term.

Ultimately, the difference reflects a deeper cultural divide, which we have encountered before. The American school, to repeat, takes its inspiration from the norms of conventional social science as developed since the late nineteenth century. Conventional social science does not deny the importance of a social conscience but insists that objective understanding must come first, in order to assure a firm foundation for any proposed change. The British school's roots, by contrast, go back much further—as noted, to the classical political economy of the eighteenth century and its links to the study of moral philosophy. As one recent commentary puts it, the foundations of IPE "are located in the value-based tradition of classical political economy" (Watson 2005, 31). Because value-based analysis puts matters of social justice front and center, it is inevitably both judgmental and inclusive. Summarizes Gills (2001, 235), in a reprise of the field:

> We should continue to strive to make a concern for human freedom and dignity . . . an intrinsic aspect of IPE. . . . We must further elaborate our shared understandings of the tensions, the contradictions and the possible harmonies between personal liberty and economic relations and investigate, as did the classical economists and moral philosophers, the conditions of human freedom. . . . We continue this tradition of fundamental enquiry in moral and political philosophy.

Broadening the Agenda

That's easier said than done, however. As in the previous chapter, matters quickly become murky once we turn to what the British school offers as an alternative. Scholars agree that the agenda must be broadened. But what else should be included in the field's problematique, and how should newer issues be studied? Here again, answers vary depending on taste, creating a traffic jam of competing research styles and programs. The British school, it turns out, is rather better at asking questions than at showing how to answer them. As one observer puts it, "The genius of [the British school] lies in problem posing, rather than problem solving" (Dickins 2006, 480).

In fact, the list of questions raised by the British school is remarkably long. Strange's call for an "open range" has been taken seriously by those who followed. The result is an agenda that admirably is nothing if not ambitious— intellectual ecumenism taken to an extreme. Writes one source, "The inclusive approach . . . spreads wider than the issues of trade, investment and monetary relations. While not ignoring those issues, attention is paid to other aspects such as militarization, development, gender, and ecology" (O'Brien 1995, 98). Writes another: "British school IPE is characterized by a concern with direct analysis of issues in the world as they appear, such as globalization, finance, trade, inequality, poverty, production, gender, race, and so on" (Phillips 2005, 12). What could be more indicative of the school's commitment to openness than that final "and so on"?

When the influential journal *New Political Economy* came out with its first issue in 1996, the editors proclaimed grandly that IPE's "key research agenda focuses on . . . the problems of transnational interest networks, governance in the world system, the collective action problems of an increasingly unified global economy and fragmented political authority, the implications of new global information and communication structures for the organization of the global economy, and the tensions between regionalism and globalism" (Gamble et al. 1996, 10). When Gills (2001, 234, 244), years after helping to found

RIPE, attempted to take stock of the IPE field, he declared that "we can affirm a set of common concerns . . . global governance, global justice, development, poverty, inequality, and the roles of labour, social movements, women and the 'global South.' " Little is left out when the subject is nothing less than the totality of human experience.

At the top of the agenda for many in the British school is the question of development along with the related issues of poverty and inequality. This is in striking contrast to the American school's relative lack of interest in the development process. Taking their cue from the radical perspective of once-popular dependency theory, British school scholars seek to explore the sources of observed distributional outcomes in the world economy. Why is development across the globe so uneven? What accounts for the wide variations we see in the wealth and poverty of particular classes, sectors, states, or regions? And what can be done about it? With the birth of IPE, Anthony Payne has suggested (2006, 7), "development political economists were challenged to come in from the ghetto of an ever more unfashionable and declining subfield and place their traditional preoccupation with equality at the centre of a bigger stage." For Gills (2001, 241), development is "the pivotal moral, political and analytical concern of the discipline."

Uneven development, in turn, raises the issue of power: Who has the capacity to determine who gets what? Power, as noted in chapter 2, was a central preoccupation for Strange—so central that one of three collections of essays published in her honor was devoted exclusively to the theme of *Strange Power* (Lawton, Rosenau, and Verdun 2000). It has also been a central preoccupation for many of those who followed her, searching in the dynamics of the world economy for underlying formations and transformations of authority. Insists Palan (2000b, 4), "Power is undoubtedly the central concept of [IPE]." Power is as essential to the analysis of historical structures or global capitalism as it is to the study of gender or race relations. Every question about the "social whole" inevitably implies, to some degree, issues of control or dominion.

With so many questions, however, how does one begin to find answers? Inclusiveness may be a virtue, but it can also lead to intellectual incoherence. Underhill is not alone in boasting that in its British version IPE "has long since burst the boundaries of traditional IR" (2000, 815). But as even one of the British school's most prominent partisans acknowledges, the school's ecumenicism is also "one of its weaknesses, in the sense that [the field's] boundaries can be notoriously hard to establish" (Phillips 2005, 10). Without established boundaries, there is no common agreement about what causal variables to look for or what methodologies to use to adjudicate among competing claims. Consequently, there is no firm basis for valid theory building or cumulative research. Nor is there any common set of standards for evaluating processes or structures—hence no firm basis for normative analysis, either. Admirably high-minded judgments are offered in the name of justice, equity, or empowerment, but on a basis that appears utterly subjective.

In short, we end up with the same lack of focus that we encountered in chapter 5. "A broad and somewhat inchoate field of study" is how Palan ruefully describes the British version of IPE (2000b, 2). Once again, it is clear that the British school's harmony of criticism of the U.S. style breaks down when it comes to providing a compelling counterpoint.

COMPLEMENTARITY, YET AGAIN

Disdain, therefore, can work both ways. The British school may be justified in criticizing the U.S. agenda as too narrow. There is no question that something is lost when the field's problematique is restricted mainly to the international-domestic research frontier of OEP. But equally, the American school might be justified in disparaging the British agenda as overly broad. Something is lost as well when the problematique is defined to encompass a holistic account of the wider social whole. Neither side is beyond reproach.

Yet again we are reminded of the complementarity of the two schools. At issue is the trade-off between parsimony and detail that is at the heart of all social science scholarship. In its allegiance to a hard-science model, the American school is content to limit itself to a range of questions that can be more or less easily addressed using the standard analytic toolkit. Other potentially related issues are set aside, and normative concerns are willingly sacrificed in the name of professional objectivity. Conversely, in its aspiration to do good in the world, the British school is prepared to forego the customary constraints of a reductionist style. No part of the real world's interlocking complexity, it is felt, should be excluded; nor should value judgments be avoided. Both trade-offs are valid, and we have learned much from each. But both also leave something to be desired.

Chapter 7

NEW BRIDGES?

The aim . . . is to start off a new generation
of bridge-builders.
—Susan Strange

THE CONSTRUCTION OF IPE is unquestionably a major accomplishment. Where once there was a dialogue of the deaf, bridges have now been built. Where once there were two insular specialties, international economics and IR, there is now a wholly new research community, an invisible college dedicated to an effective integration of disciplines. An elaborate edifice of concepts and theories has been put together. By any measure, all this represents intellectual progress.

The edifice, however, is hardly complete. As emphasized at the outset, IPE also is still very much a work in progress. Though a great deal has been learned, serious gaps remain in our understanding. The field has proved to be much better at asking questions than at providing answers. It also remains divided into factions—in the English language, best typified by the deep differences between what I have characterized as the American and British schools. More construction is needed.

But what kind of construction? Where should the field go from here? While prediction would obviously be foolhardy, it is not difficult to see where effort is most urgently called for. New bridges must be built, I would submit, in three areas in particular: between the past and the present; between rationalist and cognitive analysis; and perhaps most important, between the American and British versions of IPE. Work in these three areas would go far toward ameliorating what today may be regarded as the field's most egregious deficiencies.

THREE GENERATIONS

Back in her "Mutual Neglect" manifesto, Strange called for the construction of "bridges across the gulf" between economic and political analysis in IR. "The aim," Strange contended (1970, 315), "is to start off a new generation of bridge-builders." If this book demonstrates anything, it is that her call did not go unheeded. Nearly four decades of construction have ensued. At the risk of some oversimplification of the preceding discussion, we may speak of a succession of some three generations of bridge builders since modern IPE was born.

First, of course, was that extraordinary band of pioneers I call the Magnificent Seven. Though many others were also involved from the start, it was they more than anyone who laid the foundations of the field as we know it today. On the American side, Keohane and his colleague Nye taught us to think intuitively in terms of a world economy characterized by multiple channels of communications, an absence of hierarchy among issues, and a diminished role for military force, while Gilpin, with his three models, helped us to organize our theorizing for ready comparison and contrast. The role of hegemony and leadership was highlighted by Kindleberger as well as by Gilpin and Krasner; the role of international institutions, by Krasner and Keohane; and the role of second- and later first-image analysis, by Katzenstein. On the British side, Strange promoted a high degree of intellectual eclecticism, open to all disciplines and perspectives, while Cox legitimized both critical theory and historical materialism as valid alternatives to positivist social science.

Over the next two decades, on both sides, a Second Generation of younger scholars emerged to reinforce the architecture started by the Magnificent Seven. Many have already been noted. In the United States, important new insights on trade issues were provided by the likes of Goldstein, Milner, and Rogowski, adding considerably to our understanding of factors affecting both state preferences and system governance, while on financial issues key contributions came from Frieden and (arguably) myself, among others. Gowa and Lake inter alia helped to clarify questions posed by the prolonged debate over HST. Martin and Simmons broadened the scope of institutional theory. Odell and Ruggie made early efforts to bring cognitive analysis into the field.

In the British school, meanwhile, Gill and Gills sought to extend the kind of broad historical analysis of global systems and social transformation that had been favored by Strange and Cox. Palan turned his attention to state theory and the changing modes of governance in a globalizing world economy. Tooze explored the role of international business. Payne highlighted the complex politics of development. Cerny and Underhill brought new dimensions to the analysis of international money and financial markets.

And then, starting in the last decade of the twentieth century, came a Third Generation of even younger scholars who continue still to add to the edifice of IPE. Again, many have been noted. In the American school, Hiscox and Verdier have refined our comprehension of the domestic politics of trade, while Clark and Leblang have added fresh insights on the finance side. Andrews and Kirshner have promoted a new interest in the sources and uses of international monetary power. Koremenos has underscored the many factors involved in the rational design of international organizations. In Britain, Watson has emphasized the historical roots of IPE. Phillips has renewed focus on the question of development. Lawton has studied the evolving global production structure. Sinclair has extended the study of international credit.

The dividing line between what I call the Second and Third Generations is anything but precise. Roughly, the dichotomy separates scholars who received their graduate degrees before 1990 from those whose formal training was completed later. But it is hardly an inconsequential distinction. In the American school, in particular, the differences between the Second and Third Generations are profound. Both generations have sustained the state-centric ontology inherited from traditional IR theory. But whereas the Second Generation was largely content to work with the same kind of prosy epistemology as had Keohane and the other pioneers of the American school (indeed, many trained with one or another of the pioneers), the Third Generation has tilted far more in favor of what Galbraith called imitative scientism. Second-Generation scholars did not entirely eschew formal modeling or systematic empirical analysis; but neither were these elements central to their research efforts. Among Third-Generation scholars, by contrast, the reductionist methodology of neoclassical economics—with all its emphasis on parsimony and numeracy—has come to be the defining characteristic of the U.S. approach to IPE. The reasons for the shift in style were explored in chapter 1. No one can deny the benefits of a creeping economism, which brings both rigor and replicability to analysis. The Third Generation's penchant for professionalism should be respected. Still, as previous pages have emphasized, there has also been a cost in terms of lost ambition and shrunken horizons. The Big Picture thinking of the pioneering generation (and even some of the Second Generation) has become largely alien to the midlevel theorizers of the Third Generation.

In the British school, the differences between the two generations are less marked but nonetheless significant. The Third Generation is distinguished from the second mainly by its even greater commitment to the open range advocated by Strange. Second-Generation scholars were hardly shy about breaking down disciplinary boundaries, even as they sought to maintain a high standard of analytic rigor. But the Third Generation has been even more ecumenical in reaching out to academic traditions beyond economics and political science as well as more ambitious in defining its research agenda. Certainly, researchers cannot be faulted for the breadth of their intellectual curiosity or the depth of their normative concerns. But here too there has been a cost—an "inchoate" lack of focus, as noted in chapters 5 and 6. The British school's increasingly uncertain boundaries stand in sharp contrast to the growing standardization of American IPE's methods and problematique.

PAST AND PRESENT

"Those who cannot remember the past are condemned to repeat it," wrote the Spanish philosopher George Santayana (1905, 284). The phrase is frequently quoted, yet—in another irony—not always remembered. IPE scholarship too

often fails to pay sufficient attention to the field's own origins, where intellectual entrepreneurship played such a critical role. The indelible impact of
agency and contingency is discounted. Hence research does frequently do little
more than repeat the past, unnecessarily limiting what can be learned about
the present and the future.

The problem does not lie simply with the choice of content. Researchers
plainly are free to study whatever they want. If they pay insufficient attention
to what has come before, there is bound to be a certain amount of replication,
if not duplication, of effort. The cumulation of knowledge does not always
proceed in a straight line. Whether they realize it or not, younger scholars
frequently circle back to the preoccupations of an earlier generation. A case
in point is provided by the American school's discourse on system governance,
which after years of debate over regimes and institutional theory has more
recently returned to the study of international organizations.

Periodically, there may even be some inadvertent recycling, with ideas that
have lain dormant for years being resurrected under new, more fashionable
labels—as suggested, for example, by the Really Big Question of globalization. For many in the British school, there is no doubt that we have entered a
new age. For the mainstream of the American school, however, globalization
is little more than old wine in a new bottle—complex interdependence redux.
As Nye, reflecting back on *Power and Interdependence*, has contended (2004a,
5), "The new work on globalization [seems] to ignore the earlier literature on
interdependence ... much of the writing on these topics [is] reinventing
the wheel." Nye and the American school may not be right about the "myth"
of globalization, but the criticism is telling. Wheels do get reinvented
from time to time.

The real problem goes deeper, to underlying ontologies and epistemologies.
Students today are rarely taught much about how the field got started or why
it took the shape that it did. Thus, they have no idea of the degree to which
their specialized training is hostage to what came before—to the personalities
of key individuals and the specific historical circumstances in which those
pioneers worked. Without the Magnificent Seven, IPE might never have been
conceived; the agency of the original bridge builders was indispensable. But
how the field was then constructed was very much a matter of contingency—
of taste, experience, relationships, and location; in short, of chance. Personal
choices were made that gradually became codified as orthodoxy. Ultimately,
the process resulted in common understandings of what constitutes the legitimate study of IPE. Past standards of inquiry are now routinely passed on from
one generation to the next—a form of path dependency that conditions students
to prioritize selected questions and methodologies. Scholarship has become
increasingly blinkered, enforcing a kind of unconscious tunnel vision.

For some, the process represents progress—all part of the "maturing" of the
field, as Lake (2006) puts it. The more researchers agree on the basics, the

more their work approaches the respectability of "normal" science. But if that is the measure of maturity, perhaps we might all be better off remaining children, like Peter Pan, always seeing the world through fresh eyes. In reality, the impact of the process is anything but positive, since so much gets left out. Whatever version of IPE we are talking about, the quality of scholarship suffers when theorists automatically exclude anything that is alien to their inherited way of thinking. Our understanding of reality is impoverished.

Arguably, the best way to overcome this disability would be to spend more time exploring the intellectual history of the field, bridging the gap between the past and the present. That, of course, was precisely the motivation for this book, though as indicated I make no claim to providing the last word on the subject. The challenge is to remove the blinkers inherited from the past. Tunnel vision must be replaced by breadth of vision. Scholarship can only benefit from a greater appreciation of how and why IPE came to be constructed as it is, thereby opening up the possibility of fresh perspectives for the field's further construction in the future.

RATIONALISM AND COGNITION

A second gap in need of bridging is that between rationalist and cognitive modes of analysis in IPE. Both the American and British versions of the field suffer from a disconnect between materialist and ideational understandings of behavior.

Certainly the gap is evident in the American school where, as we saw in chapter 5, ideational factors have barely even begun to challenge the traditional dominance of neo-utilitarian rationalism. A few cognitive buds have flowered, along both the psychological and sociological tracks, but with little impact to date. Mainstream analysis still typically assumes that decision making is based on what James March and Johan Olsen (1984) called a "logic of consequences." Self-regarding actors systematically compare alternative courses of action, assessing material constraints and incentives, and choose whatever option appears to offer the most efficient means to achieve established goals. Little attention is paid to the possibility that rationality might be bounded, as emphasized by Odell (2000, 2002). Nor is allowance made for an alternative logic of appropriateness driven more by norms, identities, and social learning. Little curiosity is shown for the sources of interests, which instead are treated, for the convenience of analysis, simply as exogenous.

The gap is also evident in the British school, despite the importance attached to the power of ideas by Cox and others inspired by the musings of Gramsci. If theory is always for someone and for some purpose, as Cox was wont to insist, cognition clearly matters. But for most in the British school, working within a "historical-relativist paradigm," the values that legitimatize behavior cannot be linked analytically to any kind of rationalist interpretation. Norms and identities are embedded in specific historical contexts, defying generalization. A reductionist search for causality is useless. The psychological or sociological sources of ideas can be understood only through detailed study of a succession of world orders and social forces—a "logic of interpretation," in the words of one British constructivist, "that acknowledges the improbability of cataloging, calculating, and specifying the 'real causes'" (Campbell 1992, 4). The spirit is that of critical theory, as Cox interpreted it. Implicitly acknowledging Cox's influence, Katzenstein, Keohane, and Krasner (1999b) label the approach "critical" constructivism, in contrast to the "conventional" constructivism that is more familiar to U.S. scholars.

Can the gap be bridged? Can both materialist and ideational understandings be accommodated? Admittedly, the task is not easy. In rationalism's aspiration "to predict something large from something small," cognitivists see an incomplete or distorted view of reality. In cognitivism's hope to uncover the deeper influences on human behavior, rationalists see a lack of analytic rigor. Where rationalists see value in systematic comparisons, cognitivists stress idiosyncracy and historical contingency. Where cognitivists see merit in understanding how identities and interests are constituted, rationalists ask only how material incentives matter. Rationalists call on cognitivists to be more specific about variables and relationships. Cognitivists call on rationalists to expand their analytic foundations.

In effect, rationalists and cognitivists are speaking different languages, making even basic communication difficult. In the words of Katzenstein, Keohane, and Krasner (1999b, 38–39), "The key terms for rationalists are preferences, information, strategies, and common knowledge. The key terms for [cognitivists] are identities, norms, knowledge, and interests. Rationalist orientations do not offer a way to understand common knowledge. [Cognitive] arguments do not provide a way to analyze strategies. Yet both strategy and common knowledge are usually necessary to understand political outcomes." The challenge is to find ways to integrate strategy and knowledge in a common scholarly discourse.

Along the psychological track, an example of how this might be done is provided by Deborah Elms in a recent paper on "New Directions for IPE" (2006). Reexamining some current work in IPE through the lens of political psychology and behavioral economics, Elms demonstrates the relevance of such concepts as framing, loss aversion, and myopic time horizons for future research in the field. The literature on human behavior, she argues, is directly applicable to many of the questions addressed by mainstream IPE analysis. In similar fashion, Ethan Kapstein (forthcoming) shows how experimental evidence on the role of "fairness considerations" in strategic interactions helps to illuminate the outcomes of international trade negotiations. Personal conceptions of what might be considered an equitable or inequitable bargain appear to play a role in tempering the mercantilist forces that have traditionally been assumed to dominate state behavior.

Along the constructivist track, an example is provided by a new collection of essays coedited by Mark Blyth, an editor of RIPE, and two colleagues under the title *Constructivist Political Economy* (Blyth, Parsons, and Abdelal forthcoming). Exhibiting the research efforts of a younger generation of scholars based on both sides of the Atlantic, *Constructivist Political Economy* seeks to clarify the mechanisms through which the "social construction" of new knowledge impacts on actor strategy in the world economy. Three mechanisms of construction are identified: manipulation and rationalization; persuasion; and socialization. The contributors to the volume then put a variety of empirical methodologies to work to suggest the conditions under which each mechanism may come to shape behavior in practice. Though deeply rooted in cognitive analysis, the essays aspire to a high degree of rigor and do not hesitate to generalize. Like Helleiner in the collection on national identities that he coedited with Pickel (2005), the editors of *Constructivist Political Economy* specifically credit Katzenstein's work on security issues as an inspiration for their own efforts.

The gap between rationalism and cognitivism in IPE may never be wholly bridged, of course. As Ruggie has suggested (1999, 245), "The two approaches are not additive, and they are unlikely to meet and merge on some happy middle ground." But it is certainly possible to improve communication between the two, to the benefit of the American and British schools alike. Here too there is much room for fresh perspectives to aid in the field's further construction.

AMERICAN AND BRITISH SCHOOLS

Finally, there is the biggest gap of all. That is the persistent, even growing chasm between the two schools themselves—the new dialogue of the deaf that has emerged across the Atlantic in the years since Strange's "Mutual Neglect" manifesto. Here also difficulties of communication hamper discourse. Here too there is a need, as one source put it recently, "to renew the extensive invisible college of IPE" (Dickins 2006, 491).

That two entirely different "cultures" of IPE have developed in the English-speaking world is undeniable. The preceding chapters provide more than ample proof. In terms of ontology, the American school remains determinedly state-centric, privileging sovereign governments above all other units of interest. The British school, by contrast, treats the state as just one agent among many, if states are to be included at all. For the American school IPE is essentially a subset of IR, sharing the political science discipline's central preoccupation with public policy. The core problematique is limited to questions of state behavior and system governance. The main purpose of theory is explanation: to identify causality. The driving ambition is what Cox called problem solving: to explore possible solutions to challenges within the existing system. For the British school IPE is much more inclusive—more of a true interdiscipline in intent, open to links to many other areas of inquiry. The problematique is more ecumenical, concerned with all manner of social and ethical issues. The main purpose of theory is judgment: to identify injustice. The driving ambition is amelioration: to make the world a better place. Where the American school aspires to the objectivity of conventional social science, the British school is openly normative in the tradition of pragmatism and classical moral philosophy.

In terms of epistemology, the American school remains wedded to the principles of positivism and empiricism—the twin pillars of a hard science model. Deductive logic and parsimonious reasoning are used to seek out universal truths, in the spirit of "imitative scientism." Formal research methodologies are put to work to test hypotheses and promote the cumulation of knowledge. The British school, by contrast, embraces approaches that are more institutional and historical in nature, and more interpretative in tone. Less formal methodologies are preferred in order to accommodate the school's wider range of analytic concerns. Where the American school self-consciously restricts itself mainly to midlevel theorizing—highlighting key relationships within larger, stable structures—the British school aims for grander visions of systemic transformation or social development. Where the American school values "normal" science, the British school identifies more with critical theory's "oppositional frame of mind."

Differences like these are not necessarily undesirable—*if* they give rise to fruitful debate. Unfortunately, that does not seem to be the case here. In practice, communication between the two sides has been stunted at best, even growing weaker with time. An initial gap between the schools was understandable, given their separate starting points (both intellectual and geographic). Over time, though, their mutual insularity has only grown deeper as a result of divergent patterns of socialization. Students on either side are rarely exposed to more than one version of the field. Hence, they all too often complete their training unaware of the full range of possibilities for research. Without realizing it, they become members of a faction; the common language they acquire is more in the nature of a dialect, limiting discourse. Such factionalism is hardly unusual in a research community. But if the factions don't talk to each other, it can hardly be regarded as a sign of good health.

Can there ever be a meeting of the minds? Again, the task is not easy. On neither side is there much tolerance for the preferences of the other. For the American school, the British school's historical-relativist paradigm and normative pretensions represent a betrayal of basic principles of scientific research. For the British school, the American school's pursuit of objectivity and imitative scientism is hopelessly chimerical, an impossible dream. Scholars working in the U.S. style dismiss the likes of Strange and Cox as too eclectic, perhaps even too eccentric, to be taken seriously. Scholars working in the British style dismiss the likes of Keohane or Krasner as too limited in their vision to help us think outside the box. Each side is more comfortable confining discourse to its own faction, where there is more consensus on the underlying assumptions. Over time, as prejudices have been confirmed and reinforced, the gap has simply grown ever wider.

Yet ultimately, as I have repeatedly emphasized, the two schools are really quite complementary, the strengths of each largely balancing the weaknesses of the other. So why not seek to take the best from both, for their mutual gain? The American school could learn much from the British side's broad multidisciplinarity, which helps to import useful new insights from other academic specialties. U.S.-style IPE could benefit from a little more ambition, to combat the shrinkage of horizons that has been so noticeable in recent years. The British school, conversely, could learn much from the American side's more rigorous methodologies, which help bring consistency and replicability to theoretical analysis. British-style IPE could benefit from a little less ambition, to temper the temptation to address the totality of human experience.

Examples of how this might be done are not hard to find. For instance, I have already noted the efforts of a number of Canadian scholars to keep a foot in each camp, seeking to reconcile American empiricism with British eclecticism. That is particularly evident in Canadian approaches to the Control Gap, stressing the authoritative role of selected nonstate actors alongside states in system governance today. From the American school, I might mention my own work on currency deterritorialization (Cohen 1998, 2004), which attempts to erect a new way of thinking about the IPE of money on a traditional social science foundation. From the British school, I might mention the work of Angus Cameron and Palan on *The Imagined Economies of Globalization* (2004), which makes more systematic use of evidence to buttress a radical reinterpretation of the role of the state in economic affairs.

Fittingly, perhaps the most salient illustration comes from one of the Magnificent Seven—Katzenstein, the youngest of the seven and the only one to have received formal training on both sides of the Atlantic. Who better to build a bridge across the pond? In his recent study of *A World of Regions* (2005), Katzenstein deliberately borrowed from both the American and British traditions, combining systematic case study methodology and careful analysis of evidence with a wide-ranging integration of domestic and transnational themes on a global level. The book is not strictly confined to IPE; elements of political economy are interwoven with security and cultural analysis. Nonetheless, it offers a model of successful synthesis for the field. "In spirit," Katzenstein has written me, "this is a very British and un-American book in its intellectual openness and eclecticism, and a very American and un-British book in its development of several consistent and coherent arguments that are carefully tested." A more concise statement of the kind of bridge building that is needed between the two schools could hardly be imagined.

CONCLUSION

And so challenges remain, even after decades of construction. The story of IPE may not be quite as melodramatic as Oscar Wilde's Miss Prism warned. But neither, I like to think, has it been as horrid as Cecily feared. Inspired by the evolution of historical circumstances, ideas have competed for attention— some proving ephemeral or leading to dead ends, others enduring to influence the direction of subsequent discourse. And behind these ideas have been key individuals, intellectual entrepreneurs with the energy and ambition to promote a new scholarly enterprise. Ultimately, the story is a human one, a narrative of agency interacting with contingency to create knowledge. No curious person could possibly call it dull.

REFERENCES

Abdelal, Rawi. 2001. *National Purpose in the World Economy: Post-Soviet States in Comparative Perspective.* Ithaca, NY: Cornell University Press.

Adams, John. 1989. Review of *Production, Power, and World Order,* by Robert Cox. *Annals of the American Academy* 501 (January): 224–25.

Adler, Emanuel. 2002. "Constructivism and International Relations." In *Handbook of International Relations*, ed. Walter Carlsnaes, Thomas Risse, and Beth A. Simmons, 95–118. London: Sage Publications.

Andrews, David M. 1994. "Capital Mobility and State Autonomy: Toward a Structural Theory of International Monetary Relations." *International Studies Quarterly* 38, no. 2 (June): 193–218.

———, ed. 2006. *International Monetary Power.* Ithaca, NY: Cornell University Press.

Axelrod, Robert. 1984. *The Evolution of Cooperation.* New York: Basic Books.

Axelrod, Robert, and Robert O. Keohane. 1986. "Achieving Cooperation under Anarchy: Strategies and Institutions." In *Cooperation under Anarchy*, 226–54. Princeton, NJ: Princeton University Press.

Aydinli, Ersel, and Julie Mathews. 2000. "Are the Core and Periphery Irreconcilable? The Curious World of Publishing in Contemporary International Relations." *International Studies Perspectives* 1, no. 3 (December): 289–303.

Barkin, J. Samuel. 2003. *Social Construction and the Logic of Money: Financial Predominance and International Economic Leadership.* Albany: State University of New York Press.

Barnett, Michael, and Martha Finnemore. 2004. *Rules for the World: International Organizations in World Politics.* Ithaca, NY: Cornell University Press.

Bates, Robert. 1997. *Open-Economy Politics: The Political Economy of the World Coffee Trade.* Princeton, NJ: Princeton University Press.

Berger, Peter L., and Thomas Luckmann. 1966. *The Social Construction of Reality: A Treatise in the Sociology of Knowledge.* Garden City, NY: Doubleday.

Bergsten, C. Fred, and Lawrence B. Krause, eds. 1975. *World Politics and International Economics.* Washington, DC: Brookings Institution.

Bernhard, William T., J. Lawrence Broz, and William Roberts Clark, eds. 2003. *The Political Economy of Monetary Institutions.* Cambridge, MA: MIT Press.

Bernhard, William T., and David A. Leblang. 1999. "Democratic Institutions and Exchange Rate Commitments." *International Organization* 53, no. 1 (Winter): 71–97.

Best, Jacqueline. 2004. "Hollowing Out Keynesian Norms: How the Search for a Technical Fix Undermined the Bretton Woods Regime." *Review of International Studies* 30, no. 3 (July): 383–404.

Blyth, Mark, Craig Parsons, and Rawi Abdelal, eds. Forthcoming. *Constructivist Political Economy.*

Brecher, Michael. 1999. "International Studies in the Twentieth Century and Beyond: Flawed Dichotomies, Synthesis, Cumulation." *International Studies Quarterly* 43, no. 2 (June): 213–64.

Breuning, Marijke, Joseph Bredehoft, and Eugene Walton. 2005. "Promise and Performance: An Evaluation of Journals in International Relations." *International Studies Perspectives* 6, no. 4 (November): 447–61.

Brown, Christopher. 1973. "International Political Economy: Some Problems of an Inter-Disciplinary Enterprise." *International Affairs* 49, no. 1 (January): 51–60.

———. 1992. *International Relations Theory: New Normative Approaches.* New York: Columbia University Press.

———. 2001. " 'Our Side?' Critical Theory and International Relations." In *Critical Theory and World Politics*, ed. R. Wyn Jones, 191–204. Boulder, CO: Lynne Rienner.

Broz, J. Lawrence. 2003. "Political System Transparency and Monetary Commitment Regimes." In *The Political Economy of Monetary Institutions*, ed. William T. Bernhard, J. Lawrence Broz, and William Roberts Clark, 169–95. Cambridge, MA: MIT Press.

Bull, Hedley. 1977. *The Anarchical Society.* New York: Columbia University Press.

Burnham, Peter. 1994. "Open Marxism and Vulgar International Political Economy." *Review of International Political Economy* 1, no. 2 (Summer): 221–31.

Cameron, Angus, and Ronen P. Palan. 2004. *The Imagined Economies of Globalization.* London: Sage Publications.

Campbell, David. 1992. *Writing Security: United States Foreign Policy and the Politics of Identity.* Minneapolis: University of Minnesota Press.

Cerny, Philip G. 1990. *The Changing Architecture of Politics: Structure, Agency, and the Future of the State.* London: Sage Publications.

———. 1994a. "The Dynamics of Financial Globalization: Technology, Market Structures, and Policy Response." *Policy Sciences* 27, no. 4: 319–42.

———. 1994b. "The Infrastructure of the Infrastructure? Toward 'Embedded Financial Orthodoxy' in the International Political Economy." In *Transcending the State-Global Divide: A Neostructuralist Agenda in International Relations*, ed. Ronan P. Palan and Barry Gills, 223–75. Boulder, CO: Lynne Rienner.

Chan, Ronald. 2005. "Condoleezza Rice Taps Stephen Krasner to Assume Position of Director of Policy Planning for the State Department." *Stanford Daily,* January 31.

Chwieroth, Jeffrey M. 2007. "Neoliberal Economists and Capital Account Liberalization in Emerging Markets." *International Organization* 61, no. 2 (Spring): 443–63.

Clapp, Jennifer. 2001. *Toxic Exports: The Transfer of Hazardous Wastes from Rich to Poor Countries.* Ithaca, NY: Cornell University Press.

Clark, William Roberts. 2003. "Partisan and Electoral Motivations and the Choice of Monetary Institutions under Fully Mobile Capital." In *The Political Economy of Monetary Institutions*, ed. William T. Bernhard, J. Lawrence Broz, and William Roberts Clark, 33–57. Cambridge, MA: MIT Press.

Coase, Ronald H. 1984. "The New Institutional Economics." *Zeitschrift fur die gesamte Staatswissenschaft* [*Journal of Institutional and Theoretical Economics*] 140, no. 1: 229–31.

Cohen, Benjamin J. 1971. *The Future of Sterling as an International Currency.* London: Macmillan.

———. 1973. *The Question of Imperialism: The Political Economy of Dominance and Dependence.* New York: Basic Books.

———. 1974. "The Revolution in Atlantic Economic Relations: A Bargain Comes Unstuck." In *The United States and Western Europe: Political, Economic, and Strategic Perspectives*, ed. Wolfram Hanrieder, 106–33. Cambridge, MA: Winthrop Publishers.

———. 1976. "The Political Economy of Monetary Reform Today." *Journal of International Affairs* 30, no. 1 (Spring–Summer): 37–50.

———. 1977. *Organizing the World's Money: The Political Economy of International Monetary Relations.* New York: Basic Books.

———. 1981. *Banks and the Balance of Payments: Private Lending in the International Adjustment Process.* Montclair, NJ: Allenheld Osmun.

———. 1983a. "Balance-of-Payments Financing: Evolution of a Regime." In *International Regimes*, ed. Stephen D. Krasner, 315–36. Ithaca, NY: Cornell University Press.

———. 1983b. "An Explosion in the Kitchen? Economic Relations with Other Advanced Industrial Nations." In *Eagle Defiant: United States Foreign Policy in the 1980s*, ed. Kenneth A. Oye, Robert J. Lieber, and Donald Rothchild, 105–30. Boston: Little, Brown.

———. 1986. *In Whose Interest? International Banking and American Foreign Policy.* New Haven, CT: Yale University Press.

———. 1990. "The Political Economy of International Trade." *International Organization* 44, no. 2 (Spring): 261–81.

———. 1993. "The Triad and the Unholy Trinity: Lessons for the Pacific Region." In *Pacific Economic Relations in the 1990s: Cooperation or Conflict?* ed. Richard Higgott, Richard Leaver, and John Ravenhill, 133–58. Boulder, CO: Lynne Rienner.

———. 1996. "Phoenix Risen: The Resurrection of Global Finance." *World Politics* 48, no. 2 (January): 268–96.

———. 1998. *The Geography of Money.* Ithaca, NY: Cornell University Press.

———. 2002. "International Finance." In *Handbook of International Relations*, ed. Walter Carlsnaes, Thomas Risse, and Beth A. Simmons, 429–47. London: Sage Publications.

———. 2004. *The Future of Money.* Princeton, NJ: Princeton University Press.

Commons, John Rogers. 1934. *Institutional Economics: Its Place in Political Economy.* New York: Macmillan.

Cooper, Richard N. 1968. *The Economics of Interdependence: Economic Policy in the Atlantic Community.* New York: McGraw-Hill.

———. 1975. "Prolegomena to the Choice of an International Monetary System." In *World Politics and International Economics*, ed. C. Fred Bergsten and Lawrence B. Krause, 63–97. Washington, DC: Brookings Institution.

Cox, Robert W. 1972. "Labor and Transnational Relations." In *Transnational Relations and World Politics*, ed. Robert O. Keohane and Joseph S. Nye Jr., 204–34. Cambridge, MA: Harvard University Press.

———. 1979. "Ideologies and the New International Economic Order: Reflections on Some Recent Literature." *International Organization* 33, no. 2 (Spring): 257–302.

———. 1981. "Social Forces, States, and World Orders: Beyond International Relations Theory." *Millennium* 10, no. 2 (Summer): 126–55.

———. 1983. "Gramsci, Hegemony, and International Relations: An Essay in Method." *Millennium* 12, no. 2 (Summer): 162–75.

———. 1987. *Production, Power, and World Order: Social Forces in the Making of History.* New York: Columbia University Press.

———. 1995. "Critical Political Economy." In *International Political Economy: Understanding Global Disorder*, ed. Björn Hettne, 31–45. London: Zed Books.

———. 1996a. "Global *Perestroika*." In *Approaches to World Order*, by Robert W. Cox with Timothy J. Sinclair, 296–313. New York: Cambridge University Press.

———. 1996b. "Influences and Commitments." In *Approaches to World Order*, by Robert W. Cox with Timothy J. Sinclair, 19–38. New York: Cambridge University Press.

———. 1996c. "Realism, Positivism, and Historicism." In *Approaches to World Order*, by Robert W. Cox with Timothy J. Sinclair, 49–59. New York: Cambridge University Press.

———. 1996d. " 'Take Six Eggs': Theory, Finance, and the Real Economy in the Work of Susan Strange." In *Approaches to World Order*, by Robert W. Cox with Timothy J. Sinclair, 174–88. New York: Cambridge University Press.

———. 1999. "Conversation." *New Political Economy* 4, no. 3: 389–98.

———. 2002. "Power and Knowledge: Towards a New Ontology of World Order." In *The Political Economy of a Plural World: Critical Reflections on Power, Morals, and Civilization*, ed. Robert W. Cox with Michael G. Schechter, 76–95. New York: Routledge.

———. 2006. " 'The International' in Evolution." Paper presented at the thirty-fifth anniversary *Millennium* Conference, London, October.

Crewe, Ivor, and Pippa Norris. 1991. "British and American Journal Evaluation: Divergence or Convergence?" *PS: Political Science and Politics* 24, no. 3 (September): 524–31.

Cutler, A. Claire. 2003. *Private Power and Global Authority: Transnational Merchant Law in the Global Political Economy.* New York: Cambridge University Press.

Cutler, A. Claire, Virginia Haufler, and Tony Porter, eds. 1999. *Private Authority and International Affairs.* Albany: State University of New York Press.

DeLong, J. Bradford. 2005. "Sisyphus as Social Democrat: The Life and Legacy of John Kenneth Galbraith." *Foreign Affairs* 84, no. 3 (May–June): 126–30.

Denemark, Robert A., and Robert O'Brien. 1997. "Contesting the Canon: International Political Economy at UK and US Universities." *Review of International Political Economy* 4, no. 1 (Spring): 214–38.

Denzau, Arthur T., and Douglass C. North. 1994. "Shared Mental Models: Ideologies and Institutions." *Kyklos* 47, no. 1: 3–31.

Deutsch, Karl Wolfgang, Sidney A. Burrell, and Robert A. Kann. 1957. *Political Community and the North Atlantic Area: International Organization in the Light of Historical Experience*. Princeton, NJ: Princeton University Press.

Dickins, Amanda. 2006. "The Evolution of International Political Economy." *International Affairs* 82, no. 3 (July): 479–92.

Doremus, Paul N., William W. Keller, Louis W. Pauly, and Simon Reich. 1998. *The Myth of the Global Corporation*. Princeton, NJ: Princeton University Press.

Dunne, Timothy. 1998. *Inventing International Society: A History of the English School*. Basingstoke, UK: Macmillan.

Economist. 2006. "Obituary: John Kenneth Galbraith," May 6, 90.

Editors. 1994. "Editorial: Forum for Heterodox International Political Economy." *Review of International Political Economy* 1, no. 1 (Spring): 1–12.

Eichengreen, Barry. 1989. "Hegemonic Stability Theories of the International Monetary System." In *Can Nations Agree? Issues in International Economic Cooperation*, Richard N. Cooper, Barry Eichengreen, Gerald Holtham, Robert D. Putnam, and C. Randall Henning, 255–98. Washington, DC: Brookings Institution.

———. 1999. "Dental Hygiene and Nuclear War: How International Relations Looks from Economics." In *Exploration and Contestation in the Study of World Politics*, ed. Peter J. Katzenstein, Robert O. Keohane, and Stephen D. Krasner, 353–72. Cambridge, MA: MIT Press.

Elms, Deborah Kay. 2006. "New Directions for IPE: Drawing from Behavioral Economics." Paper presented at the inaugural meeting of the International Political Economy Society, Princeton, NJ, November.

Emmanuel, Arghiri. 1972. *Unequal Exchange: A Study of the Imperialism of Trade*. New York: Monthly Review Press.

Evans, Peter B., Harold K. Jacobson, and Robert D. Putnam, eds. 1993. *Double-Edged Diplomacy*. Berkeley: University of California Press.

Fearon, James D. 1998. "Bargaining, Enforcement, and International Cooperation." *International Organization* 52, no. 2 (Spring): 269–305.

Feis, Herbert. 1930. *Europe: The World's Banker, 1870–1914*. New Haven, CT: Yale University Press.

Finkelstein, Lawrence S., ed. 1969. "The United States and International Organization: The Changing Setting." Special issue, *International Organization* 23, no. 3 (Summer).

Finnemore, Martha. 1996. *National Interests in International Society*. Ithaca, NY: Cornell University Press.

Frank, Andre Gunder. 1967. *Capitalism and Underdevelopment in Latin America*. New York: Monthly Review Press.

Frey, Bruno. 1984. "The Public Choice View of International Political Economy." *International Organization* 38, no. 1 (Winter): 199–233.

Frieden, Jeffry A. 1991. "Invested Interests: The Politics of National Economic Policies in a World of Global Finance." *International Organization* 45, no. 4 (Autumn): 425–51.

Frieden, Jeffry A., and Lisa L. Martin. 2002. "International Political Economy: Global and Domestic Interactions." In *Political Science: State of the Discipline*, ed. Ira Katznelson and Helen V. Milner, 118–46. New York: W. W. Norton.

Friedman, Thomas L. 2005. *The World Is Flat: A Brief History of the Twenty-first Century.* New York: Farrar, Straus and Giroux.

Galbraith, John Kenneth. 1970. *Economics, Peace, and Laughter.* Harmondsworth, UK: Penguin.

Gamble, Andrew, Anthony Payne, Michael Dietrich, Ankie Hoogvelt, and Michael Kenny. 1996. "Editorial: New Political Economy." *New Political Economy* 1, no. 1 (March), 5–11.

Garand, James C., and Michael W. Giles. 2003. "Journals in the Discipline: A Report on a New Survey of American Political Scientists." *PS: Political Science and Politics* 36, no. 2 (April): 293–308.

Garrett, Geoffrey. 2000. "The Causes of Globalization." *Comparative Political Studies* 33, nos. 6–7 (August–September): 941–91.

Germain, Randall D. 1997. *The International Organization of Credit: States and Global Finance in the World-Economy.* New York: Cambridge University Press.

Gill, Stephen, and David Law. 1988. *The Global Political Economy: Perspectives, Problems, and Policies.* Baltimore, MD: Johns Hopkins University Press.

———. 1989. "Global Hegemony and the Structural Power of Capital." *International Studies Quarterly* 33, no. 4 (December): 475–99.

Gill, Stephen, and James H. Mittelman. 1997. Preface to *Innovation and Transformation in International Studies*, ed. Stephen Gill and James H. Mittelman, xv–xx. New York: Cambridge University Press.

Gills, Barry K. 2001. "Re-Orienting the New (International) Political Economy." *New Political Economy* 6, no. 2 (June): 233–45.

Gilpin, Robert. 1962. *American Scientists and Nuclear Weapons Policy.* Princeton, NJ: Princeton University Press.

———. 1968. *France in the Age of the Scientific State.* Princeton, NJ: Princeton University Press.

———. 1972. "The Politics of Transnational Economic Relations." In *Transnational Relations and World Politics*, ed. Robert O. Keohane and Joseph S Nye Jr., 48–69. Cambridge, MA: Harvard University Press.

———. 1975a. "Three Models of the Future." In *World Politics and International Economics*, ed. C. Fred Bergsten and Lawrence B. Krause, 37–60. Washington, DC: Brookings Institution.

———. 1975b. *U.S. Power and the Multinational Corporation.* New York: Basic Books.

———. 1981. *War and Change in World Politics.* New York: Cambridge University Press.

———. 1987. *The Political Economy of International Relations.* Princeton, NJ: Princeton University Press.

———. 2001. *Global Political Economy: Understanding the International Economic Order.* Princeton, NJ: Princeton University Press.

Goldstein, Judith L. 1993. *Ideas, Interests, and American Trade Policy.* Ithaca, NY: Cornell University Press.

Goldstein, Judith L., Miles Kahler, Robert O. Keohane, and Anne-Marie Slaughter. 2001. *Legalization and World Politics*. Cambridge, MA: MIT Press.

Goldstein, Judith L., and Lisa L. Martin. 2001. "Legalization, Trade Liberalization, and Domestic Politics: A Cautionary Note." In *Legalization and World Politics*, ed. Judith L. Goldstein, Miles Kahler, Robert O. Keohane, and Anne-Marie Slaughter, 219–48. Cambridge, MA: MIT Press.

Gourevitch, Peter. 1978. "The Second Image Reversed: The International Sources of Domestic Politics." *International Organization* 32, no. 4 (Autumn): 881–911.

———. 2002. "Domestic Politics and International Relations." In *Handbook of International Relations*, ed. Walter Carlsnaes, Thomas Risse, and Beth A. Simmons, 309–28. London: Sage Publications.

Gowa, Joanne. 1994. *Allies, Adversaries, and International Trade*. Princeton, NJ: Princeton University Press.

Greider, William. 1997. *One World, Ready or Not: The Manic Logic of Global Capitalism*. New York: Simon and Schuster.

Grieco, Joseph M. 1988. "Anarchy and the Limits of Cooperation: A Realist Critique of the Newest Liberal Institutionalism." *International Organization* 42, no. 3 (Summer): 485–507.

Griffiths, Martin. 1999. *Fifty Key Thinkers in International Relations*. New York: Routledge.

Haas, Ernst B. 1958. *The Uniting of Europe: Political, Social, and Economic Forces, 1950–1957*. Palo Alto, CA: Stanford University Press.

Haggard, Stephan, and Beth A. Simmons. 1987. "Theories of International Regimes." *International Organization* 41, no. 3 (Summer): 491–517.

Hall, Michael G. 2005. *Exchange Rate Crises in Developing Countries: The Political Role of the Banking Sector*. Burlington, VT: Ashgate.

Hall, Rodney Bruce, and Thomas J. Biersteker, eds. 2002. *The Emergence of Private Authority in Global Governance*. New York: Cambridge University Press.

Halliday, Fred. 1998. "New World Orders: Susan Strange." *Guardian*, November 14, 24.

Haufler, Virginia. 1997. *Dangerous Commerce: Insurance and the Management of International Risk*. Ithaca, NY: Cornell University Press.

Hefeker, Carsten. 1997. *Interest Groups and Monetary Integration: The Political Economy of Exchange Regime Choice*. Boulder, CO: Westview.

Helleiner, Eric. 2005. "The Meaning and Contemporary Significance of Economic Nationalism." In *Economic Nationalism in a Globalizing World*, ed. Eric Helleiner and Andreas Pickel, 220–34. Ithaca, NY: Cornell University Press.

Helleiner, Eric, and Andreas Pickel, eds. 2005. *Economic Nationalism in a Globalizing World*. Ithaca, NY: Cornell University Press.

Hermann, Margaret. 1998. "One Field, Many Perspectives: Building the Foundations for Dialogue." *International Studies Quarterly* 42, no. 4 (December): 605–24.

Hirschman, Albert O. 1945/1969. *National Power and the Structure of Foreign Trade*. Berkeley: University of California Press.

Hiscox, Michael J. 2002. *International Trade and Political Conflict: Commerce, Coalitions, and Mobility*. Princeton, NJ: Princeton University Press.

Hoffmann, Stanley. 1989. "A Retrospective." In *Journeys through World Politics: Autobiographical Reflections of Thirty-four Academic Travelers*, ed. Joseph Kruzel and James N. Rosenau, 263–78. Lexington, MA: Lexington Books.

Institute of International Studies, University of California at Berkeley. 2003. "Sovereignty: Conversation with Stephen D. Krasner." Available at http://globetrotter.berkeley.edu/people3/Krasner.

———. 2004. "Theory and International Institutions: Conversation with Robert O. Keohane." Available at http://globetrotter.berkeley.edu/people4/Keohane.

International Relations. 2005. "Conversations in *International Relations*: Interview with Robert Gilpin." *International Relations* 19, no. 3 (September): 361–72.

James, Scott C., and David A. Lake. 1989. "The Second Face of Hegemony: Britain's Repeal of the Corn Laws and the American Walker Tariff of 1846." *International Organization* 43, no. 1 (Winter): 1–29.

Jervis, Robert. 1976. *Perception and Misperception in International Politics*. Princeton, NJ: Princeton University Press.

———. 1983. "Security Regimes." In *International Regimes*, ed. Stephen D. Krasner, 173–94. Ithaca, NY: Cornell University Press.

Johnson, Harry G. 1971. "The Keynesian Revolution and the Monetarist Counter-Revolution." *American Economic Review* 61, no. 2 (May): 1–14.

Jones, R. J. Barry. 1995. *Globalisation and Interdependence in the International Political Economy: Rhetoric and Reality*. London: Pinter Publishers.

Kahler, Miles. 1990. "A Look at the International Political Economy." In *Sea-Changes: American Foreign Policy in a World Transformed*, ed. Nicholas X. Rizopoulos, 94–109. New York: Council on Foreign Relations.

———. 2002. "The State of the State in World Politics." In *Political Science: State of the Discipline*, ed. Ira Katznelson and Helen V. Milner, 56–83. New York: W.W. Norton.

Kahler, Miles, and David A. Lake, eds. 2003. *Governance in a Global Economy: Political Authority in Transition*. Princeton, NJ: Princeton University Press.

Kapstein, Ethan B. Forthcoming. "Fairness Considerations in World Politics: Lessons from International Trade Negotiations."

Katzenstein, Peter J. 1976. "International Relations and Domestic Structures: Foreign Economic Policies of Advanced Industrial States." *International Organization* 30, no. 1 (Winter): 1–45.

———, ed. 1978a. *Between Power and Plenty: Foreign Economic Policies of Advanced Industrial States*. Madison: University of Wisconsin Press.

———. 1978b. "Conclusion: Domestic Structures and Strategies of Foreign Economic Policy." In *Between Power and Plenty: Foreign Economic Policies of Advanced Industrial States*, ed. Peter J. Katzenstein, 295–336. Madison: University of Wisconsin Press.

———. 1978c. "Introduction: Domestic and International Forces and Strategies of Foreign Economic Policy." In *Between Power and Plenty: Foreign Economic Policies of Advanced Industrial States*, ed. Peter J. Katzenstein, 3–22. Madison: University of Wisconsin Press.

———. 1985. *Small States in World Markets: Industrial Policy in Europe*. Ithaca, NY: Cornell University Press.

————. 1996a. *Cultural Norms and National Security: Police and Military in Postwar Japan*. Ithaca, NY: Cornell University Press.

————, ed. 1996b. *The Culture of National Security: Norms and Identity in World Politics*. New York: Columbia University Press.

————. 1996c. "Introduction: Alternative Perspectives on National Security." In *The Culture of National Security: Norms and Identity in World Politics*, ed. Peter J. Katzenstein, 1–32. New York: Columbia University Press.

————. 1996d. Preface to *The Culture of National Security: Norms and Identity in World Politics*, ed. Peter J. Katzenstein, xi–xv. New York: Columbia University Press.

————. 2005. *A World of Regions: Asia and Europe in the American Imperium*. Ithaca, NY: Cornell University Press.

Katzenstein, Peter J., Robert O. Keohane, and Stephen D. Krasner, eds. 1999a. *Exploration and Contestation in the Study of World Politics*. Cambridge, MA: MIT Press.

————. 1999b. "*International Organization* and the Study of World Politics." In *Exploration and Contestation in the Study of World Politics*, ed. Peter J. Katzenstein, Robert O. Keohane, and Stephen D. Krasner, 5–45. Cambridge, MA: MIT Press.

Keohane, Robert O. 1979. "U.S. Foreign Economic Policy toward Other Advanced Capitalist States: The Struggle to Make Others Adjust." In *Eagle Entangled: U.S. Foreign Policy in a Complex World*, ed. Kenneth A. Oye, Donald Rothchild, and Robert J. Lieber, 91–122. New York: Longman.

————. 1980. "The Theory of Hegemonic Stability and Changes in International Economic Regimes, 1967–1977." In *Change in the International System*, ed. Ole R. Holsti, Randolph M. Siverson, and Alexander L. George, 131–62. Boulder, CO: Westview Press.

————. 1983. "The Demand for International Regimes." In *International Regimes*, ed. Stephen D. Krasner, 141–71. Ithaca, NY: Cornell University Press.

————. 1984. *After Hegemony: Cooperation and Discord in the World Political Economy*. Princeton, NJ: Princeton University Press.

————. 1988. "International Institutions: Two Approaches," *International Studies Quarterly* 32, no. 4 (December): 379–96.

————. 1989a. *International Institutions and State Power: Essays in International Relations Theory*. Boulder, CO: Westview Press.

————. 1989b. "A Personal Intellectual History." In *Journeys through World Politics: Autobiographical Reflections of Thirty-four Academic Travelers*, ed. Joseph Kruzel and James N. Rosenau, 403–15. Lexington, MA: Lexington Books.

————. 1993. "The Analysis of International Regimes: Towards a European-American Research Programme." In *Regime Theory and International Relations*, ed. Volker Rittberger, 23–45. Oxford: Clarendon Press.

————. 1997. "Problematic Lucidity: Stephen Krasner's 'State Power and the Structure of International Trade.'" *World Politics* 50, no. 1 (October): 150–70.

————. 2000. Foreword to *Strange Power: Shaping the Parameters of International Relations and International Political Economy*, ed. Thomas C. Lawton, James N. Rosenau, and Amy C. Verdun, ix–xvi. Aldershot, UK: Ashgate.

Keohane, Robert O. 2002. *Power and Governance in a Partially Globalized World*. New York: Routledge.

Keohane, Robert O., and Lisa L. Martin. 1995. "The Promise of Institutionalist Theory." *International Security* 20, no. 1 (Summer): 39–51.

———. 2003. "Institutional Theory as a Research Program." In *Progress in International Relations Theory: Appraising the Field*, ed. Colin Elman and Miriam Fendius Elman, 71–107. Cambridge, MA: MIT Press.

Keohane, Robert O., and Helen V. Milner, eds. 1996a. *Internationalization and Domestic Politics*. New York: Cambridge University Press.

———. 1996b. "Internationalization and Domestic Politics: A Conclusion." In *Internationalization and Domestic Politics*, ed. Robert O. Keohane and Helen V. Milner, 243–58. New York: Cambridge University Press.

———. 1996c. "Internationalization and Domestic Politics: An Introduction." In *Internationalization and Domestic Politics*, ed. Robert O. Keohane and Helen V. Milner, 3–24. New York: Cambridge University Press.

Keohane, Robert O., and Joseph S. Nye Jr., eds. 1972. *Transnational Relations and World Politics*. Cambridge, MA: Harvard University Press.

———. 1975. "International Interdependence and Integration." In *International Politics*, ed. Fred I. Greenstein and Nelson W. Polsby, 363–414. Reading, MA: Addison-Wesley.

———. 1977. *Power and Interdependence: World Politics in Transition*. Boston: Little, Brown.

———. 1987. *"Power and Interdependence* Revisited." *International Organization* 41, no. 4 (Autumn): 725–53.

———. 2001. *Power and Interdependence*. 3rd ed. Boston: Little, Brown.

Keynes, John Maynard. 1936. *The General Theory of Employment, Interest, and Money*. New York: Harcourt, Brace.

Kindleberger, Charles P. 1970. *Power and Money: The Politics of International Economics and the Economics of International Politics*. New York: Basic Books.

———. 1973. *The World in Depression, 1929–1939*. Berkeley: University of California Press.

———. 1991. *The Life of an Economist: An Autobiography*. Cambridge, MA: Basil Blackwell.

Kirshner, Jonathan. 1995. *Currency and Coercion: The Political Economy of International Monetary Power*. Princeton, NJ: Princeton University Press.

———. 2003. "The Inescapable Politics of Money." In *Monetary Orders: Ambiguous Economics, Ubiquitous Politics*, ed. Jonathan Kirshner, 3–24. Ithaca, NY: Cornell University Press.

Knorr, Klaus. 1947. "Economics and International Relations: A Problem in Teaching." *Political Science Quarterly* 62, no. 4 (December): 552–68.

Koremenos, Barbara, Charles Lipson, and Duncan Snidal, eds. 2003a. *The Rational Design of International Institutions*. New York: Cambridge University Press.

———. 2003b. "The Rational Design of International Institutions." In *The Rational Design of International Institutions*, ed. Barbara Koremenos, Charles Lipson, and Duncan Snidal, 1–40. New York: Cambridge University Press.

Krasner, Stephen D. 1973. "The Great Oil Sheikdown." *Foreign Policy* 13 (Winter): 123–38.

———. 1976. "State Power and the Structure of International Trade." *World Politics* 28, no. 3 (April): 317–47.

———. 1978a. *Defending the National Interest: Raw Materials Investments and U.S. Foreign Policy.* Princeton, NJ: Princeton University Press.

———. 1978b. "United States Commercial and Monetary Policy: Unraveling the Paradox of External Strength and Internal Weakness." In *Between Power and Plenty: Foreign Economic Policies of Advanced Industrial States*, ed. Peter J. Katzenstein, 51–87. Madison: University of Wisconsin Press.

———, ed. 1983a. *International Regimes.* Ithaca, NY: Cornell University Press.

———. 1983b. Preface to *International Regimes*, ed. Stephen D. Krasner, vii–ix. Ithaca, NY: Cornell University Press.

———. 1983c. "Regimes and the Limits of Realism: Regimes as Autonomous Variables." In *International Regimes*, ed. Stephen D. Krasner, 355–68. Ithaca, NY: Cornell University Press.

———. 1983d. "Structural Causes and Regime Consequences: Regimes as Intervening Variables." In *International Regimes*, ed. Stephen D. Krasner, 1–21. Ithaca, NY: Cornell University Press.

———. 1989. "Fortune, Virtue, and Systematic versus Scientific Inquiry." In *Journeys through World Politics: Autobiographical Reflections of Thirty-four Academic Travelers*, ed. Joseph Kruzel and James N. Rosenau, 417–27. Lexington, MA: Lexington Books.

———. 1991. "Global Communications and National Power: Life on the Pareto Frontier." *World Politics* 43, no. 3 (April): 336–66.

———. 1996. "The Accomplishments of International Political Economy." In *International Theory: Positivism and Beyond*, ed. Steve Smith, Ken Booth, and Marysia Zalewski, 108–27. New York: Cambridge University Press.

———. 1999. *Sovereignty: Organized Hypocrisy.* Princeton, NJ: Princeton University Press.

Krätke, Michael R., and Geoffrey R. D. Underhill. 2006. "Political Economy: The Revival of an 'Interdiscipline.' " In *Political Economy and the Changing Global Order*, ed. Richard Stubbs and Geoffrey R. D. Underhill, 24–38. 3rd ed. New York: Oxford University Press.

Krugman, Paul. 1996. *Development, Geography, and Economic Theory.* Cambridge, MA; MIT Press.

Lairson, Thomas D., and David Skidmore. 2003. *International Political Economy: The Struggle for Power and Wealth.* 3rd ed. Belmont, CA: Wadsworth/Thomson Learning.

Lake, David A. 1993. "Leadership, Hegemony, and the International Economy: Naked Emperor or Tattered Monarch with Potential?" *International Studies Quarterly* 37, no. 4 (December): 459–89.

———. 2006. "International Political Economy: A Maturing Interdiscipline." In *The Oxford Handbook of Political Economy*, ed. Barry R. Weingast and Donald A. Wittman, 757–77. New York: Oxford University Press.

Lawton, Thomas C., James N. Rosenau, and Amy C. Verdun, eds. 2000. *Strange Power: Shaping the Parameters of International Relations and International Political Economy*. Aldershot, UK: Ashgate.

Leblang, David A. 1999. "Domestic Political Institutions and Exchange Rate Commitments in the Developing World." *International Studies Quarterly* 43, no. 4 (December): 599–620.

Lenin, Valdimir Ilyich. 1917. *Imperialism: The Highest Stage of Capitalism*. Petrograd: Parus Publishers.

Linklater, Andrew, and Hidemi Suganami. 2006. *The English School of International Relations: A Contemporary Reassessment*. New York: Cambridge University Press.

Long, David. 1995. "The Harvard School of Liberal International Theory: A Case for Closure." *Millennium* 24, no. 3: 489–505.

Lorentzen, Jochen. 2002. Preface to *Markets and Authorities: Global Finance and Human Choice*, ed. Jochen Lorentzen and Marcello de Cecco, viii–ix. Cheltenham, UK: Edward Elgar.

Lorentzen, Jochen, and Marcello de Cecco, eds. 2002. *Markets and Authorities: Global Finance and Human Choice*. Cheltenham, UK: Edward Elgar.

Magdoff, Harry. 1969. *The Age of Imperialism: The Economics of U.S. Foreign Policy*. New York: Monthly Review Press.

Mansfield, Edward D. 1994. *Power, Trade, and War*. Princeton, NJ: Princeton University Press.

Mansfield, Edward D., Helen V. Milner, and Peter Rosendorff. 2000. "Free to Trade: Democracies, Autocracies, and International Trade." *American Political Science Review* 94, no. 2 (June): 305–21.

March, James G., and Johan P. Olsen. 1984. "The New Institutionalism: Organizational Factors in Political Life." *American Political Science Review* 78, no. 3 (September): 734–49.

Martin, Lisa L. 2002. "International Political Economy: From Paradigmatic Debates to Productive Disagreements." In *Conflict, Security, Foreign Policy, and International Political Economy: Past Paths and Future Directions in International Studies*, ed. Michael Brecher and Frank P. Harvey, 244–51. Ann Arbor: University of Michigan Press.

Martin, Lisa L., and Beth A. Simmons. 1999. "Theories and Empirical Studies of International Institutions." In *Exploration and Contestation in the Study of World Politics*, ed. Peter J. Katzenstein, Robert O. Keohane, and Stephen D. Krasner, 89–117. Cambridge, MA: MIT Press.

Maxfield, Sylvia. 2002. "International Development." In *Handbook of International Relations*, ed. Walter Carlsnaes, Thomas Risse, and Beth A. Simmons, 462–79. London: Sage Publications.

McDermott, Rose. 2004. *Political Psychology in International Relations*. Ann Arbor, MI: University of Michigan Press.

McNamara, Kathleen R. 1998. *The Currency of Ideas: Monetary Politics in the European Union*. Ithaca, NY: Cornell University Press.

Milner, Helen V. 1997a. "Industries, Governments, and Regional Trade Blocs." In *The Political Economy of Regionalism*, ed. Edward D. Mansfield and Helen V. Milner, 77–106. New York: Columbia University Press.

———. 1997b. *Interests, Institutions, and Information: Domestic Politics and International Relations*. Princeton, NJ: Princeton University Press.

———. 2002a. "International Trade." In *Handbook of International Relations*, ed. Walter Carlsnaes, Thomas Risse, and Beth A. Simmons, 448–61. London: Sage Publications.

———. 2002b. "Reflections on the Field of International Political Economy." In *Conflict, Security, Foreign Policy, and International Political Economy: Past Paths and Future Directions in International Studies*, ed. Michael Brecher and Frank P. Harvey, 207–23. Ann Arbor: University of Michigan Press.

Milner, Helen V., and Keiko Kubota. 2005. "Why the Move to Free Trade? Democracy and Trade Policy in the Developing Countries." *International Organization* 59, no. 1 (Winter): 107–43.

Milner, Helen V., and David B. Yoffie. 1989. "Between Free Trade and Protectionism: Strategic Trade Policy and a Theory of Corporate Trade Demands." *International Organization* 43, no. 2 (Spring): 239–72.

Mittelman, James H. 1998. "Coxian Historicism as an Alternative Perspective in International Studies." *Alternatives* 23, no. 1 (January–March): 63–92.

Modelski, George. 1987. *Long Cycles in World Politics*. London: Macmillan.

Morgan, Roger, Jochen Lorentzen, Anna Leander, and Stefano Guzzini, eds. 1993. *New Diplomacy in the Post-Cold War World: Essays for Susan Strange*. New York: St. Martin's Press.

Murphy, Craig N. 2000. "Global Governance: Poorly Done and Poorly Understood." *International Affairs* 76, no. 4 (October): 789–803.

Murphy, Craig N., and Douglas R. Nelson. 2001. "International Political Economy: A Tale of Two Heterodoxies." *British Journal of Politics and International Relations* 3, no. 3 (October): 393–412.

Murphy, Craig N., and Roger Tooze. 1991. "Getting beyond the 'Common Sense' of the IPE Orthodoxy." In *The New International Political Economy*, ed. Craig N. Murphy and Roger Tooze, 11–31. Boulder, CO: Lynne Rienner.

Nisonger, Thomas E. 1993. "A Ranking of Political Science Journals Based on Citation Data." *Serials Review* 19, no. 4 (Winter): 7–14.

Norris, Pippa. 1997. "Towards a More Cosmopolitan Political Science?" *European Journal of Political Research* 31, nos. 1–2 (February): 17–34.

Norris, Pippa, and Ivor Crewe. 1993. "The Reputation of Political Science Journals: Pluralist and Consensus Views." *Political Studies* 41, no. 1 (March): 5–23.

North, Douglass C. 1981. *Structure and Change in Economic History*. New York: W. W. Norton.

Nye, Joseph S., Jr. 1965. *Pan Africanism and East African Integration*. Cambridge, MA: Harvard University Press.

———. 1989. "Studying World Politics," In *Journeys through World Politics: Autobiographical Reflections of Thirty-four Academic Travelers*, ed. Joseph Kruzel and James N. Rosenau, 199–212. Lexington, MA: Lexington Books.

———. 1990. *Bound to Lead: The Changing Nature of American Power*. New York: Basic Books.

———. 2002. *The Paradox of American Power: Why the World's Only Superpower Can't Go It Alone*. New York: Oxford University Press.

Lake, David A. 2004a. *Power in the Global Information Age: From Realism to Globalization.* New York: Routledge.

———. 2004b. *Soft Power: The Means to Success in World Politics.* New York: Public Affairs.

Oatley, Thomas H. 1997. *Monetary Politics: Exchange Rate Cooperation in the European Union.* Ann Arbor: University of Michigan Press.

O'Brien, Robert. 1995. "International Political Economy and International Relations: Apprentice or Teacher?" In *Boundaries in Question: New Directions in International Relations,* ed. John MacMillan and Andrew Linklater, 89–106. London: Pinter.

O'Brien, Robert, and Marc Williams. 2004. *Global Political Economy: Evolution and Dynamics.* New York: Palgrave Macmillan.

Odell, John S. 1979. "The U.S. and the Emergence of Flexible Exchange Rates: An Analysis of Foreign Policy Change." *International Organization* 33, no. 1 (Winter): 57–81.

———. 1982. *U.S. International Monetary Policy: Markets, Power, and Ideas as Sources of Change.* Princeton, NJ: Princeton University Press.

———. 2000. *Negotiating the World Economy.* Ithaca, NY: Cornell University Press.

———. 2002. "Bounded Rationality and the World Political Economy." In *Governing the World's Money,* ed. David M. Andrews, C. Randall Henning, and Louis W. Pauly, 168–93. Ithaca, NY: Cornell University Press.

Ohmae, Kenichi. 1990. *The Borderless World: Power and Strategy in the Interlinked Economy.* New York: HarperPerennial.

Olson, Mancur. 1965. *The Logic of Collective Action.* Cambridge, MA: Harvard University Press.

Onuf, Nicholas. 1989. *World of Our Making: Rules and Rule in Social Theory and International Relations.* Columbia: University of South Carolina Press.

Palan, Ronen P., ed. 2000a. *Global Political Economy: Contemporary Theories.* London: Routledge.

———. 2000b. "New Trends in Global Political Economy." In *Global Political Economy: Contemporary Theories,* ed. Ronen P. Palan, 1–18. London: Routledge.

———. 2003. "Pragmatism and International Relations in the Age of Banker's Capitalism: Susan Strange's Vision for a Critical International Political Economy." In *International Relations at LSE: A History of 75 Years,* ed. Harry Bauer and Elisabetta Brighi, 117–38. London: Millennium Publishing Group.

Palan, Ronen P., and Jason Abbott. 1996. *State Strategies in the Global Political Economy.* London: Pinter.

Palan, Ronen P., and Barry Gills, eds. 1994. *Transcending the State-Global Divide: A Neostructuralist Agenda in International Relations.* Boulder, CO: Lynne Rienner.

Parker, Richard. 2005. *John Kenneth Galbraith: His Life, His Politics, His Economics.* New York: Farrar, Straus and Giroux.

Paul, Darel E. 2006. "Teaching Political Economy in Political Science: A Review of International and Comparative Political Economy Syllabi." *Perspectives on Politics* 4, no. 4 (December): 729–34.

Pauly, Louis W. 1995. "Capital Mobility, State Autonomy, and Political Legitimacy." *Journal of International Affairs* 48, no. 2 (Winter): 369–88.

———. 1997. *Who Elected the Bankers? Surveillance and Control in the World Economy.* Ithaca, NY: Cornell University Press.

———. 1999. "Good Governance and Bad Policy: The Perils of International Organizational Overextension." *Review of International Political Economy* 6, no. 4 (Winter): 401–24.

Payne, Anthony. 2005. "The Study of Governance in a Global Political Economy." In *Globalizing International Political Economy*, ed. Nicola Phillips, 55–81. New York: Palgrave Macmillan.

———. 2006. "The Genealogy of New Political Economy." In *Key Debates in New Political Economy*, ed. Anthony Payne, 1–10. New York: Routledge.

Peterson, Susan, Michael J. Tierney, and Daniel Maliniak. 2005. "Inside the Ivory Tower." *Foreign Policy* (November–December): 58–64.

Phillips, Nicola. 2005. " 'Globalizing' the Study of International Political Economy." In *Globalizing International Political Economy*, ed. Nicola Phillips, 1–19. New York: Palgrave Macmillan.

Polanyi, Karl. 1944. *The Great Transformation: The Political and Economic Origins of Our Time.* Boston: Beacon Press.

Porter, Tony. 2005. *Globalization and Finance.* Malden, MA: Polity Press.

Putnam, Robert D. 1988. "Diplomacy and Domestic Politics: The Logic of Two-Level Games." *International Organization* 42, no. 3 (Summer): 427–60.

Putnam, Robert D., and C. Randall Henning. 1989. "The Bonn Summit of 1978: A Case Study in Coordination." In *Can Nations Agree? Issues in International Economic Cooperation*, by Richard N. Cooper, Barry Eichengreen, Gerald Holtham, Robert D. Putnam, and C. Randall Henning, 12–140. Washington, DC: Brookings Institution.

Ravenhill, John, ed. 2005. *Global Political Economy.* New York: Oxford University Press.

Rittberger, Volker. 1993. "Research on International Regimes in Germany: The Adaptive Internalization of an American Social Science Concept." In *Regime Theory and International Relations*, ed. Volker Rittberger, 3–22. Oxford: Clarendon Press.

Robinson, William I. 2004. *A Theory of Global Capitalism: Production, Class, and State in a Transnational World.* Baltimore, MD: Johns Hopkins University Press.

Rogoff, Kenneth. 1985. "Can International Monetary Policy Cooperation Be Counterproductive?" *Journal of International Economics* 18, nos. 3–4 (May): 199–217.

Rogowski, Ronald. 1989. *Commerce and Coalitions: How Trade Affects Domestic Political Alignments.* Princeton, NJ: Princeton University Press.

Rosenau, James N. 1992. "Governance, Order, and Change in World Politics." In *Governance without Government: Order and Change in World Politics*, ed. James N. Rosenau and Ernst Otto Czempiel, 1–29. New York: Cambridge University Press.

Rosendorff, B. Peter, and Helen V. Milner. 2003. "The Optimal Design of International Trade Institutions: Uncertainty and Escape." In *The Rational Design of*

International Institutions, ed. Barbara Koremenos, Charles Lipson, and Duncan Snidal, 69–97. New York: Cambridge University Press.

Roy, Ravi K., Arthur T. Denzau, and Thomas D. Willett, eds. 2007. *Neoliberalism: National and Regional Experiments with Global Ideas.* New York: Routledge.

Ruggie, John Gerard. 1975. "International Responses to Technology: Concepts and Trends." *International Organization* 29, no. 3 (Summer): 557–83.

———. 1983. "International Regimes, Transactions, and Change: Embedded Liberalism in the Postwar Economic Order." In *International Regimes,* ed. Stephen D. Krasner, 195–231. Ithaca, NY: Cornell University Press.

———. 1999. "What Makes the World Hang Together? Neo-Utilitarianism and the Social Constructivist Challenge." In *Exploration and Contestation in the Study of World Politics,* ed. Peter J. Katzenstein, Robert O. Keohane, and Stephen D. Krasner, 215–45. Cambridge, MA: MIT Press.

Rupert, Mark, and M. Scott Solomon. 2006. *Globalization and International Political Economy: The Politics of Alternative Futures.* New York: Rowman and Littlefield.

Russett, Bruce. 1985. "The Mysterious Case of Vanishing Hegemony; or, Is Mark Twain Really Dead?" *International Organization* 39, no. 2 (Spring): 207–31.

Samuelson, Paul A. 1947. *Foundations of Economic Analysis.* Cambridge, MA: Harvard University Press.

Santayana, George. 1905. *The Life of Reason.* Vol. 1 of *Introduction and Reason in Common Sense.* New York: Scribner's.

Schechter, Michael G. 2002. "Critiques of Coxian Theory: Background to a Conversation." In *The Political Economy of a Plural World: Critical Reflections on Power, Morals, and Civilization,* by Robert W. Cox with Michael G. Schechter, 1–25. New York: Routledge.

Schelling, Thomas. 1978. *Micromotives and Macrobehavior.* New York: W. W. Norton.

Seabrooke, Leonard. 2006. *The Social Sources of Financial Power: Domestic Legitimacy and International Financial Orders.* Ithaca, NY: Cornell University Press.

Sen, Gautam. 1998. "Obituary: Professor Susan Strange." *Independent,* December 8, 6.

Shaw, Martin. 2000. *Theory of the Global State: Globality as an Unfinished Revolution.* New York: Cambridge University Press.

Simmons, Beth A. 1994. *Who Adjusts? Domestic Sources of Foreign Economic Policy during the Interwar Years.* Princeton, NJ: Princeton University Press.

———. 2001. "The Legalization of International Monetary Affairs." In *Legalization and World Politics,* ed. Judith L. Goldstein, Miles Kahler, Robert O. Keohane, and Anne-Marie Slaughter, 189–218. Cambridge, MA: MIT Press.

Simmons, Beth A., and Lisa L. Martin. 2002. "International Organizations and Institutions." In *Handbook of International Relations,* ed. Walter Carlsnaes, Thomas Risse, and Beth A. Simmons, 192–211. London: Sage Publications.

Simon, Herbert A. 1997. *Models of Bounded Rationality.* Vol. 3 of *Empirically Grounded Economic Reason.* Cambridge, MA: MIT Press.

Sinclair, Timothy J. 1996. "Beyond International Relations Theory: Robert W. Cox and Approaches to World Order." In *Approaches to World Order*, by Robert W. Cox with Timothy J. Sinclair, 3–18. New York: Cambridge University Press.

———. 2005. *The New Masters of Capital: American Bond Rating Agencies and the Politics of Creditworthiness*. Ithaca, NY: Cornell University Press.

Snidal, Duncan. 1985. "The Limits of Hegemonic Stability Theory." *International Organization* 39, no. 4 (Autumn): 579–614.

Stegemann, Klaus. 1989. "Policy Rivalry among Industrial States: What Can We Learn from Models of Strategic Trade Policy." *International Organization* 41, no. 1 (Winter): 73–100.

Stein, Charles. 2003. "Obituary: Charles Kindleberger." *Boston Globe*, July 8, D17.

Stiglitz, Joseph E. 2002. *Globalization and Its Discontents*. New York: W. W. Norton.

Stopford, John, and Susan Strange. 1991. *Rival States, Rival Firms: Competition for World Market Shares*. New York: Cambridge University Press.

Strange, Susan. 1970. "International Economics and International Relations: A Case of Mutual Neglect." *International Affairs* 46, no. 2 (April): 304–15.

———. 1971. *Sterling and British Policy: A Political Study of an International Currency in Decline*. London: Oxford University Press.

———. 1979. Review of *Organizing the World's Money*, by Benjamin J. Cohen. *International Affairs* 55, no. 1 (January): 107–9.

———. 1983. "*Cave! hic dragones*: A Critique of Regime Analysis." In *International Regimes*, ed. Stephen D. Krasner, 337–54. Ithaca, NY: Cornell University Press.

———, ed. 1984a. *Paths to International Political Economy*. London: George Allen and Unwin.

———. 1984b. Preface to *Paths to International Political Economy*, ed. Susan Strange, ix–xi. London: George Allen and Unwin.

———. 1985. "International Political Economy: The Story So Far and the Way Ahead." In *An International Political Economy*, ed. W. Ladd Hollist and F. LaMond Tullis, 13–25. Boulder, CO: Westview Press.

———. 1986. *Casino Capitalism*. Oxford: Basil Blackwell.

———. 1987. "The Persistent Myth of Lost Hegemony." *International Organization* 41, no. 4 (Autumn): 551–74.

———. 1988a. Review of *Production, Power, and World Order*, by Robert Cox. *International Affairs* 64, no. 2 (Spring): 269–70.

———. 1988b. *States and Markets*. London: Pinter Publishers.

———. 1989 "I Never Meant to Be an Academic." In *Journeys through World Politics: Autobiographical Reflections of Thirty-four Academic Travelers*, ed. Joseph Kruzel and James N. Rosenau, 429–36. Lexington, MA: Lexington Books.

———. 1991. "An Eclectic Approach." In *The New International Political Economy*, ed. Craig N. Murphy and Roger Tooze, 33–49. Boulder, CO: Lynne Rienner.

Strange, Susan. 1994. "Wake Up, Krasner! The World *Has* Changed." *Review of International Political Economy* 1, no. 2 (Summer): 209–19.

———. 1995. "ISA as a Microcosm." *International Studies Quarterly* 39, no. 3 (September): 289–96.

———. 1996. *The Retreat of the State: The Diffusion of Power in the World Economy.* London: Cambridge University Press.

———. 1998a. *Mad Money.* Manchester, U.K.: Manchester University Press.

———. 1998b. "Why Do International Organizations Never Die?" In *Autonomous Policy Making by International Organizations*, ed. Bob Reinalda and Bertjan Verbeek, 213–20. London: Routledge.

Stubbs, Richard, and Geoffrey R. D. Underhill, eds. 2006. *Political Economy and the Changing Global Order.* 3rd ed. New York: Oxford University Press.

Swidler, Ann, and Jorge Arditi. 1994. "The New Sociology of Knowledge." *Annual Review of Sociology* 20: 305–29.

Synnott, Thomas W., III. 2003. "Charles P. Kindleberger, 1910–2003: In Memoriam." *Business Economics* 38, no. 14 (October): 6.

Tabb, William K. 2004. *Economic Governance in the Age of Globalization.* New York: Columbia University Press.

Tétreault, Mary Ann, Robert A. Denemark, Kenneth P. Thomas, and Kurt Burch, eds. 2003. *Rethinking Global Political Economy: Emerging Issues, Unfolding Odysseys.* London: Routledge.

Tooze, Roger. 1984. "Perspectives and Theory: A Consumers' Guide." In *Paths to International Political Economy*, ed. Susan Strange, 1–22. London: George Allen and Unwin.

———. 1985. "International Political Economy." In *International Relations: British and American Perspectives*, 108–25. Oxford: Basil Blackwell.

Tooze, Roger, and Christopher May. 2002. *Authority and Markets: Susan Strange's Writings on International Political Economy.* Basingstoke, UK: Palgrave Macmillan.

Tsygankov, Andrei P. 2001. *Pathways after Empire: National Identity and Foreign Economic Policy in the Post-Soviet World.* Lanham, MD: Rowman and Littlefield.

Uchitelle, Louis. 2006. "Students Are Leaving the Politics out of Economics." *New York Times*, January 27, C3.

Underhill, Geoffrey R. D. 2000. "State, Market, and Global Political Economy: Genealogy of an (Inter?) Discipline." *International Affairs* 76, no. 4 (October): 805–24.

———. 2006. "Introduction: Conceptualizing the Changing Global Order." In *Political Economy and the Changing Global Order*, ed. Richard Stubbs and Geoffrey R. D. Underhill, 3–23. 3rd ed. New York: Oxford University Press.

Verdier, Daniel. 1998. "Democratic Convergence and Free Trade?" *International Studies Quarterly* 42, no. 1 (March): 1–24.

Vernon, Raymond. 1971. *Sovereignty at Bay: The Multinational Spread of U.S. Enterprises.* New York: Basic Books.

———. 1989. "The Foundations Came Last." In *Journeys through World Politics: Autobiographical Reflections of Thirty-four Academic Travelers*, ed. Joseph Kruzel and James N. Rosenau, 437–45. Lexington, MA: Lexington Books.

Veseth, Michael. 2005. *Globaloney: Unraveling the Myths of Globalization*. Lanham, MD: Rowman and Littlefield.

Viner, Jacob. 1948. "Power versus Plenty as Objectives of Foreign Policy in the Seventeenth and Eighteenth Centuries." *World Politics* 1, no. 1 (October): 1–29.

Wallerstein, Immanuel. 1984. *The Politics of the World-Economy*. New York: Cambridge University Press.

Waltz, Kenneth N. 1959. *Man, the State, and War*. New York: Columbia University Press.

———. 1979. *Theory of International Politics*. Reading, MA: Addison-Wesley.

Watson, Matthew. 2005. *Foundations of International Political Economy*. New York: Palgrave Macmillan.

Webb, Michael C. 1995. *The Political Economy of Policy Coordination: International Adjustment since 1945*. Ithaca, NY: Cornell University Press.

Webb, Michael C., and Stephen D. Krasner. 1989. "Hegemonic Stability Theory: An Empirical Assessment." *Review of International Studies* 15 (Spring): 183–98.

Weiss, Linda. 1998. *The Myth of the Powerless State*. London: Policy Press.

Wendt, Alexander. 1992. "Anarchy Is What States Make of It: The Social Construction of Power Politics." *International Organization* 46, no. 2 (Spring): 391–425.

———. 1999. *Social Theory of International Politics*. New York: Cambridge University Press.

Willett, Thomas D., ed. 1988. *Political Business Cycles: The Politics of Money, Inflation, and Unemployment*. Durham, NC: Duke University Press.

Willett, Thomas D., and Roland Vaubel, eds. 1991. *The Political Economy of International Organizations*. Boulder, CO: Westview Press.

Williamson, Oliver E. 1985. *The Economic Institutions of Capitalism: Firms, Markets, Relational Contracting*. New York: Free Press.

Young, Oran R. 1983. "Regime Dynamics: The Rise and Fall of International Regimes." In *International Regimes*, ed. Stephen D. Krasner, 93–113. Ithaca, NY: Cornell University Press.

———. 1986. "International Regimes: Toward a New Theory of Institutions." *World Politics* 39, no. 1 (October): 104–22.

Zuckerman, Mortimer B. 1998. "A Second American Century." *Foreign Affairs* 77, no. 3 (May–June): 18–31.

Zürn, Michael. 2002. "From Interdependence to Globalization." In *Handbook of International Relations*, ed. Walter Carlsnaes, Thomas Risse, and Beth A. Simmons, 235–54. London: Sage Publications.

INDEX